Thinking the Inexhaustible

SUNY series in Contemporary Italian Philosophy
―――――
Silvia Benso and Brian Schroeder, editors

Thinking the Inexhaustible

Art, Interpretation, and Freedom in the
Philosophy of Luigi Pareyson

Edited by
Silvia Benso and Brian Schroeder

Foreword by
Dennis J. Schmidt

Published by State University of New York Press, Albany

© 2018 State University of New York

All rights reserved

No part of this book may be used or reproduced in any manner whatsoever without written permission. No part of this book may be stored in a retrieval system or transmitted in any form or by any means including electronic, electrostatic, magnetic tape, mechanical, photocopying, recording, or otherwise without the prior permission in writing of the publisher.

For information, contact State University of New York Press, Albany, NY
www.sunypress.edu

Library of Congress Cataloging-in-Publication Data

Names: Benso, Silvia, editor. | Schroeder, Brian, editor.
Title: Thinking the inexhaustible : art, interpretation, and freedom in the
  philosophy of Luigi Pareyson / edited by Silvia Benso and Brian Schroeder.
Description: Albany, NY : State University of New York, 2018. | Series: SUNY
  series in contemporary Italian philosophy | Includes bibliographical
  references and index.
Identifiers: LCCN 2017034948 | ISBN 9781438470252 (hardcover) |
  ISBN 9781438470269 (pbk.) | ISBN 9781438470276 (ebook) Subjects: LCSH:
Pareyson, Luigi.
Classification: LCC B3636.P364 T45 2018 | DDC 195—dc23
LC record available at https://lccn.loc.gov/2017034948

10 9 8 7 6 5 4 3 2 1

Contents

Acknowledgments — vii

Foreword — ix
    Dennis J. Schmidt

Introduction: Thinking the Inexhaustible — 1
    Silvia Benso and Brian Schroeder

1. Luigi Pareyson: A Master in Italian Hermeneutics — 11
    Silvia Benso

2. When Transcendence Is Finite: Pareyson, the Person, and the Limits of Being — 29
    Antonio Calcagno

3. Pareyson's Role in Twentieth-Century Italian Aesthetics — 43
    Paolo D'Angelo

4. Pareyson vs. Croce: The Novelties of Pareyson's 1954 *Estetica* — 61
    Umberto Eco

5. On Pareyson's Interpretation of Kant's Third Critique — 81
    Massimo Cacciari

6. Pareyson's Aesthetics as Hermeneutics of Art — 93
    Federico Vercellone

7. The Unfamiliarity of Kindredness: Toward a Hermeneutics of Community — 105
    Robert T. Valgenti

8. Truth as the Origin (Rather Than Goal) of Inquiry 123
   Lauren Swayne Barthold

9. The "I" Beyond the Subject/Object Opposition: Pareyson's Conception of the Self Between Hegel and Heidegger 139
   Paolo Diego Bubbio

10. From Aesthetics to the Ontology of Freedom 159
    Gianni Vattimo

11. Evil in God: Pareyson's Ontology of Freedom 169
    Martin G. Weiss

12. Philosophy and Novel in the Later Pareyson 185
    Sergio Givone

Bibliography 201

Contributors 205

Index 211

Acknowledgments

We are deeply appreciative for the encouragement and support of this volume that we have received from many people. We are especially grateful to Prof. Claudio Ciancio, president of the Centro Studi Filosofico-Religiosi Luigi Pareyson in Turin, Italy; and Dr. Antonella Galbiati at Mursia Editore. Their assistance was invaluable in helping us secure the rights for the English translation of some of the essays contained in this volume and already published in Italian as part of the 2011 issue of the *Annuario Filosofico*, the philosophy yearly journal founded by Pareyson and some others in 1985.

We are, as always, indebted to Andrew Kenyon and the staff at SUNY Press for their enthusiastic backing of this volume and their unfailing support of the Series in Contemporary Italian Philosophy.

We also extend our most sincere appreciation to the contributors of this volume for their excellent work and patience. Without them this work would not have been possible.

It is noteworthy that the publication of this volume occurs during the centennial of Luigi Pareyson's birth. May this timing be an auspicious testimony to and gesture of appreciation for the significance of his philosophical thought.

Foreword

Dennis J. Schmidt

One realizes the importance of translation in the history of philosophy when one discovers an original body of work that has not had the same impact outside its native language as it has had in its original language. Because linguistic borders are difficult to cross, significant contributions to philosophy that have had a profound influence in their own linguistic sphere can go largely unnoticed in other languages. Until quite recently, such was the fate of the work of Luigi Pareyson, who is undeniably one of the singular and key voices in post–World War II Italian thought yet who has remained mostly a rumor in the Anglophone world. Fortunately, thanks to recent translations and to this volume of essays, that fate has changed and Pareyson will now be more accessible.[1]

The essays in this volume will do much to unfold the complexities of Pareyson's work and to engage the wide range of his contribution to philosophy. Nonetheless, a few remarks situating Pareyson's thought in its larger contexts might help to further introduce him to those as yet unfamiliar with his complex and original philosophical project. The scope of Pareyson's thought spanned over five decades from the end of the Second World War through the student movements of the late 1960s up to the late 1980s; he wrote books about themes such as existentialism, aesthetics, German Idealism, truth, religion, evil, and freedom, as well as on figures such as Vico, Jaspers, Fichte, Schelling, and Dostoevsky. In short, his career cuts a broad path through key concerns of our times as well as pivotal figures in intellectual history. Deeply committed to the relevance of philosophy and what Pareyson calls the "vindication" of truth in the world, Pareyson brings to the tradition that has come to be labeled as "continental philosophy" an important point of view and potent reminders of issues that are not always remembered today.

Presenting ideas or a body of work by identifying them with a label always risks being reductive. However, situating a body of work as coming out of traditions can be a helpful way of entering it. In Pareyson's case, his self-identification with the hermeneutic tradition as well as its more contemporary form offers an excellent entrée into his thought.

The word "hermeneutics" has a long history that has moved through disciplines as seemingly diverse as theology, jurisprudence, psychology, pedagogy, anthropology, and philosophy. Its history reaches back to the ancient Greek conception of hermeneutics as concerned with the structure of language and moves through medieval debates about interpreting biblical texts as well as legal debates about the proper application of law. Since its first formulations, the idea of hermeneutics as a way of addressing problems of interpretation has evolved and expanded its reach, and it has never disappeared from debates it enters: hermeneutics invariably hones in upon the way in which interpretation lodges itself as a constitutive moment in every claim to truth, whether that claim concerns a text, the word of God, or the true application of a law. However, nothing in this history and none of the issues within the long tradition of hermeneutics from Aristotle to Schleiermacher could have prepared one for the revolution in the idea of hermeneutics that would define the early twentieth century when "hermeneutics" would name a radical transformation in the very idea and task of philosophy. Indeed, it is fair to say that the formulation of a genuinely philosophical hermeneutic theory that understood itself to be an ontology was one of the defining events of the last century and that the shock waves of this revolution are still being felt today. It was Heidegger who would take this word, "hermeneutics," that hitherto had been enlisted to refer to more specialized problems of interpretation—of translation, of scriptural and textual exegesis, and of the legal problem of judgment—and demonstrate how these themes were to be understood as epiphenomenal problems rooted in what Heidegger described as the hermeneutics of factical life. The task of interpretation that had long been the theme of hermeneutic practices was no longer regarded as a special theoretical or practical problem, but as the most elemental account of how we experience the riddle of existence. We live in the world interpretively. Our way of being in the world is constituted such that we cannot escape interpreting: we look at the sky and interpret the movement of clouds, we interpret the body language of others, we try to make sense of what is said, what we read, what we see. In *Being and Time*, Heidegger explains this by saying that we live in the world understandingly.[2] Philosophy, he argues, is the radicalization of this way of being and so it is fitting that he describes philosophy as a "hermeneutic of existence." Pareyson will further unfold this point and say that once philosophy recognizes this "originality of interpretation," it is able to release the "inexhaustibility" and "richness" of existence itself. In short, the hermeneutic question of interpretation was no longer considered to be a specialized matter, but was seen as defining the very fabric of existence as such.

Until Heidegger, hermeneutics was typically described as a practice or "method," but Heidegger's account of the most radical force of the problem of interpretation made clear that hermeneutics has always been the name for reflection upon that which resists being submitted to any rule-bound practice or methodology.[3] Indeed, what unites all of the various forms of hermeneutic practices is that they are devoted to what calls for interpretation, what resists conceptual clarity, and what is inexhaustible in possibilities. So, the first themes of hermeneutics were centered upon the word of God, the translation across languages, the application of the rule of law, the riddle of memory, and the interpretation of texts from different epochs and cultures. If there has been a common theme holding together all the diverse ways in which the word "hermeneutics" has been invoked throughout history, then one might say that it has always been concerned with the strange, the foreign, and that which challenges understanding. The contemporary form of hermeneutics has both intensified and universalized this theme.[4]

The claim that hermeneutic problems are not confined to regional concerns or disciplines, but that they are rooted in the structure of existence and thus need to be understood as universal, radically challenges the dominant conception of philosophy that, since modernity, has taken method as a primary concern. From its first formulation, this new way of speaking of hermeneutics was understood as opening genuinely original avenues for philosophical reflection, and the word "hermeneutics," which had been used for millennia, suddenly became the name of a philosophical sensibility that shifted the possibilities of philosophy.

Curiously, Heidegger, who opened the door for this new and universal sense of philosophical hermeneutics, would largely abandon all talk of hermeneutics after *Being and Time*. So it would fall to others to advance the promises of philosophical hermeneutics.

During the second half of the twentieth century, the project of philosophical hermeneutics would receive important creative impulses, and three figures would be most significant here: Gadamer, Ricoeur, and Pareyson worked in three different languages and cultural contexts but would—each in his own way—develop the prospects of such a new path of thinking in original ways. They were contemporaries, but they did not work collaboratively even though their independent efforts were clearly congenial, motivated by shared concerns, and pointed in similar directions.

Perhaps the most basic theme uniting Pareyson with Gadamer and Ricoeur is their shared sense that truth is not a matter of correspondence or correctness, but rather one of interpretation.[5] Furthermore, they all agree that such a claim does not relativize or subjectivize truth: the struggle of understanding, which is the real goal of hermeneutic truth, is never cut loose from history, from the nuances of language, or from the logic of text and contexts. Pareyson put the point this way: "of truth, there is only ever interpretation, and there is no interpretation lest it be of truth."[6] To speak of truth as interpretation is to acknowledge both the complexity and the inexhaustibility of truth, and to think of truth as an ongoing task rather than a finished result. Pareyson again: "Truth resides in its formulation not as the object of a completed statement, but as the stimulus for an unending revelation . . . in a continual and unending discourse."[7] Thus, the truth proper to understanding is best described as the process of interpretation, of engaging again and again to make sense of what is to be understood. Interpretation always involves a repetition, a gradual peeling back of the layers of a text or the deepening of a question, and this repetition does not leave the interpreter outside of this process because understanding is never fully distinguished from the self-understanding of the interpreter (as one's understanding evolves, the task of interpretation itself changes, and this process continues to repeat itself). This repetition is what is named by the celebrated notion of the hermeneutic circle. In the end, truth, which seems to take on the character of being a verb rather than a noun, is a form of discourse. Pareyson's way of making this point is to say that "[t]ruth is not the object, but the origin of philosophical discourse, and philosophical discourse is not the enunciation, but the site of truth . . . truth is present *in* discourse."[8]

There are several consequences of these developments in hermeneutic theory. Perhaps the most far-reaching of these consequences is that once the hermeneutic sense of truth is set free from the presumption that truth needs to be modeled on the idea of truth governing the natural sciences, it becomes possible to understand how truth belongs to the work of art. To find truth in literature, painting, music, and the arts generally flies in the face of the long history of philosophy that has relegated the questions of art to that philosophical ghetto of aesthetics and has reduced art to matters of feeling and contingent pleasure—art is almost never taken as a matter of truth—at best it might be said to illustrate a truth established by conceptual reason. It is thus no surprise that Kant's *Critique of Judgment*, which is the most significant exception to this philosophical habit, is a work of considerable importance for contemporary hermeneutic philosophers. While Kant himself does not explicitly develop the kinship of art and truth, he does make the necessity of such a kinship evident so that after Kant—in Hegel, Schelling, Schopenhauer, and Nietzsche—we find the move to think the real achievement of the work of art as a work of truth. Philosophical hermeneutics will explore this kinship of art and truth so powerfully that it will prove to be one of the ways in which the very idea of truth is reconceived in this new tradition: once it is granted its elemental force, the truth of art lets the character of truth itself be better understood. In setting art free to be a site of truth, philosophy, as Pareyson puts it, lets "art truly [be] art and not aestheticism."[9] This liberation of the achievement of art to be itself recoils upon the sense of truth, pressing us forward to open ourselves up to its largest horizons.

There are, of course, other themes central to the project of philosophical hermeneutics that deserve special note. Language, especially forms of language that are not captured by the logic of the concept—poetic language and metaphor, for instance—is one of the persistent concerns of hermeneutics. Translation, which is not simply an experience of language but of history as well, is a problematic that exposes the foreign in unique ways. Tradition, and the task of grasping for the weight of history and prejudice in understanding, also binds various hermeneutic theories. These themes—language, translation, and tradition—expose that which Pareyson described as the "unsaid," and, as the "source of infinite possibilities," they remain hallmarks of the contemporary hermeneutic sensibility. But, while it can be helpful to point out how Gadamer, Ricoeur, and Pareyson stand together in forging this new philosophical tradition that bears the name of hermeneutics and finds its roots in Heidegger, it is also important not to reduce them to a collective point of view. Each is too original and too passionate about different issues for that to make sense. The chapters that follow in this volume go far to distinguish Luigi Pareyson and to highlight his unique voice and inspiring philosophical imagination.

NOTES

1. The two books with translations of Pareyson's essays are Luigi Pareyson, *Existence, Interpretation, Freedom: Selected Writings*, trans. A. Mattei, ed. P. D. Bubbio (Aurora, CO: Davies Group, 2009); and Luigi Pareyson, *Truth and Interpretation*, trans. R. Valgenti, ed. S. Benso (Albany: State University of New York Press, 2013). Both of these volumes include very helpful introductory essays that provide fine overall accounts of Pareyson's life and work.

2. See, for instance, Martin Heidegger, *Being and Time*, trans. J. Stambaugh and D. Schmidt (Albany: State University of New York Press, 2010), sections 31 and 32. For one of the earliest discussions of hermeneutics in Heidegger, see Martin Heidegger, *Ontology—The Hermeneutics of Facticity*, trans. J. van Buren (Bloomington: Indiana University Press, 2008).

3. One of the foundational texts of recent philosophical hermeneutics, Gadamer's *Truth and Method*, makes this point by beginning the formulation of hermeneutic theory by contrasting the idea of method in the natural sciences with the inappropriateness of any such method in the humanities. Gadamer makes clear that this rejection of method is not in any sense meant to signal a lack of rigor or any disregard for truth; rather, he argues that the natural scientific conceptions of truth and of method are inadequate for thinking through the questions not addressed to those that already fit the framework of scientific concerns.

4. Pareyson makes a point of nuancing this sense of the foreign by distinguishing it from "othering": "[o]thering is the concept most detrimental to an exact understanding of hermeneutics" (Pareyson, *Truth and Interpretation*, 55). In saying this and thus somewhat domesticating the sense of the strangeness of existence, Pareyson separates himself a bit from Heidegger.

5. There are many works one could refer to in order to elaborate on and defend such a claim, but the following sets of essays can serve as starting points: Luigi Pareyson, *Truth and Interpretation*; Paul Ricoeur, *The Conflict of Interpretations*, trans. D. Ihde (Evanston, IL: Northwestern University Press, 2007); Hans-Georg Gadamer, *Philosophical Hermeneutics*, trans. D. Linge (Berkeley: University of California Press, 2008).

6. Pareyson, *Truth and Interpretation*, 47.
7. Ibid., 66.
8. Ibid., 179.
9. Ibid., 174.

Introduction

Thinking the Inexhaustible

Silvia Benso and Brian Schroeder

What if the *inexhaustible*, the concept invoked by the title of this volume, were the only mode of self-revelation of truth—beyond all conceptions that reduce truth and being to either truth without evidence (as in subjectivism, relativism, perspectivism, and ideologies) or evidence without truth (as in objectivism, positivism, dogmatism, and scientism), but also beyond all ontologies of presence, meontologies, ontologies of the ineffable, the obscure, and the mystery that preclude human beings from any possibility of a meaningful access to the truth? The question of the inexhaustibility of truth, and its relation to being and interpretation, is the challenge posed by the philosophy of the prominent Italian thinker Luigi Pareyson (1918–1991). "That which is not possessed as *inexhaustible*," writes Pareyson, "and that is explicated in a definitive enunciation is not truth; and that which, in order to possess truth, thinks that it must eliminate every unsaid, completing the discourse with a perfect and complete totality, is not interpretation. As a sign of its presence, truth points out precisely the unending and always ulterior nature of discourse; the enunciation of truth in a complete exposition would be the very sign of the inability to grasp it. *Only as inexhaustible does truth give itself to its formulations*."[1] Within the perspective of the inexhaustibility of truth, art, religion, history, philosophy, and various other sociocultural manifestations including politics become modes of such formulations, which presuppose freedom—both human and divine—as that which initiates and gives form to all possible interpretations.

This volume comprises a collection of essays devoted to Pareyson's hermeneutic philosophy. In Europe and South America, the figure of this remarkable Italian thinker is often aligned with the more renowned German philosopher Hans-Georg Gadamer and the equally famous French thinker Paul Ricoeur; as Dennis J. Schmidt notes in his foreword to the present volume, though, Pareyson's philosophical position has remained largely unknown to the Anglophone readership. This collection aims to remedy such neglect and oversight through a critical engagement and, at times, an overview of the most salient aspects of Pareyson's philosophical proposal.

Art, the interpretation of truth, and the theory of being as ontology of both inexhaustibility and freedom constitute the main themes of Pareyson's distinctive form of philosophical hermeneutics. This volume explores these (and other) themes in the complexity of their interpretation as provided by Pareyson on the basis of another fundamental concept operative in his philosophy, namely, that of personhood understood in the radically existentialist sense of the human being. In the end, Pareyson's philosophy proves to be a philosophy of the inexhaustibility of truth, being, and the human being alike. While establishing itself as such a mode of thinking, Pareyson's philosophy of inexhaustibility engages in a conversation with major figures in Western intellectual history—from Croce to Valéry, Dostoevsky, and Berdyaev; from Kant to Fichte, Hegel, and German Romanticism; and from Pascal to Schelling, Kierkegaard, Marcel, Jaspers, and Heidegger.

Of the twelve essays collected here, six (by the well-known Italian thinkers Paolo D'Angelo, Umberto Eco, Massimo Cacciari, Federico Vercellone, Gianni Vattimo, and Sergio Givone) were initially presented as invited lectures at a conference commemorating the twentieth anniversary of Pareyson's death. They appear here for the first time in their English translation.[2] The essay by Silvia Benso is a slightly revised version of a previously published essay under the same title.[3] The other five essays have been written specifically for this volume. The twelve contributions have been organized to follow the unfolding of the various stages of Pareyson's position. Altogether they provide a superb, extensive overview of the philosophy of a thinker whose activity spans well over half a century and has been highly influential for world-renowned philosophers such as Umberto Eco, Mario Perniola, and Gianni Vattimo, among others.

The volume opens with Benso's essay, "Luigi Pareyson: A Master in Italian Hermeneutics," which serves as a general introduction to the work of Luigi Pareyson and to which, to avoid unnecessary repetition here, the reader should refer for a general overview of Pareyson's philosophy.

Benso retraces the biographical and theoretical unfolding of Pareyson's lines of thought from existentialism to hermeneutics to ontology of freedom and exposes the lived, incarnated, deep hermeneutic character of his philosophical stance. Demonstrating how his hermeneutic attitude affects both his biography and his theory, Benso situates Pareyson's status as an original thinker in Italian hermeneutics, one whose work stands in clear distinction to that of more familiar hermeneuticians such as Gadamer and Ricoeur.

Examining Pareyson's claims about the person, a concept that appears most prominently in Pareyson's initially existentialist stage but that runs continuously throughout his thinking, Antonio Calcagno argues in "When Transcendence Is Finite: Pareyson, the Person, and the Limits of Being" that the being revealed by the relations that constitute personhood cannot possibly manifest the broad, unified sense of being with which human beings are in solidarity, as Pareyson maintains. Rather, what we find, maintains Calcagno, is a more limited, finite form of being constituted by the collective dwelling of persons with one another, other nonhuman living beings, and the world. Determinations of the being of the person need not necessarily be absolutized or totalized, thereby resulting in a finite and reductive understanding of human persons. Determinations can instead be understood as Kantian limits that ultimately generate possibilities of further determinations, which can lead to greater self-understanding and collective well-being. Pareyson correctly understands determination and situatedness as important for the being of persons, but the open-ended nature of determination he advocates, which must be understood as the possibility of nondetermination or transcendence, runs the risk of undermining his view of the singularity of the person. Specific determinations that condition and shape singularity must not be read therefore simply as limiting or conditioning, but as creating possibilities for initiative (*iniziativa*) and being without recourse to infinite transcendence. Instead of viewing personal determinations as pointing to transcendence, Calcagno contends that we need to see them as operating within a situation, intensely complexifying and differentiating it and ultimately producing layers of meaningful determination.

Paolo D'Angelo's contribution, "Pareyson's Role in Twentieth-Century Italian Aesthetics," follows Pareyson's theoretical move from personhood to art by focusing on the fundamental role that his aesthetics played in twentieth-century Italian philosophy. Pareyson's main work in this field, *Estetica. Teoria della Formatività* [*Aesthetics: Theory of Formativity*], represents the first systematic aesthetic theory written in Italy from a non-Crocean standpoint and marks a notable turning point in twentieth-century Italian philosophy, which had been deeply influenced in the first fifty years by Croce's new idealism and historicism. The first part of D'Angelo's essay gives an account of the main differences between Pareyson's and Croce's views on aesthetics, emphasizing the different solutions concerning the nature of aesthetic activity and the different views concerning the role of emotions in art, the function of interpretation, and the relation between philosophical aesthetics and poetics. The second part of D'Angelo's essay reconstructs the influence of Pareyson's aesthetics on Italian philosophy in the second half of the twentieth century and discusses the reasons why, despite the great international success of hermeneutics, the importance of Pareyson's aesthetics (an important constituent of his interpretation theory) is not entirely acknowledged, even if several significant Italian philosophers such as Vattimo and Eco receive substantial inspiration from it.

Aesthetic themes are taken up also by Umberto Eco in his posthumous contribution, "Pareyson vs. Croce: The Novelties of Pareyson's 1954 *Estetica*." Eco describes the main innovations of Pareyson's aesthetics in comparison with Croce's theory of art. Eco emphasizes the separation that Croce establishes between the moment of intuition-expression and the moment of technical-material manifestation as well as the attention Pareyson pays to the concrete experiences of the artist and the importance of matter and pointers implied in his aesthetic formativity. This new concept of formativity introduced by Pareyson considers the nexus (ingrained in all artworks) between *forming* form and *formed* form in light of the notions of process and attempt. Whereas Croce views execution as the faithful realization of a work or the expression of the executor's personality, Eco points out that for Pareyson an essential dialectics is at work between faithfulness to the work and freedom of interpretation. Finally, with regard to Croce's question of "structure," Eco stresses that not only does Pareyson consider structure as an essential moment of the formative project, but he also pays close attention to the associated fillers or wedges [*zeppa*], regarding them as fundamental joints that enable each part to connect with the others. Thinking of wedges not only as failed attempts, but also as something that the interpretation sets aside as a latent stimulus for further interpretations, Eco concludes by drawing a connection, in light of the wedge, between Pareyson's aesthetics and his ontology of freedom with its related theme of a God who overcomes the negative but, at the same time, preserves it within himself as a trace.

In his "On Pareyson's Interpretation of Kant's Third Critique," Massimo Cacciari points to the disclosure, which Pareyson realizes, of the theoretical and systematic pregnancy and significance of Kant's *Critique of Judgment* for critical philosophy as a whole. Such relevance appears quite evidently on the basis of at least two basic themes: First, on the basis of the teleological principle, on which the aesthetic judgment is based (this principle is in fact operative also as a general condition of all intellectual judgments); and second, on the basis of the concept of the imagination, which retains a not merely aesthetic value. Imagination as considered from the point of view of the third *Critique* must be read and understood in unity with the imagination that is operative in the construction of schemas of transcendental schematism, which may be said to represent the main problem of the first *Critique*. It is the same faculty that in the *Critique of Pure Reason* images (in the sense of putting-into-images) the concepts and in the *Critique of Judgment* images the ideas of reason. These two dimensions of the faculty of imagination cannot be separated. This is precisely what allows one to understand the great level of immanence that the "a-logical" (that is, *pathos*, feeling or sentiment) has in the constitution of the faculty of judgment as a whole.

The move from art to hermeneutics in the evolution of Pareyson's philosophy is approached by Federico Vercellone in his essay "Pareyson's Aesthetics as Hermeneutics of Art." Pareyson's long engagement with aesthetics mainly concerns the first phase of his work even if he never abandons art as the object of his theoretical reflections. If the trajectory of Pareyson's thought within aesthetics were to be traced, it could be described, albeit with a certain degree of uncertainty, as the move from a hermeneutics of art to a hermeneutics of myth. In his *Estetica*, Pareyson proposes a conception that stands outside the classic structure of the philosophy of art and establishes instead a close connection between aesthetics and hermeneutics. Here Pareyson develops a dynamic idea of form that allows him to articulate a critical comparison with Croce. By rejecting Croce's idea of immediate identity, that is, a relation between intuition and expression that is not process based, Pareyson makes the move that allows him to closely approach contemporary art. On the basis of this approach, Pareyson is also able to advance the concept of the indeterminateness of form, which anticipates the idea of "open work" later developed by Eco.

Robert T. Valgenti explores the social and political possibilities of Pareyson's aesthetic concepts by offering an examination of the concept of "kindredness" [*congenialità*] in Pareyson's work in his essay "The Unfamiliarity of Kindredness: Toward a Hermeneutics of Community." Valgenti reflects on the possibilities for this concept to work as the basis for a hermeneutics of community, a community that understands its formation and identity as an act of interpretation. Valgenti begins by tracing the development of community starting with the concept of "exemplarity" in Pareyson's earliest works on aesthetics and proceeding to the development of his aesthetics of formativity as the model for interpretative human activity. In the course of this development, it becomes clear that the shared element in human production—as exemplified in the work of art—is the very ability to undertake an activity that forms its own rules of development and value. Through an analysis of this development and of the idea of "kindredness" that finally emerges in *Truth and Interpretation*, Valgenti argues that the basis for community can be found in the tension between the subjectivity of individual taste and the consensual recognition of the kindred element that brings together human production and interpretation.

Pareyson's refusal to take up the standard epistemic trope for truth, namely, as the goal or aim of inquiry, is the starting point of Lauren Swayne Barthold's "Truth as the Origin (Rather Than Goal) of Inquiry." Accordingly, if truth is not our goal, then it does not make sense to attempt to articulate a method or criteria that secure it, as is the aim of traditional analytic approaches to truth. Pareyson insists rather that truth is fundamentally our starting point, our origin. His general hermeneutic commitment can be seen in the way he defines interpretation as the human expression, indeed revelation, of our fundamental relation with being and truth. Yet Barthold argues that this general hermeneutic approach, which defines truth in terms of human "being" rather than human "doings" (that is, formulating beliefs and propositions), goes further than either Heidegger's or Gadamer's positions insofar as Pareyson defends the human being's origin in truth as the condition for freedom. Pareyson's explication of truth is unique within the hermeneutic tradition because of its ability to demonstrate how the instrumentalization of human reason as a means to achieve truth-as-end leads to domination and oppression. If, as Pareyson insists, our only interest is to reduce truth to its criterion for measuring human doings, then we miss something more fundamental about truth and human existence, namely, its ability to promote human freedom. To unpack and demonstrate the significance of Pareyson's change of metaphor regarding truth and its connection to freedom that distinguishes him from other hermeneutic thinkers, Barthold focuses on Pareyson's comments in *Truth and Interpretation* regarding truth's relation to interpretation, being, and ideology.

According to Paolo Diego Bubbio, Pareyson's work features a deep understanding of the issues and problems of Hegel's philosophy as well as a critical proximity with Heidegger's existential and hermeneutic project. In his essay "Pareyson's Conception of the Self Between Hegel and Heidegger," Bubbio argues that one of the reasons for Pareyson's interest in these philosophical traditions, sometimes hidden and yet very prominent in his work, is the centrality of the notion of the "I." Cartesian philosophy led to a conception of the "I" marked with subjectivism. Bobbio contends that Pareyson captures the attempts made by Hegel to overcome a *subjectivist* account of the self. In the first section, Bubbio considers Pareyson's interpretation of Hegel, paying close attention to the notion of the self. In the second section, he focuses on Pareyson's interpretation of Heidegger and shows that Pareyson considers Heidegger as being similarly concerned with the subjectivism of the "I," but also critical of the "solitary self" emerging from the German philosopher's analysis of *Dasein*. Bubbio concludes with the claim that Pareyson develops a mode of philosophizing about the "I" that goes beyond the traditional notion of subjectivity, avoids the regression of Heidegger's analysis of *Dasein* to a solitary self, and eventually contributes to a richer understanding of the self.

Gianni Vattimo highlights the deep continuity between Pareyson's "aesthetics of formativity" and the later religious developments of his philosophy in his contribution, "From Aesthetics to Ontology of Freedom." According to Vattimo, from the very start Pareyson's aesthetics involves a theory of interpretation in which the expression of the artist's personal creativity and the presence of a transcendent "legality" coincide completely. Such identification makes understandable the nonarbitrariness of both creation and critical approach to the work. It is on this basis, Vattimo contends, that Pareyson later develops his "ontology of freedom."

The theme of the ontology of freedom, which constitutes one of the arrival points of Pareyson's intellectual trajectory, is further explored by Martin G. Weiss in "Evil in God: Pareyson's Ontology of Freedom." According to Weiss, in addition to being a hermeneutic thinker, Pareyson is also the author of an intriguing modern theodicy. The first part of Weiss' essay is focused on this aspect. Pareyson refutes the classical Christian definition of evil as mere lack of being or goodness and tries to combine the Manichean insight into the violent reality of evil and suffering with the Christian (but still Aristotelian) doctrine that there can be only one first principle or cause of reality, namely, God. If God, however, is the first principle and evil is real, then God must be considered the principle of evil. Following Schelling, Pareyson emphasizes that the concepts of both good and evil are intrinsically connected to the concept of freedom because when we speak of evil, we in fact mean chosen evil (that is, bad in the presence of a good alternative), and when we speak of good, we actually mean a chosen good (that is, good in the presence of a bad alternative). Neither necessity nor contingency but rather freedom is associated with good and bad. God is therefore good not because this is God's necessary nature, as traditional onto-theology claims, but because God chose, in an absolute past that was never present, to be good (that is, to exist) by rejecting the possibility of being bad (that is, not to exist). Thus evil is truly in God, although only as mere possibility. This possibility was however realized by the human being, as Pareyson states in line with the Christian tradition. The second part of Weiss' essay attends to the question of how this Christian narration, according to Pareyson's peculiar *thelogia crucis*, may assist one to understand (and perhaps even to accept) real evil, and therefore overcome what Pareyson terms "modern consolatory atheism."

The volume concludes with Sergio Givone's "Philosophy and Novel in the Later Pareyson," which offers an analysis of the themes that interest Pareyson in his later years, namely, the narrative character of truth as disclosed in myths and narrations. Pareyson leaves his readers with important suggestions for a philosophical theory of the novel and of the narrative essence of truth that are not present in his earlier existentialist writings or in his *Estetica*, but rather in his later works *Dostoevskij: Filosofia, romanzo ed esperienza religiosa* [*Dostoevsky: Philosophy, Fiction, and Religious Experience*] and *Ontologia della libertà* [*Ontology of Freedom*]. According to Pareyson, interpretation (and philosophy is for him essentially interpretation) has no other object than truth. Emerging through the interpretation of tales and stories because reality is not a chain of facts, truth is an eventful horizon where freedom is more significant than necessity. When searching for truth—not truth in itself, but truth for us, truth that reveals to us a possible meaning of the human life and world—we find it in that original form of revelation that is the myth. Novels are nothing else than myths, Pareyson claims; secularized myths, we could add, for modern times. Moving from this conviction, Pareyson engages Dostoevsky's novels and discloses in them not only a variety of philosophical problems, but also a real chance for a new philosophy of freedom and the sense of being.

"Being inexhaustible," writes Pareyson in *Truth and Interpretation*, "truth resides in words without being identified with them, but always holding itself in reserve. . . . It is a presence that does not identify itself with explication and thus opens the possibility of an ulterior and always new discourse. . . . Inexhaustibility is that thanks to which, instead of presenting itself under the false appearance of concealment, absence, or obscurity, ulteriority shows its true origin, that is, its richness, fullness, and excess, through its inexhaustibility: not nothingness, but Being;

not *steresis* [lack], but *hyperoche* [pre-eminence]; not *Abgrund* [abyss], but *Ungrund* [ungrounded ground]; not the *mystikos gnophos tes agnosias* [mystical darkness of the lack of knowledge], but the *anexichniaston ploutos* [unsearchable richness]; not the mysticism of the ineffable, but the ontology of the inexhaustible."[4] We editors think that the inexhaustibility of truth shines forth in the works of Luigi Pareyson, and that the scholarly contributions contained in this volume respond to and continue the work of such inexhaustible truth. If the reader takes up some of the suggestions contained in Pareyson's philosophy and highlighted in such contributions, then the inexhaustibility of truth will have made a step forward—not toward its own dissolution but toward dialogical enrichment. Philosophy, says Pareyson, "creates dialogue because, in the very act in which it endlessly multiplies the personal interpretations of truth, it unites all of them in the common awareness of their possessing truth without exhausting it but rather nourishing themselves on it continually."[5] The specific dialogue that philosophy forms and embraces is precisely what this volume wishes to foster by reflecting on the thought of Luigi Pareyson.

NOTES

1. Luigi Pareyson, *Truth and Interpretation*, trans. Robert Valgenti (Albany: State University of New York Press, 2013), 67, emphasis added.

2. The 2011 conference *Luigi Pareyson e l'estetica* [*Luigi Pareyson and Aesthetics*] was organized in Turin by the Centro di Studi Filosofico-Religiosi Luigi Pareyson. These lectures were published in *Annuario Filosofico* 27 (2011). *Annuario Filosofico* is the yearly journal published by Mursia, founded by Pareyson in 1985 with a group of scholars close to his philosophical position, and is currently edited by Claudio Ciancio. We wish to thank Mursia for the permission to publish these essays in this volume.

3. In *Philosophy Today* 49, no. 4 (Winter 2005): 381–90; republished here by kind permission.

4. Pareyson, *Truth and Interpretation*, 19–24.

5. Ibid., 182.

I

Luigi Pareyson

A Master in Italian Hermeneutics

Silvia Benso

"Philosophical thinking is hermeneutic in a full sense because it is at the same time interpretation of experience and interpretation of truth, and it cannot be the one without the other: it is ontological and revelatory as well as historical and personal, together, indissolubly."

—Luigi Pareyson, "Pensiero ermeneutico e pensiero tragico"[1]

RADICAL HERMENEUTICS

The vicissitudes of hermeneutics, broadly understood as philosophy of interpretation, are long and complex. Nowadays, "hermeneutics" has become mostly synonymous with the positions of twentieth-century thinkers such as Martin Heidegger, Hans-Georg Gadamer, and Paul Ricoeur.

Yet this identification is limiting in many ways. First, hermeneutics is not a historical trend that can be restricted to the twentieth century only, as, for example, Friedrich Schleiermacher's interest in interpretation attests. Second, "hermeneutics" is not a specific philosophical label under which to classify this or that philosopher, this or that movement, in an exclusive manner. Rather, and especially in the twentieth century, "hermeneutics" names a theme—namely, interpretation, with its problems and difficulties—that is assumed as the privileged modality of human beings' being in their relation to existence, truth, and the world. Such a human way of being or attitude toward being that is grounded on interpretation can be approached through various registers of understanding; this yields to hermeneutic variations in relation to the broader, but also more idiosyncratic, context within which the theme of interpretation is inserted. Such variations span well beyond the positions of Heidegger, Gadamer, or Ricoeur. Within the Italian scene, one can mention Enrico Castelli's, Alberto Caracciolo's, and Italo Mancini's hermeneutics, where hermeneutics intersects with philosophy of religion; Carlo Sini's hermeneutics, where hermeneutics and semiotics (mainly Peirce) are interwoven; Umberto Eco's hermeneutics, where it is hermeneutics and semiology that interact; Gianni Vattimo's hermeneutics, where hermeneutics unfolds in conversation with metaphysics or foundational thinking; and the hermeneutics of a thinker whose thought has been more appreciated abroad than in Italy, namely, Emilio Betti, where the notion of interpretation develops in relation to the concept of rights or objectivity.

For Luigi Pareyson, the twentieth-century Italian thinker to whom this book is devoted, hermeneutics is not simply a theme within a broader context of approach and interests. For him, hermeneutics is the radical element, the deeply rooted matrix that nourishes and sustains his entire philosophical path. For him, thinking itself is interpretation through and through, to its very *radices*, its roots—hence, the radicality of hermeneutics. As he says, philosophy is "hermeneutic in a full sense" because existence itself is hermeneutic.

Who is Luigi Pareyson? In a way, he is one of the venerable "forerunners" of contemporary Italian philosophy. His legacy is demonstrated by the impressive list of his successful students, now well-established professors in the Italian academia and renowned scholars within the international philosophical picture.[2] The stature and relevance of his philosophical figure is readily acknowledged through essays, quotations, and references even by philosophers who were not formed at his school or within the "Turin school" within which he was active after World War II with other remarkable thinkers of various philosophical orientations (most notably Augusto Guzzo, Nicola Abbagnano, Norberto Bobbio, Pietro Chiodi, and Augusto Del Noce). The number of dissertations written on him in philosophy departments of very different lineages all over Italy counts as additional evidence of his ongoing appeal, recognition, and reputation.[3]

Oddly enough, despite various translations of his works in French, German, Portuguese, and especially Spanish, Pareyson's name and thought are largely unknown to the Anglophone philosophical audience.[4] This regrettable neglect is only partially mitigated by the somewhat recent publication of two volumes translating (some of) Pareyson's work. Yet, as another prominent contemporary Italian philosopher, Gianni Vattimo, stated in a 2001 article in the Italian daily newspaper *La Stampa* ten years after the death of his teacher, Pareyson's thought retains an "anticipatory, if not definitely prophetic relevance"[5] for philosophy. It is precisely this prophetic character, which may need to be explored further, that renders Pareyson's philosophy still timely—for us, today, in the world.

A PHILOSOPHICAL BIO/BIBLIOGRAPHY

Pareyson's philosophical career officially starts the year in which possibly the greatest catastrophe in twentieth-century history also begins—1939. In that year, Pareyson graduates at twenty-one years of age from the Università di Torino under the guidance of Augusto Guzzo with a dissertation (published in 1940) on Karl Jaspers, with whom he had studied in Heidelberg in 1936 and 1937.[6] Already two years before that publication, that is, in 1938, the first of Pareyson's publications had appeared in the prestigious *Giornale critico della filosofia italiana* (directed by the famous Italian philosopher Giovanni Gentile). The title of the essay was "Note sulla filosofia dell'esistenza [Notes on the Philosophy of Existence]." The intellectual background of Pareyson's philosophy is in fact existentialism. Pareyson's philosophical existentialism is not purely a theoretical position. It is rather nourished by the concrete experience of the suffering and devastation of the war, which Pareyson endures while teaching at the humanities-based high school, the Liceo Classico, in Cuneo, a major town southwest of Turin. There Pareyson forms some of the leaders of the Italian resistance brigades (*Giustizia e Libertà*) and becomes himself part of the antifascist movement, *Partito d'Azione*, until he is arrested for a few days and suspended from teaching in 1944. From 1946 until 1988, the year of his retirement, Pareyson teaches at the Università di Torino, first aesthetics (1945–1964), then theoretical and moral philosophy (1964–1983). He dies in 1991, after having been appointed member of the prestigious Italian national academy, the *Accademia Nazionale dei Lincei*.

Existentialism, which Pareyson has the merit of introducing into Italy, is the background of Pareyson's initial speculation as revealed by his first works of the 1950s—in addition to those mentioned above, one should cite *Studi sull'esistenzialismo* [Studies on Existentialism] (1943, 1950) and the collection of essays *Esistenza e persona* [Existence and Person]

(1950).[7] Pareyson engages existentialism both in its German variations (Jaspers, Barth, Heidegger, Kierkegaard) as well as its French interpretations (especially Marcel and Lavelle but also Maritain and, later, Pascal, although the latter is not canonically an existentialist). From the French existentialists, Pareyson borrows especially the personalistic stance, which was also congenial to his teachers Augusto Guzzo and Armando Carlini.

In parallel to the existentialist production, and dating back to the same years, Pareyson endeavors to reread the history of German Romanticism and classical idealism in manners that release their representatives (most notably Fichte and later Schelling, but also Schiller and Novalis) from subordination to Hegel. Such a subservient position is taken for granted in the neo-idealistic tradition that in Italy finds major (albeit opposed) representatives in Croce and Gentile on one side and Gramsci on the other. Still in the 1950s, Pareyson publishes two major essays, *L'estetica dell'idealismo tedesco* [*Aesthetics of German Idealism*] (1950) and *Fichte: Il sistema della libertà* [*Fichte: The System of Freedom*] (1950). The essays on German idealism also attest to Pareyson's increasing interest in aesthetic themes.

As is likewise the case for some of his previous production, Pareyson's concern with aesthetics is partly tied to his hermeneutic endeavor to renovate the historical categories through which to read pre-Hegelian philosophy. The 1968 volume *L'estetica di Kant* [*Kant's Aesthetics*] is a clear demonstration of this. Earlier than this work on Kant, though, specifically in 1954, Pareyson publishes his fundamental aesthetic work *Estetica: Teoria della formatività* [*Aesthetics: Theory of Formativity*]. In it, Pareyson deeply challenges Croce's then-dominating aesthetic theory of expression through the novel notion of "formativity." According to the *Estetica*, "the artist's doing is a doing that, while it does, also invents what is to be done, and the way of doing it." In other terms, in the process of its creation, the work of art also determines the language of its own interpretation. Stated more radically, all artistic doing is an interpretative act. Formativity is, for Pareyson, indeed the main and primary property of all artistic doing. Additionally though, for Pareyson, formativity also characterizes all human activities including knowledge, which always retains an interpretative character. The path to a conception of art (and consequently of myths and religion as creative products) as place of interpretation of truth, and thus as hermeneutic site, is also cleared and developed by Pareyson in later works such as *Teoria dell'arte* [*Theory of Art*] (1965), *I problemi dell'estetica* [*Problems of Aesthetics*] (1966), *Conversazioni di estetica* [*Conversations on Aesthetics*] (1966), and *L'esperienza artistica* [*The Aesthetic Experience*] (1974).

In 1971, independently from and yet somewhat in parallel with Ricoeur's and Gadamer's[8] main works, Pareyson returns explicitly to the theme of interpretation and its necessary connection with ontology and truth in his highly original and innovative book *Verità e interpretazione* [*Truth and Interpretation*]. This is undoubtedly the most important Italian essay in hermeneutics. Truth is here understood as something not ineffable (as in Heidegger, who thus walks down the "dead end" of an ontology of the ineffable or "negative ontology") but rather inexhaustible (*inesauribile*). Quoting Pareyson's most famous claim, made against all objectivistic and thereby scientific notions of truth, "of truth there can only be interpretations; and all interpretations can only be of truth."[9] Because of its inexhaustibility, truth constantly spurs new interpretations, that is, new relations to itself.

As Pareyson argues, any interpretation is, ultimately, a matter of a historical and personal decision in favor of either faithfulness to truth and being or betrayal of both. Thus, all interpretations involve a risk. As a consequence, the theme of interpretation develops, in Pareyson's most recent years and up to the time of his death, in the direction of the ontology of freedom. The move to the ontology of freedom occurs through the publication of various works: in 1975, a volume on *Schelling*; in 1989, the volume *Filosofia della libertà* [*Philosophy of Freedom*]; and, in the philosophical journal he had directed since 1985 (*Annuario filosofico*), a series of essays later collected in the volume *Ontologia della libertà* [*Ontology of Freedom*], which was edited posthumously by some of Pareyson's students (1995).

The ontology of freedom locates the possibility for freedom within the human being. However, through the reading of Schelling and Dostoevsky (reading that produces the volume *Dostoevskij*, published postmortem in 1993), the ontology of freedom also situates freedom, as both beginning and choice, in God. The God that is called into the picture here is not the God of metaphysics but rather the biblical God, the God of Christianity, God who is abandoned by God and dies on the cross, God against God, a tragic God who does not explain but rather assumes upon himself death, doubt, anguish, and atheism. For Pareyson, the core of reality is freedom and ambiguity, suffering, pain, and evil, as suggested by the title of the latest, posthumously published volume, the 1998 *Essere libertà ambiguità* [*Being Freedom Ambiguity*]. This ultimately tragic core is also disclosed through a philosophical hermeneutics of the Christian religious experience. Pareyson dies in 1991 while still working on the question of eschatology, which thus remains as an uncompleted theme in his thought.

HERMENEUTIC COILS

From existentialism to hermeneutics to ontology (of freedom): this is, in Pareyson's own description,[10] the three-step path along which his philosophical itinerary unfolds. In Pareyson's thought the unfolding is neither, allegedly à la Heidegger, a matter of a turn (or two turns) nor, à la Hegel, a question of progression achieved through the sublimation of previous positions. Rather, the unfolding is itself a hermeneutic matter; that is, it is the return upon itself of a thinking that, by making interpretation the core of the speculative project, constantly revisits itself—not to deny or bring new truth to the old truth of previous positions, but to both enlighten and be enlightened anew by them. In the 1988 Naples lectures "In cammino verso la libertà [On the Way to Freedom]," contained in *Ontologia della libertà*, Pareyson refers to the last stage of his own itinerary, that of the philosophy of freedom, as a moment of faithfulness and loyalty "to Schelling's genuine spirit and deep program." The Schellingian program has, however, been modified thanks to the "experience of nihilism and existentialism" that was Pareyson's starting point.[11] That is to say, Pareyson's initial existentialism is still there "on his way to freedom" (one should note the Heideggerian polemic flavor of this title), and yet, in the later reflections, it is no longer there in its originary form because of Pareyson's own having passed through Schelling; and for Pareyson, Schelling is never simply the historical Schelling precisely because of Pareyson's own initial existentialism. In other words, the later Pareyson refers back to the earlier Pareyson to modify as well as be modified by it.

Let us briefly follow the unfolding of Pareyson's theoretical lines of thought to appreciate the lived, incarnated, deeply hermeneutic character of his philosophical position—hermeneutic character, both biographical and theoretical, that truly elevates Pareyson to being a "master" in Italian hermeneutics.

Pareyson's initial existentialism, self-understood as a prosecution of Kierkegaardian instances as the only viable alternative to Hegel, unfolds in the direction of an "ontological personalism"[12] that paradoxically (that is, nondialectically) and historically (that is, within time) keeps together particular and universal, immanence and transcendence, self-relation and hetero-relation. On the one hand, for Pareyson, the human being is self-relation, free and autonomous being, power of self-creation and foundation. This does not mean that the human being is simply an individual, an a priori transcendental or existential subject, or a function of its society. More properly and fundamentally, the human being is historicity, situatedness, this-concrete-existing-human-being *hic et nunc*—in a word, a person (*persona*).[13] On the other hand, and at the same time, for Pareyson, the human being is also opening toward being, in relation to which it understands itself; it is not only creation but also revelation of being, hetero-relation, transcendence, that is, relation with the other (and, in this sense, possible site of religious experience). In other words, for Pareyson, existentialism—existence being the only access to reality—can only be personalism, but personalism can only be ontological, that is, rooted in being; lest each existence closes itself upon itself and its intimacy, lest it dissolve into the ephemerality of its own position and the nihilism of the will to power.[14] "Between human being and being there is an originary solidarity, an initial complicity, which manifests itself on the one hand in the constitutive ontologicity of human beings, on the other in the inseparability of existence and transcendence," Pareyson writes.[15]

Pareyson's initial existentialism is thus oriented, already in *Esistenza e persona*, in the ontological direction. More specifically, it is an ontology of the inexhaustible (*ontologia dell'inesauribile*) in which the hermeneutic component is primary. "The originary ontological relation is in and by itself hermeneutic," Pareyson writes.[16] Pareyson in fact understands the person in its relation to being as a specific interpretation of truth, so that there is an originary relation in place between person and truth. "To say that the human being *is* relation with being is as if to say that the human being is interpretation of truth, that each particular human being is *an* interpretation of truth," Pareyson claims.[17] The relation is ontological because the person is a perspective on truth; it is personal because the only way to access the truth is one's own personal situatedness. Yet, as Pareyson emphasizes in *Truth and Interpretation*, interpretation is "the never definite possession of an infinite";[18] therefore, in any interpretation, the truth is present in its whole and yet in its inexhaustibility that thus calls for even further quests for truth, or for new interpretations. What remains one, inexhaustible, supratemporal is truth, whereas philosophy or metaphysics, as hermeneutic knowledge of the truth, is constitutively "multiple and temporal, plural and historical, or, to say it better, always particular and personal."[19] In this way, Pareyson is able to avoid both dogmatism and relativism while achieving an ontological foundation for the need for dialogue and pluralism—an important asset for our current philosophical time marked by the exigencies of multiculturalism and globalization.

The ontology of freedom, at which Pareyson's later thought arrives, is already foreshadowed in this understanding of the inextricable *nexus* binding together person, being, and truth. Each interpretation is, in fact, a risk and the result of a free choice—in favor of or against being and truth. In this sense, interpretation is one and the same as freedom. There are entire epochs, Pareyson remarks, "that remain without truth."[20] This is the case both because "not the whole of time is revelatory, since being forsakes those who betray it,"[21] but also because of human beings' betrayal of truth in its inexhaustibility (as it happens in dogmatism, for example). Already in *Truth and Interpretation*, we read that the heart of the ontological relation to truth is "theory and practice at the same time, in the sense that . . . theoretically it is revelation of truth and practically it is decision for being, and it is not one thing without the other, since the revelation of truth, as personal interpretation of it, is an originary act of freedom, and there is no act of freedom more originary than the decision for being itself."[22]

The possibility of human freedom, in turn, that is, the possibility for the occurrence of evil, which our century witnesses and which, according to Pareyson, neither atheism nor nihilism can confront in its seriousness, is rooted in a more fundamental freedom located at the heart of reality—the freedom of God, who is not goodness (as in metaphysical discourse) but chosen goodness.[23] "Being and the good are not primary: primary are being that has been willed and the good that has been chosen," Pareyson claims.[24] That is, primary is freedom, even in God.

God chooses the good of truth and being; evil remains though as "a shadow," an obscure, opaque trace in God's own being, Pareyson claims. Evil appears as a challenge, a temptation, a provocation that the human being actualizes and concretizes, and that God himself accepts by subjecting himself to it in the figure of Christ. Here, in the hermeneutics of Christian thought[25] where, in the figure of Christ, God takes evil and suffering upon himself without explaining or justifying them, Pareyson's philosophy encounters tragic thought. The encounter occurs primarily through a sustained and inspired reading of Dostoevsky.

According to tragic thought, reality is, at its core, ambivalence, ambiguity, contradiction, possibility of both goodness and evil. Moreover, identifying freedom with the essence of reality means not only asserting ambiguity and conflict, but also, in Pareyson's words, "supposing a ground that always denies itself as ground, and insisting on the inseparability of positivity and negation."[26] Thus, "hermeneutic thought, insofar as it refers to the ontology of freedom, is strictly connected to tragic thought."[27] Yet tragic thought is itself a form of hermeneutics capable of giving an account of "two principles . . . First of all, that evil is not privation of being, lack of reality, but rather reality, positive reality in its negativity. . . . Secondly, there is an indissoluble knot between evil and suffering. . . . Evil and suffering are at the core of the universe, and the heart of reality is tragic and suffering."[28]

As in Pareyson's existentialist beginnings, which reappear here but enriched with novel reverberations, the Kierkegaardian tension between opposite categories persists in the later manifestations of Pareyson's thought. Earlier, there was the tension within the person, the opposition between particular and universal, between self-relation and hetero-relation that existence nevertheless keeps together. Later, there is the conflict between good and evil, positivity and negativity—a radicalized conflict, as it is situated at the center of reality. One position explains and finds its deeper meaning and truth in the other and vice versa. This is the supreme enactment and sanctioning of hermeneutics in Pareyson's own thought.

That Pareyson's philosophy is hermeneutic not only as for its themes but also and primarily in its very unfolding is suggested by Pareyson himself (and here, against Hegel, there is both a subscription to—philosophy is practice—and a strike at—philosophy is not simply practice—the Feuerbachian/Marxian emphasis on practice in opposition to theory). In an interview with the Italian theologian Sergio Quinzio, while reflecting on the arrival point of his own speculation, namely, the hermeneutics of the Christian myth as a philosophical site of the ontology of freedom, Pareyson claims that such an arrival point in his philosophy "is not a break (*cesura*) but rather a return, even, a never interrupted continuity. My first studies had to do with a religious problematic: the philosophy of existence, Kierkegaard, Karl Barth."[29] And elsewhere, in a self-interpretation of his philosophical path, Pareyson says that "in a living development of thinking, it is not the initial stage that contains the meaning of subsequent stages; rather, the reversal occurs: explaining the afterward with the beforehand is too reductivistic whereas considering the beforehand in the light of the afterwards is much more enlightening and revealing."[30] Taken together, the two claims reveal something essential with respect to Pareyson's relation to truth and being both ontologically/ hermeneutically (that is, in terms of his philosophical understanding of the relation between philosophy and truth/being in general) and ontically/ existentially, as it were (that is, more specifically in terms of Pareyson's own philosophical biography or historiography).

Pareyson's philosophy definitely stands against perspectivism and its most recent development, deconstructionism. In such positions, truth (and being as truth's ontological counterpart) is abandoned to a series of discrete stances that are to be read side by side (as breaks, *cesure*) and/or is consigned to deferrals that ultimately dissolve the very possibility of truth and being but also the possibility of accounting for the radicalness and scandal of evil. Where there is no God, everything is in fact allowed, and nothing is any longer a scandal, according to Pareyson. Pareyson's philosophy also stands against historicism and scientism (or technicism), which explain the afterwards with the beforehand (or, in teleology, vice versa) in a linear development that reads truth and being as a process of causal connections and explanations that progressively exhaust the origin (or the *telos*) by objectifying it in its historical concretizations.

What Pareyson advocates is indeed a continuity of truth and being. Yet this continuity proceeds not through linearity (as in Hegel and scientism) but through the circularity of a return that goes back onto the before only to enrich it with a new meaning that was not there at the beginning, and which thus constitutes a new beginning. In this sense, Pareyson speaks of the "originariness of the tradition" (*originarietà della tradizione*). This is what Kierkegaard, one of Pareyson's favorite but also sharply criticized authors, would name "repetition." This is nothing else than the hermeneutic circle in which Pareyson's philosophy is deeply steeped, first of all in its specific, historical, biographical unfolding.

The hermeneutic circle in which Pareyson is caught is very peculiar. It is a hermeneutic circle in which the relation to truth is never dissolved—in Pareyson, ontology and hermeneutics are one and the same. Thus, truth (and being) is not dissolved by or in the historical interpretations to which it gives rise. Rather, historical interpretations can only be such (that is, they can be interpretations) because they relate to truth. They are interpretations *of* and *they are* (or claim to be, but in their claim they are) the truth. And yet each of these interpretations, in which alone truth offers itself, does not exhaust truth. Hermeneutics yields not to the dissolution of truth but to an ontology of the inexhaustible (*ontologia dell'inesauribile*) in which it is truth itself that, precisely because of its inexhaustibility, demands dialogue and conversation among its different interpretations and interpreters. In other words, the connection between particular and universal is never relinquished, but also never solved or resolved. Conflicts are kept side by side, in tension, and acquire their innermost meaning and significance from the incommensurable relation that exists between them. It is this incommensurable relation that, properly, constitutes hermeneutics, at least in its Pareysonian version. As Pareyson phrases it, "hermeneutic thinking is at the same time thinking of being and discourse on beings, in tension between a deep ontological rooting and an immense experiential opening . . . It is in this discourse, both singular and double at once, that hermeneutic thinking resides."[31]

ATHEISM, NIHILISM, AND CHRISTIANITY, THAT IS, PHILOSOPHY AND RELIGION

The appeal or timeliness of Pareyson's hermeneutics in comparison with other contemporary philosophical options possibly lies precisely in this ability, even demand to keep tensions in place exactly as tensions—in a proximity that grants meaning to them all.

By Pareyson's own admission, his is a case of dialectical thinking, though his dialectical thinking is centered on a dialectics of freedom, not of necessity.[32] When added to Pareyson's timeliness, this feature not of conciliation but of tensions that are held together in freedom also constitutes Pareyson's specificity—namely, the connection he establishes between hermeneutic and tragic thought, the latter understood as the truest, most faithful interpretation of the core of being and reality.

Already at the beginning of his meditation, in *Esistenza e persona*, Pareyson reads Kierkegaard (and religious existentialism) and Feuerbach (and atheism) as two opposed moments in the dissolution of Hegelianism. In front of these two moments, one must inevitably choose. Pareyson chooses Kierkegaard.

The superiority of the Kierkegaardian standpoint lies, for Pareyson, in the ability Kierkegaard's position retains to encompass within itself Feuerbach's atheism as well as Feuerbach's more recent epigones, from Marxism to nihilism. Such encompassing is possible because of Kierkegaard's conception of existence as self-relation that, when closed upon itself, as sickness onto death leads to despair and, when open to transcendence, that is, to the religious dimension, is able to account for the very questions of atheism. The choice, always actual, between atheism and theism is not a choice between the death of God and God, between God's absence and God's presence. Rather, it is a choice between an option capable of accounting for the complexity and contradictoriness of reality and an alternative option that, by eliminating one horn of the alternative (God), also eliminates the possibility of conflict and the radicalness of evil—evil that, for Pareyson, retains its meaning only in the presence of the good.

The good to which Pareyson refers cannot be, of course, the metaphysical God, the God of theodicy (but also of theology and ontotheology), the God based on powerfulness and necessity, who claims to explain evil by in fact denying evil's reality. Against such a God, atheism has an easy way by insisting precisely on the reality and concreteness of evil (for Pareyson, though, atheism has no viable outcome because, having dissolved God, it also dissolves evil and turns into consolatory nihilism, comforting atheism). Against such a God, as Nietzsche understands very well, secularization is, for Pareyson, an obligation.

The Christianity onto which Pareyson ultimately lands through his reading of both Schelling and Dostoevsky is a non-triumphant Christianity, "a Christianity that is non-consolatory, non-habituated, non-reconciled, non-sweet, not meek and easy (Kierkegaard), non-safe (Luther), non-whiny (about the powerlessness of God)."[33] Rather, it is a tragic Christianity, in which the existence of God is not incompatible with, is even inseparable from the reality of evil. In a long passage worth reproducing in its entirety, Pareyson writes that

> it is a great and terrible mystery, profound and unfathomable, that on the one hand the act by which God redeems suffering by taking it upon himself is also the act by which God opposes himself to himself, insurrects against himself, is pitiless toward the Son; that is, he aggravates, increases, extends suffering in the world to the point of turning it, from human, into cosmic and theogonic suffering. On the other hand, the act by which God opposes himself to himself, wants to suffer and die, forsakes his Son remaining silent in front of his uttermost suffering and even destroys himself by himself by giving himself to the triumphant powers of pain and death, is also the act by which he conquers suffering, redeems humanity, and confirms himself. The atheistic moment of the godhead is also its theistic moment.[34]

Here is precisely where art and religion, ancient (and modern) tragedy, and Christian myth come together as material for philosophical hermeneutics, because a myth is "a revelatory narration about things that cannot be said except in this manner."[35]

In the essay "L'esperienza religiosa e la filosofia [Religious Experience and Philosophy]," Pareyson argues in favor of the superiority of myths (which speak in symbols) in comparison to philosophical concepts (which speak the language of objectification) when it comes to the ability to render adequately the ambiguity and richness of reality in its "transcendence and presence, ulteriority and availability, concealment and revelation: the unobjectifiable as *geheimnisvoll offenbar*."[36] Philosophical activity can only be a hermeneutics of myths, in which "thought poetry and religion meet, indistinct but not thereby less vigorous and powerful."[37] Against much technicism occurring even in philosophy, Pareyson maintains that "truth cannot give itself to human beings if not through a fervid human faculty such as the imagination [*fantasia*], both poetic and speculative, which however would lose itself in the whims of fancy if it did not make of itself an appropriate site for truth, which offers and even imposes itself to the imagination. . . . One cannot possess the truth if not in the form of being possessed by it."[38] The conclusion to which Pareyson is led is a retrieval of Kant's distinction between *kennen* and *denken* while at the same time echoing Ricoeur: a symbol is an image that "gives raise to much thinking (*viel zu denken veranlasst*)."[39]

Inadequate philosophical positions are, for Pareyson, those that display lack of dialogue and confrontation between philosophy (understood as either atheistic or rational moment) and religion (meant as either its theistic or its mythological counterpart) as well as those that present lack of dialogue between secularized philosophy (whether humanistically, Marxistically, or nihilistically oriented) and philosophy that is religiously, that is, generally theologically or at least metaphysically inspired. That is, the isolation of either, whether philosophy or religion, into its own specific linguistic and thematic domain is ultimately an unsuccessful stance. The lack of dialogue Pareyson chastises has characterized much of the Italian philosophical scenario until rather recently. Pareyson's verdict does not affect only Italian philosophy and religion, though, but extends further to cover all those philosophical (or theological) positions that duplicate a similar narrowness and eliminate the other from the scene of the epistemic and ontological conversation. Such positions are failures not because they are nonviable, contradictory, or inconsistent within themselves (it is not a problem of logic or methodology), but rather because, in their unilaterality, limitedness, and exclusion of the other, they pre-empty the meaning and richness of the reality they claim to describe (it is a problem of ontology and existence).

Of course, as Pareyson is very well aware, one can seek refuge in a consolatory position in which there is neither God nor suffering, and everything is a play or deferral of interpretations. Such a position does not do justice, though, to the seriousness of major tragedies within our times. As Pareyson already claims in his 1950 *Esistenza e persona*, "when confronted with the ruins of modern culture, there arises the problem of a new culture, a new world to be built, in which we all have to live . . . , and it is here that the choice for or against Christianity becomes crucial [*decisiva*]."[40] The way in which Italian philosophers have most recently responded to the challenge put forth by Pareyson's understanding of Christianity cannot be a topic of consideration here. Suffice to say that the responses have come from figures who in the past had more closely aligned themselves with the atheistic/nihilistic line of development such as Gianni Vattimo and Massimo Cacciari, who more recently have returned to the themes of God and religion.

FRENCH? GERMAN? NO, ITALIAN

"Since the beginning of my activity as a scholar I have always moved within the perspective of a European philosophy so that it is difficult for me to understand the expression 'Italian philosophy' if not in the rather general sense of an anagraphic or geographic delimitation," Pareyson asserts.[41] Leaving aside Pareyson's own dismissal of the appropriateness of the question of his national philosophical belonging, the issue of a national identity for Italian philosophy may seem debatable, if not dangerous or even obsolete, given the contemporary world scenario of boundary crossing, transculturalism, transnationalism, and globalization. Yet it seems important to raise the question with respect to Pareyson's hermeneutics not to condemn him to some "province" of universal or European philosophy, but rather to differentiate his thought from that of two other, more world-established hermeneuticians, namely, Ricoeur and Gadamer, and to establish the specificity, uniqueness, and originality of his position in a philosophical context in which, to use Vattimo's expression, hermeneutics has become the *koiné*.[42]

It should be clear from what has been said in the previous pages that Pareyson's philosophy develops in constant dialogue with some major figures in both the French and German traditions: Kant, Schiller, Schelling, Kierkegaard, Jaspers, and Heidegger, but also Pascal, Marcel, and Maritain (especially on the notion of art as making). It also develops in conversation with Russian philosophy, especially Berdyaev, and with arguably the greatest of the Russian novelists, at least as far as a description of the human soul is concerned: Dostoevsky. In addition to situating itself in an ongoing conversation with major international thinkers, Pareyson's thinking evidently does not disdain finding its sources in material other than philosophy strictly defined. Rather, in the last stage of his thinking, Pareyson explicitly thematizes a return to myths and to a hermeneutics of the religious experience captured in myths as perhaps the only possible way to access a truth that cannot be demonstrated, objectified, explained, but only narrated. In this sense, myths appear not as escape from reason into arbitrariness, irrationality, and superstition. Rather, myths are an aid to philosophy (which nevertheless remains rational and rigorous thinking) so as to talk about reality and problematize, question, and universalize its truth. Pareyson draws elements, suggestions, and inspirations from many names and places in a philosophical gathering that is multicultural and interdisciplinary, transnational and transcultural (although mainly Western).

I argue that Pareyson's conversation with various thinkers yields to his own personal and innovative philosophy, one that differs rather radically first of all from other existentialist trends, which, especially in the German variations, maintain a conception of existence and the finite as negativity (for example, Barth). Pareyson's entire speculative itinerary emphasizes the positivity of the finite, of human existence, which, in the risk entailed in freedom, posits new beings into existence and is itself positivity, creativity, beginning, origin, and creation. Pareyson also distances himself from other, especially French Christian existentialist thinkers in that, in his ontological personalism, there is, in his own words, "that hermeneutic and thereby ontological undertone of personalism that separates [him] from any form of spiritualism of idealistic or intimistic origin."[43] The link with truth and being in their transcendence, or the hermeneutic character of existentialism, is never lost on Pareyson.

More specifically, though, Pareyson's thought differs also from the perspectives reached more or less at the same time by two other philosophers who, often in conversation with the same authors Pareyson engages, nevertheless achieve a different understanding of philosophy as hermeneutics: his longtime friend Hans-Georg Gadamer and Paul Ricoeur, whose thought Pareyson claimed he did not know until much later in his development.[44] Being a scholar neither of Gadamer nor of Ricoeur, I would like simply to indicate two features that appear to me as two main points of Pareyson's divergence from the two other hermeneuticians.

First, Pareyson's hermeneutics is linked to the ontology of truth. It is being and truth that ensure, and even bring to hermeneutics, a dimension of universality. It is only the universal dimension, in fact, that grants that the historical truths in which truth each time gives itself, in its wholeness yet inexhaustibility, do not fall into ideology or ephemerality. It is only truth, Pareyson claims, that "insulates [philosophy] from all attempts, today increasingly widespread, to reduce it to merely historic and pragmatic, technical and instrumental, empirical and ideological thinking."[45] Philosophy is not simply a conflict of interpretations, each abandoned to itself. The unifying context that holds such interpretations together is not simply the tradition; rather, it is truth and being themselves. Given the philosophical scenario coeval to his thinking, Pareyson is very well aware not simply of the unpopularity, but moreover of the difficulty of the path he has chosen when remaining loyal to the concept of truth understood not simply as expressive but also as revelatory; and he is fully conscious of the audacity and courage that such a risk involves. Yet as he says, quoting Schelling, "Wer wahrhaft philosophieren will, muss aller Hoffnung, alles Verlangens, aller Sensucht los sein; er muss nichts wollen, nichts wissen, sich ganz bloss und arm fühlen, alles dahingeben, um alles zu gewinnen."[46]

Second, as the previous quote announces in its evocation of the figure of Christ, Pareyson's hermeneutics leads, as already examined, to tragic rather than ludic thinking in which freedom, both human and divine, constitutes the core of a reality that is fundamentally pain and suffering.

These two differentiating features—basically, ontology and tragedy—allow us to speak of Pareyson as a specific, original, and creative case of Italian hermeneutics, whether existential or ontological (but can they be distinguished in Pareyson?), and not simply as a variation of its European counterparts.

NOTES

1. Luigi Pareyson, "Pensiero ermeneutico e pensiero tragico," in *Dove va la filosofia italiana?*, ed. J. Jacobelli (Rome-Bari: Laterza, 1986), 136.

2. Among Pareyson's students one should name at least Claudio Ciancio, Sergio Givone, Aldo Magris, Diego Marconi, Maurizio Pagano, Mario Perniola, Ugo Perone, Gianni Vattimo, and the later Umberto Eco, Francesco Moiso, and Valerio Verra.

3. For an impressive bibliography of works by and on Luigi Pareyson, see Francesco Tomatis, *Bibliografia pareysoniana* (Turin: Trauben, 1998).

4. To be fair, one should mention the translation of his essays "The Unity of Philosophy," *Cross Currents* (1953): 57–69; "Pointless Suffering in *The Brothers Karamazov*," *Cross Currents* (1987): 271–86: the volume by Diego Bubbio, ed., *Existence, Interpretation, Freedom: Selected Writings* (Aurora, CO: Davies Group, 2009); the recent translation of Luigi Pareyson, *Truth and Interpretation* (Albany: State University of New York Press, 2013); and a couple of sessions or individual contributions at IAPL and SPEP, respectively, in recent years.

5. Gianni Vattimo, "Pareyson, esistenzialismo no global," in *La Stampa*, 8 settembre 2001.

6. The dissertation was published in 1940 with the title *La filosofia dell'esistenza e Carlo Jaspers*. It is perhaps interesting to notice that also one of Paul Ricoeur's first works, which he compiled with Michel Dufrenne, is devoted to *Karl Jaspers and the Philosophy of Existence* (1947).

7. In this chapter, I mainly mention books. For more complete bibliographical information, see the volume by Francesco Tomatis quoted above.

8. Paul Ricoeur's *The Conflict of Interpretation* appeared in 1969, whereas Hans-Georg Gadamer's *Truth and Method* was published in 1960.

9. Luigi Pareyson, *Verità e interpretazione* (Milan: Mursia, 1971), 53. All references in this essay are to the Italian translation; all translations into English are my own.

10. Luigi Pareyson, *Esistenza e persona*, (Genoa: Il Melangolo, 1985). All quotations are from this 4th edition, which contains as an addition the important autobiographical essay "Dal personalismo esistenziale all'ontologia della libertà."

11. Luigi Pareyson, *Ontologia della libertà* (Turin: Einaudi, 1995), 61, fn. 1.

12. Pareyson, *Esistenza e persona*, 14ff.

13. Here the polemic reference is Heidegger's existential analytic, which develops in the sense of an existential (not an existentiell, that is ontic) analysis aimed at retracing the a priori structures of existence, not of the existent human being. From this comes Heidegger's neglect of ethics, according to Pareyson.

14. In *Esistenza e persona*, Pareyson differentiates his version of personalism from other variations of it when saying: "Independently from other forms of personalism, such as Italian personalism of actualistic descent, or German personalism of a phenomenological kind, or French personalism both spiritualistic and communitarian, my intention was to present an existentialist version of personalism, which on the one hand arose from the crisis of metaphysical rationalism, . . . and on the other emerged from the dissolution of Hegelism . . . and culminated in a real form of ontological personalism"; see Pareyson, *Esistenza e persona*, 14.

15. Pareyson, *Esistenza e persona*, 17.

16. Ibid., 23.

17. Ibid., 20.

18. Pareyson, *Verità e interpretazione*, 73.

19. Ibid., 159.

20. Ibid., 43.

21. Ibid.

22. Ibid., 106.

23. "To say that the good is chosen means to say that such a choice has been made in opposition, in the presence of the possibility for the opposite choice, that is, of the choice for evil, for the negative choice. Thus evil is in God—obviously as possibility . . . Meontology is, albeit as the other side of ontology, its inseparable companion"; see Pareyson, *Ontologia della libertà*, 55.

24. *Ontologia della libertà*, 66.

25. And, Pareyson adds, also "in the hermeneutics of ancient and modern tragedy"; see Pareyson, "Pensiero ermeneutico e pensiero tragico," 140.

26. "Pensiero ermeneutico e pensiero tragico," 137.

27. Ibid., 139.

28. Ibid., 140.

29. Luigi Pareyson, *Essere Libertà Ambiguità* (Milan: Mursia, 1998), 169.

30. Pareyson, *Esistenza e persona*, 25–26.

31. Pareyson, "Pensiero ermeneutico e pensiero tragico," 136.

32. On Pareyson's dialectical thinking in his distinction from Hegel's, see especially the characterization he himself hints at in the section "Frammenti sull'escatologia," in Pareyson, *Ontologia della libertà*, 331–38 especially.

33. Pareyson, "Frammenti sull'escatologia," in *Ontologia della libertà*, 343.

34. Paresyon, "La sofferenza inutile in Dostoevskij," *Giornale di metafisica* 6, no. 1 (1982): 168–69.

35. Pareyson, *Ontologia della libertà*, 52.

36. Ibid., 104.

37. Ibid., 116.

38. Ibid., 115.

39. Ibid., 107.

40. Pareyson, *Esistenza e persona*, 12.

41. Pareyson, "Pensiero ermeneutico e pensiero tragico," 134.

42. See Gianni Vattimo, "Perché 'debole,'" in *Dove va la filosofia italiana?*, 187.

43. Pareyson, *Verità e interpretazione*, 10.

44. This is at least according to some personal sources of mine who worked in close proximity and friendship with Pareyson.

45. Pareyson, *Verità e interpretazione*, 8.

46. Ibid., 11.

2

When Transcendence Is Finite

Pareyson, the Person, and the Limits of Being

Antonio Calcagno

In *Esistenza e persona* [*Existence and Person*],[1] Luigi Pareyson announces that his work seeks to recover a strong sense of personalism in which the human person can be grasped in her or his full liberty and ontological reality (EP 11–12). His argument for the importance and viability of personhood is embedded in a historical and critical analysis of modern philosophy, existentialism, and Marxist materialist history. He also notes that there are various forms of personalism, for example, Italian-Christian personalism, which views the person as an act; phenomenological personalism; and French spiritual or communal personalism (EP 12); they, however, all fail to capture what he sees as the foundational aspects of personhood. Pareyson sees the person as a "coincidence of auto-relation and hetero-relation, that is, the human being as coincidence of relation with itself and with being. An originary solidarity exists between the human being and being, an original intertwining that displays itself on the one hand in the constitutive ontological character of the human being and on the other in the inseparability of existence and transcendence. In this intertwining one finds the fundamental concept of the unobjectifiability of being, which requires us to abandon ontic metaphysics and adopt a critical ontology" (EP 14–15). Personhood is relational and defined by the very relations of persons to themselves and others.

But Pareyson maintains that such relations reveal a deeper, nonobjectifiable foundation in being, a ground of solidarity that can manifest itself through interpretation.

Because the person is inextricably linked to being, and being is understood as exceeding and transcending the ontic descriptions and understanding we ascribe to it, traditional understandings of the person, such as substance; individual; material, historical subject; bearer of a soul, psyche, and spirit; and as a pure freedom fail to capture the ontological excess of the person, understood as transcendent being. This chapter examines Pareyson's claim and argues that the being revealed by the relations that constitute personhood cannot possibly manifest the broad, unified sense of being with which, he claims, human beings are in solidarity; rather, what we find is a more limited, finite form of being constituted by the collective dwelling of persons with one another, other non-human living beings, and the world. Determinations of the being of the person need not necessarily be absolutized or totalized, thereby resulting in a finite and reductive understanding of human persons; rather, determinations can be understood as Kantian limits that ultimately generate possibilities of further determinations, which can lead to greater self-understanding and collective well-being. Pareyson is correct in understanding determination and situatedness as important for the being of persons, but the open-ended nature of determination he advocates, which must be understood as the possibility of non-determination or transcendence, runs the risk of undermining his view of the singularity of the person. Specific determinations that condition and shape singularity must not be read then simply as limiting or conditioning, but as creating possibilities for initiative (*iniziativa*) and being without recourse to infinite transcendence. Rather than view personal determinations as pointing to transcendence, I maintain that we need to see them as operating within a situation, intensely making it more complex and differentiating it, ultimately producing layers of meaningful determination.

THE PERSON

Luigi Pareyson was deeply formed by his early studies on existentialism, especially the work of Karl Jaspers.[2] In his *Studi sull'esistenzialismo* [*Studies on Existentialism*],[3] Pareyson identifies determination or limits as key for understanding nineteenth- and twentieth-century forms of existentialism. "In existentialism, the personalist stance is articulated through the precise awareness of limits, which, far from presenting spirit as a univocal tendency, marks it with a fracture, thereby highlighting spirit's deep character as choice."[4] One of the key tenets of French existentialist thought, according to Pareyson, is freedom to choose, to respond to the exigencies or limits of the situation within which one finds oneself. This choice is always self-referential, however, and does not admit the possibility that other conditions are involved in subjective decision making that exceed or transcend freedom of choice and the situation: the person is more than a situated (limited) subject or freedom who enacts his or her existence through his or her choices.

For Pareyson, the person is neither an object nor a concept: the person is a historical reality who poses a central problem for contemporary philosophy. "The problem of personhood is central in contemporary philosophy, as attested to by the great interest provoked by its various treatments and the emergence everywhere of forms of personalism and humanism. The urgency of the problem of personhood is rooted in the consciousness that the contemporary crisis, when seen in its hidden and profound meaning, is a philosophical crisis. Various conceptions of the human being conflict with one another, and the conscious taking on of a position cannot be defined except through a conscious adherence to a determined concept of the human being" (EP 163). The legacy of two world wars and a divided Europe, concomitant with the death of the Enlightenment ideal of the human subject, provoked a crisis in our understanding of ourselves. Pareyson argues that the exigency of responding to the questions of who and what we are must be set within the frameworks of history and interpretation: we are interpretative/interpreted historical beings. History and interpretation ground persons in situations and give them cultural and historical contexts with which to live, understand, and form themselves. But persons are more than historical and interpretative beings; they are ontologically constituted in intersubjective relations that ultimately culminate in the person being understood as opening onto infinity and God.

Pareyson views the person as a unique and unrepeatable singularity. The traditional characterization of the person as an individual or as being understood in terms of genus and species (whole and part) is inadequate for capturing the existence of the person (EP 165). Individuation, especially in modern philosophy (one could read Locke, for example) excludes universality, but universality is not to be understood as some universal genus or species. "Individuality excludes universality: if the person is an individual, then it is simply one among many, and the normative aspect in the concept of humanity is lost. Particularity excludes totality: if the person is a part, then it simply is a fragment of the whole and the aspect of the totality of the person is lost. Instead, in the singularity of the person both universality and totality are present. This grants us the two fundamental features of a form of personalism capable of grounding our respect for the person. Universality and totality do not lie outside the person; rather, they are inside him or her" (EP 165–66). Individuation reduces the person to one among many, thereby undermining the possibility of guaranteeing any universal respect for the singularity of the individual. Likewise, if the person is viewed simply as a particularity, then the person is seen as a fragment incapable of securing any more encompassing view of humanity that is not reducible to a sum total of parts: personhood comes to shape humanity, and what we understand by personhood is not simply a synthesis of the various elements constitutive of personhood. The person is a whole that truly exceeds the parts of its being, for the person is related to others and being.

Pareyson claims that a person is both singular and universal. How can this be? Is this claim not contradictory? Pareyson justifies his position by arguing that persons have a unique capacity, namely, initiative, that allows them to singularize and universalize their humanity. Initiative, *iniziativa* in Italian, is a polyvalent word. It easily translates to initiative, understood as the capacity to begin, create, or undertake something (before anyone else), but it also has the senses of interdependence as well as drive or impetus. When Pareyson uses the term to describe what lies at the core of the human person, the sense of force, power, or drive is palpable in his descriptions. He observes, "The unique ground of the person's singularity and universality is initiative. On the one hand, initiative concretizes and therefore singularizes the person. On the other hand, it gives value to and hence universalizes the person. Initiative is simultaneously an exigency, a decision, and a valuing: decision offers determination to the exigency, thus concretizing and singularizing exigency; valuing locates such a determination within the domain of values, giving the determination its value while universalizing it" (EP 168).

A person's situation, whether it is historical, local, or in the relations to oneself, others, and God, imposes demands. These demands or exigencies, in turn, call forward a free, decisive response to the exigencies of the situation. "The more the person freely shapes and defines its profile, the more its decisions become circumscribed (even if they are never constrained) by the historical concreteness within which the person acquires its own consistency. The process of singularization is a process of election and selection, that is, of originary and progressive qualification in which the person's uniqueness [*irripetibilità*] is increasingly affirmed. Such uniqueness, understood as a determination of initiative, is never a pure quality precisely because it is an axiological determination" (EP 169). The decisions that flow freely from one's own initiative singularize and concretize the person, giving the person a more defined profile. Yet—and this is where Pareyson differs from more traditional French existentialist accounts of the person—decisions produce effects on the situation, which, in turn, involve and affect others: values are given to the situation, and the person can be seen as valuing.

The valuing and values created are communicable and can be handled, investigated, accepted, or struggled against, and even rejected. This means that these values take on the form of objects and can even be shared; in other words, they can be universalized. "Initiative is also the ground of the universality of the person insofar as it gives the person value. Initiative is exigency, that is, a demand for value. Initiative simultaneously posits, solves, and discriminates an alternative such that the specific result of any decision emerges as judged in terms of its value and dis-value. This is the process through which the person universalizes itself; that is, the person acquires a validity that can be recognized by all because each of its acts contains a valuing that recognizes its validity and which allows it to be recognized as such" (E 169–170). Persons see one another as valuing, and they judge one another vis-à-vis their respective and shared values. This shared recognition by persons of the valuing/valued judgments of persons is seen by Pareyson as true universalization. It is not simply a formal universalism, but one that is concretely lodged in the articulation of values and in judgments by singular persons on values of other valuing persons. He observes, "The person constitutes itself historically in a validity that perennially demands recognition, that continuously requires being judged, that in its wake arouses value judgments. In each moment of its existence, a person is what it succeeds in making of itself; each moment recapitulates and condenses the entire history of the person and carries within itself its complete valuing. This comprehensive valuing, which is contained in each instant, highlights the person's validity, which is inscribed in a specific and unmistakable profile. In this way, validity is not defined simply as value but as concrete value, that is, as a historical and determined value" (EP 170). Initiative, then, must be understood as the unique foundation of both the universality and singularity of the human person.

Pareyson notes that a problem arises with the aforementioned position insofar as the person is viewed as acting at one moment in time in which the present situation demands a response, and in giving a response, the person auto-determines her- or himself within the dialectics of valuing; but this always happens within the moment of the present, or so the description suggests. As a temporal being, one's future decisions can bend back and undo one's initiatives of the present moment, which suggests that initiatives are always incomplete or unfinished as they are subject to future revision.

> The person, insofar as s/he is always enclosed in a present instant, is a totality; that is, s/he is the unity of a multiplicity, the punctuated concentration of a succession of acts and the decisions of various deeds, a living and concrete plexus of multiple determinations that have coalesced in her or his historical existence, the condensation of a series of variations and inflections that have been concretized in the present, the permanence underlying constant change, the overall integrity of an indefinite activity. Yet, insofar as no one instant can possibly define the whole person, for each instant of the person is only one of his or her instants (that is, insofar as each instant is, in the person, always one of its instants, then the person is insufficient and incomplete), [the person is] then a perennial revision of the past and a constant opening toward the future, a never-ending differentiation of instants, always unsatisfied and awaiting completion, a retrocession into the past of the actual and conclusive instant. This is the case because the person is viewed as provisional and inadequate: [in the flow of time] there occurs a reversal of the process that completes the entire history of the person with an actual instant; rather, [time] converts completed instants into a process of a [flow of a series] of infinite instants awaiting completion. (EP 171)

The aforementioned citation explains two important aspects about the human person. First, the human person is a temporal being. In *Truth and Interpretation*, Pareyson specifically views the person as a historical being who is capable of understanding itself, others, and the world as a being subject to time. The act of interpretation opens up possibilities of being. "[Truth] is a call that demands an answer and a witnessing, not an imposition that oppresses or constrains; it is an appeal that places human beings in front of their responsibilities and urges them freely to commit the self-assertive act that confirms their own being, recovers their origin, and indissolubly fastens the bind between person and truth: *he alethetheia eleutherosei humas* [the truth will set you free]."[5]

Second, and this is most important for our purposes here, the various personal determinations that arise from initiative are always incomplete or insufficient because of the nature of time: the future may undo what was concretized in the present—an instant of the present is always being conditioned by a future anticipation, and the past merges as an instant of having been that acquired its very status of having been through the negation of the present by a future's coming to be. Following a long line of philosophers, including Heraclitus, Pareyson argues that time changes the nature of instants insofar as they can never be complete instants. If time is conceived as a flow of instants, it conditions the temporal appearing of the object and the object may be seen to change temporally, but the determinations enacted by the person through initiative do not only have a temporal status: they also have an ontological reality in and of themselves. Personal determinations also perdure, despite the flow of the instants of time. For example, one may find oneself in a situation of perduring oppression: the determinations of oppression remain, though the instants of time continue to carry out their very production of the lived experiences of the moments of past, present, and future. In short, the flow of time does not always necessarily guarantee insufficiency, as there are real moments of duration that resist Pareyson's account of instantaneous time.

Despite the foregoing critique of Pareysonian time, one must keep in mind a deeper point: initiative, though it gives determinations, does not always create initiatives that are absolute or complete. There is an inherent contradiction within initiative: it determines, yet its determinations are always subject to change. The determinations are always insufficient unto themselves. A limit is exposed within the very structure of initiative. Yet, and perhaps following the insight of Viktor Frankl when he discusses the power of *Trotzmacht*, the person is conscious of this limit and still tires to exceed it, to transcend this limit of incompleteness or insufficiency of initiative. The desire to leap over the very limit contained within the determining capacity of initiative manifests, for Pareyson, the real possibility of transcendence.

> There can only be one rational solution to the problem created by the aforementioned contradiction: transcendence. As a form of indigence, insufficiency is limit; the limit refers back to the other, but to an other that limits my being only insofar as it fulfils my being; that is, [such an other] is the principle that grounds my being. Initiative has a beginning, it is given by itself, it is a dative that makes itself nominative. So much so that I *must* decide but also I *cannot but* decide. There is an initial "necessity" that is the mark of my having had an origin [or cause of my being—*principiato*]. (EP 173)

Transcendence is understood, then, as the possibility of making a singular decision despite the fact that it might change or be revised, despite the fact that it might always be incomplete.

Furthermore, though an initiative compels decisions, initiative itself is not reducible simply to the act of taking the personal initiative. As a structure, initiative is not solely dependent upon the person, but is a self-given reality that bespeaks an initial principle that gives initiative, which Pareyson will identify with God.

It is the aforementioned sense of transcendence, which lies at the heart of initiative, that makes possible relations to others (including God and other persons in society) that are not simply reducible to my own projections. The singular person can be modified by another person or God, especially when it comes to values and value making. Insofar as we are insufficient to ourselves and incomplete, an ontological space is opened where others and God can come to condition and determine our existence: we are not solipsistic beings. "More precisely, it is a matter of the transcendence of a God that is, simultaneously, Value and Person. God is value because otherwise he would not be the ground of an initiative. Were He not Value, God would then be only principle of being and not the initiator of an ought to be. He could perhaps justify a world of individuals but not the history of persons . . . Decision itself is valid only if it is constituted as an obedience to what is first stimulated in us and as the observance of an originary law, that is, only insofar as the principle of action is a God-value. Valuing can consist in judging validity only insofar as valuing is rendered possible by the highest criterion, namely, the Value that is source of all validity . . . Only if God is Person can He treat the human person as person, recognizing the person's independence and totality" (EP 173–174).

For Pareyson, the person comes to manifest her- or himself through initiative. Initiative reveals that one is never sufficient to oneself; a gap becomes manifest between oneself and what is yet unfinished or incomplete; one is not self-sufficient and requires the other, understood as God and other persons, in order to exist. But the being of oneself is insufficient for carrying out the work of initiative (one is never a totality onto oneself) as well as the being of God and others. Persons are theandric (*teandrico*) beings (EP 158). Pareyson remarks, "The person's validity is guaranteed by the fact that s/he is initiative. The person's independence is guaranteed by the fact that s/he is in relation with God. Determined by value, initiative places the person on an axiological plane. The relation with God, insofar as it completes the person's insufficiency, determines the goal toward which the person is ordered" (EP 175). The being of the person is marked by a deep relation to others and God, and the relationship between person, others, and God opens onto an axiological plane where values become primary. God is understood as the ultimate value and person (*Valore, Persona*) (EP 174). The insufficiency and poverty (*indigenza*) of the being of the person makes a person desire to be whole, a desire that is a value (EP 174–175). Values are neither private nor individual; rather, they can be shared and, hence, are viewed by Pareyson as societal. "Person and society are born together. It is neither possible to presuppose the person without society nor society without the person" (EP 176). Values are not to be understood merely in a normative or prescriptive sense; rather, we must understand values in their literal sense as something shared or social which we care about. The relationships of person to others and God make manifest things we care about in our existence, which is marked by the indigence and insufficiency of being.

Having discussed the fundamental structure of the person as self-relational and related to others, Pareyson claims that there exist four fundamental ways in which the person comes to be further defined or determined: existence, task, a work, and as an I. First, the person must be understood as existence insofar as s/he comes to exist through the dialectics of unity and duality, passivity and activity, and determination and infinity. The person experiences her- or himself as a unity insofar as initiative makes clear that one is deciding or acting for oneself. At the same time, however, the revelation of the limit of initiative and the opening unto the desire to transcend one's own indigence and insufficiency makes one recognize that one needs others and God. Hence, one is both a unity and a duality insofar as otherness is co-constitutive of one's personhood (EP 185). Furthermore, the situation one finds oneself in while undertaking an initiative reveals that the person is both active and passive. One actively decides to respond to the exigencies of a situation, but in doing so, one also becomes aware of how one is informed by the lack that passively informs one's being and by the relationship to others and God in society. I become subject to the values we share, either in law or societal expectations (EP 186). Finally, the person is both determined (or defined) and infinite, understood as both exceeding determination and as unfinished or incomplete. Pareyson maintains, "The person is finite insofar as initiative is caused. My ability not to decide is the mark of my being caused, that is, of my being not God but human. The determination of living within a situation cannot only be described as a 'finitude,' but can also be understood as inexhaustible infinity and indefinite development: infinity of development and situational delimitation are inextricably joined and coessential" (EP 186).

The person as task means that s/he must be considered to exist in a concrete dialectics of plasticity and determined ordering (*programmazione*), dedication and obligation, freedom and necessity. Plasticity and determined ordering both refer to one's relationship to history. As one notes in *Truth and Interpretation*, history is vital for Pareyson's thinking, for not only is it an important mode for understanding the movement of philosophy, but it also determines how and why we exist in a certain way in the world and in society. The person is conditioned and determined by history, but is not simply a product or construction of it. A person can respond to the exigencies of the times of a situation, ultimately creating a unique, changing (plastic) response to a historical situation, but one can never completely extricate oneself from one's historical epoch. Dedication and obligation are modes of comportment that flow from the values we share and that flow from God working in society: they are moral techniques, Pareyson says (EP 187), which impose on us the duty of responding to ethical demands. Freedom and necessity are ontological categories that play themselves out when we will or do not will to carry out our duties and obligations. In choosing or refusing to choose or accept our duties, we exercise our freedom to become or not become that which we will. Pareyson observes, "The persons one would like to be are often many, they change over time, and they can be replaced such that, in a sense, a person truly becomes a 'mask,' that is, the peculiar character that one assumes or puts down or replaces as one's task or ideal" (EP 187).

The person understood as a work (*opera*) is seen as living the dialectics between universality and singularity, totality and insufficiency, and newness and exemplarity. It should be remarked that the descriptors Pareyson inserts here for a work remind one of categories invoked to describe the creation and interpretation of the work of art in his work *Estetica. Teoria della formatività* [*Aesthetics: Theory of Formativity*].[6] We have already touched upon the first two dialectical movements in the preceding analysis, and they form the core of Pareyson's view of the person. Newness, understood as a historical value, stems from the person being an original product of history who ultimately enriches reality but is not reducible to pure economic measurement or quantification (EP 188). Furthermore, the newness of the person is viewed as paradigmatic, and it can serve as an example for future new productions and undertakings.

Regarding the final personal descriptor, namely, the person as an I, I-ness is produced through the dialectics of person and work, substance and responsibility, and universality and person. Concerning the first dialectics, Pareyson argues that given that the person produces a work and that work bends back to define the person, one's personal existence is shaped by the possession of the work and the work's possession of its author. He notes, "The I is the possession and directing of one's own life, the presence of myself as an agent of my works that are incorporated within myself, the consciousness that I am what I do, and that I am what I am because of myself" (EP 188). On the relation between responsibility and substance, Pareyson observes that my response to the exigencies and determinations of a situation not only informs one, but also permits one to respond to the very demands for oneself. "A person is what it is insofar as it not only accepts but also demands that it be responsible for itself" (EP 189). Finally, the universality of personhood, that is, insofar as all human beings are persons, means that all human persons are endowed with personality. The personal uniqueness of single human beings does not mean that the uniqueness of personhood is reducible to the private. On the contrary, recalling what Pareyson said about value and its universality, the person is societal and oriented toward God. Furthermore, reason facilitates communication between persons and affords a common understanding. Reason allows us to share in the experience of a universal humanity (EP 189).

THE PROBLEM OF INFINITY, TRANSCENDENCE, AND THE PERSON

I have presented thus far a very brief sketch of the major elements of Pareyson's concept of the person. Central in all of his descriptions is the dialectics between determining and transcending, infinite and open-ended realities, including infinity, God, and being. Unquestionably, our relationships to ourselves and others, and the open-ended (understood as the incomplete or unfinished because of our finite becoming in a situation) being of these relations, influence who we are as persons. I see these determinations, however, as unfolding within the playing out of finitude, that is, our temporal finitude in a given historical situation.

According to Pareyson, initiative manifests a tension between finitude and infinity. Time can only concretize itself in particular instants or moments insofar as these moments can individuate themselves against a flowing forward of time. Time, then, helps the being of a person individuate her- or himself in a given situation. For example, my decision to respond to the demand of a situation, say, an ethical dilemma, is possible only to the extent that I can circumscribe the dilemma as a moment in time against which I can make the effort or use my personal force to respond to it in the way I choose, always in relation to myself and others, including God. The moment of the dilemma is set up against a temporal flow that keeps unfolding, an unfinished or infinite flow. The tension between a defined moment and the flow of time as becoming creates the energy that drives initiative. Time is central for Paryeson, as it manifests transcendence and, ultimately, being. One certainly sees here the influence of the early Heidegger on Pareyson's thought.

I wonder, however, whether time conditions the determination and conditioning of the person in the way Pareyson presents. Though time and being may be opened up by initiative, there is nothing to say that time and being necessarily manifest transcendence, infinity, liberty, and God in the way Pareyson describes. Rather, I argue that the very *content* of the determination of a situation itself, and not the flowing forward of time, exerts pressure on a person to respond in a decisive manner, and the response itself is a further determination. Each determination is an additional definition of one's person vis-à-vis others and the world, and while the process of determination can reveal liberty, especially as one can freely decide to respond in the way one can and wills, this dialectic of determination and response to determination must be understood within the framework of finitude. Persons condition one another by the choices and responses they give to the determinations of their being, which can be imposed from within and/or from outside oneself. The particularity of the content of the ethical dilemma discussed above, to continue with our example, makes a demand upon me. My personhood takes on shape or acquires determination not only through the effect the dilemma has on me, but also through the response I choose to give to it. Though questions of practical timing (as opposed to time or temporality) may emerge, the content and force of the determining effect and response to the dilemma in a given historical situation is what drives the initiative, not time. Time, in my view, is simply a horizon against which action and response, both to the self and others, play themselves out. The real driving force behind initiative lies in the freedom of the person and the very particular content of the determination. What individuates the relations of the person, what personalizes the person, is the content of the determinations, be they chosen as responses or felt as effects. The specificity and demands of the determination are what can trigger or launch initiative.

But persons are mortal: they live for finite periods of time. Science informs us that the universe is finite: it had a beginning and will end. The temporality that Pareyson sees as infinite, justified by the very becoming of time and its flowing forward, is precisely a feeling, and perhaps it is truly felt as being infinite, transcending, and open-ended. However, if we consider time as a horizon, as we did above, and we are conscious of the finitude that marks the human person and his or her life, then we have to rethink the claims of infinity and transcendence. Concerning the latter, the robust sense of transcendence of being that makes God manifest has to be limited. If we are truly finite, the force of the determinations that condition personal being must be understood as transcendent insofar as they are not simply projects or responses of an isolated person; however, the fact that we can determine each other and the world we live in means that our thoughts, actions, decisions, and initiatives really are mutually influencing and conditioning: they transcend our own realms of personhood. Finitude establishes limits, which, in turn, exert demands and pressures on our person to respond, thereby further determining our personhood. The auto- and hetero-relationality of personhood that Pareyson sees as constitutive of personhood requires transcendence in order for initiative and determinations to play themselves out, but this transcendence plays itself out within the dialectics of finite freedoms in finite persons.

Concerning the former, a pure or absolute infinity, as contained and manifested in Pareyson's view of God, is a religious possibility, a possibility registered in one's own faith system, but it is hard to say that the infinity of God is revealed in the very transcendence opened up by Pareysonian initiative, if we understand it outside the rubric of Pareyson's Christian commitment. Specific finite determinations may demand particular finite decisions, but they are always bound by our mortality and the mortality of people in a given historical situation. Persons can continue to be affected and respond to the determinations of others across time, but not infinitely so, for we all die. With our death comes the end of our determination and our relationality and, ultimately, all possibility of transcendence.

In the end, what is both beautiful and affirming about Pareyson's personalism is the centrality he gives to relationality and determination. Intersubjective or, more precisely, interpersonal determination need not be so excruciatingly nihilating or sadomasochistic as it is for Sartre. In fact, one sees in Pareyson's view of interpersonal relationality a robust possibility of affirming the creation and creativity, indeed the *formatività*, of the person through initiative. But his view of time, as opposed to the force generated by the particular personalized (through personality) content of a determination coming into relation with determined selves and others, who also are determined by the specific content of the being as persons, ascribes to time a power that it does not have, especially if we consider time simply as a horizon that conditions the flows of person's lives from a present that experiences a person's having been and anticipates its future coming to be. The finite limits that personal determinations can generate act as the impetus for initiatives, which continue to condition the deep interpersonal relations that constitute the core of Luigi Pareyson's personalism.

NOTES

1. Luigi Pareyson, *Esistenza e persona* (Genoa: Il Melangolo, 2002). Hereafter parenthetically cited as EP. English translation by Silvia Benso and Antonio Calcagno.

2. Luigi Pareyson, *La filosofia dell'esistenza e Carlo Jaspers* (Naples: Loffredo, 1940). Republished as *Karl Jaspers* (Turin: Marietti, 1983).

3. Luigi Pareyson, *Studi sull'esistenzialismo* (Milan: Mursia, 2001).

4. Ibid., 23.

5. Luigi Pareyson, *Truth and Interpretation*, trans. Robert T. Valgenti (Albany: State University of New York Press, 2013), 27.

6. Luigi Pareyson, *Estetica. Teoria della formatività* (Florence: Sansoni, 1974), 219–318.

3

Pareyson's Role in Twentieth-Century Italian Aesthetics

Paolo D'Angelo

PAREYSON'S AESTHETICS AND THE RENEWAL OF AESTHETICS AFTER CROCE

Pareyson's place within twentieth-century Italian aesthetics can be most briefly established by saying that his aesthetics has been the first systematic non-Crocean aesthetics that was published in Italy. The first point that must be emphasized is that Pareyson's *Estetica. Teoria della formatività* [*Aesthetics: Theory of Formativity*][1] is a systematic aesthetics, that is, a complete treatise in aesthetics that aims at organically encompassing all main issues within such discipline. During the same period when the work was published (the *Estetica* came out in subsequent issues of the journal *Filosofia* between 1950 and 1954), many essays on aesthetics appeared in Italy in sharp discontinuity with Benedetto Croce's approach. Examples include Guido Morpurgo-Tagliabue's *Il concetto dello stile* [*The Concept of Style*][2] in 1951, Gillo Dorfles' *Il discorso tecnico delle arti* [*The Technical Discourse of Arts*][3] in 1952, Dino Formaggio's *Fenomenologia della tecnica artistica* [*Phenomenology of Artistic Technique*][4] in 1953, and Galvano Della Volpe's *Verosimile filmico* [*Filmic Verisimile*][5] in 1954. None of these books, however, possesses the systematic and complete character that belongs to Pareyson's work, and none aims at an inquiry into the entire field of aesthetics; rather, they advanced an alternative to Croce relative to specific albeit important aspects.

A second point must be expanded to substantiate the claim with which we started, namely, that Pareyson's systematic aesthetics is elaborated in a deliberately anti-Crocean perspective. Previous to Pareyson's *Estetica*, at least two very meaningful systematic aesthetics had been published: Cesare Brandi's 1945 work *Carmine o della pittura* [*Carmine or On Painting*],[6] which despite its title is a general aesthetics, and Guido Calogero's *Estetica. Semantica. Istorica* [*Aesthetics, Semantics, Historics*],[7] which was written during the last years of World War II and published in 1947. Although they deeply renewed the way of considering aesthetics, neither of these works meant to break definitively the continuity with Croce's aesthetics. Gianfranco Contini's remark that the effort of his generation was to "be post-Crocean without being anti-Crocean" applies perfectly.[8] Such a remark could not be repeated in the case of Pareyson, however, who not only is post-Crocean but also was formed in an environment alien to the idealism in which Brandi and Calogero had matured. Pareyson's aesthetics is not only post-Crocean; it is also non-Crocean and even anti-Crocean.

Someone could remark, of course, that attempts at breaking away from Croce's hegemony within the aesthetic field had occurred already before World War II. In addition to some other problems, the famous (and tendentious) claim that idealism exercised a dictatorship on Italian culture in the first half of the twentieth century risks neglecting those authors who, in the first fifty years of the century, walked paths different from and irreducible to those of Croce and Gentile. It is true that, in the first thirty years of the twentieth century, it is difficult to point to aesthetic works capable of successfully opposing Croce's theories, and alternative voices have to be found either among outsiders who only later become famous (such as Carlo Michelstaedter and Giuseppe Rensi) or among escapees from Croceanism (such as Giuseppe Antonio Borgese). Nevertheless, at least starting in the 1930s, autonomous theoretical approaches emerge more sharply, and with time they become increasingly successful. I am thinking of the philosophy of the sensible by Adelchi Baratono (1934),[9] Anceschi's important book *Autonomia ed eteronomia dell'arte* [*Art's Autonomy or Heteronomy*] (1936),[10] and Antonio Banfi's writings on aesthetics (which in their prewar formulation reveal, because of their Kantian matrix, a proximity with Croce that will become unsurpassable distance only when they are rewritten later).

Not grasping the deep difference between the historical function of these works and Pareyson's *Estetica* would mean to portray a completely falsified picture of twentieth-century Italian aesthetics. The difference is immediately apparent when one considers that Anceschi's or Banfi's works from the 1930s only marginally affected the Crocean hegemony. Conversely, Pareyson's work and the other essays from the beginning of the 1950s mentioned at the outset initiated a process by which the Italian culture distanced itself from Croce. Such a process was substantially accomplished by the beginning of the 1960s and was as fast as it was radical. In a little over ten years, new orientations (phenomenological and Marxist aesthetics, hermeneutics) produced an almost complete eclipse of Crocean thinking. Little by little, even literary criticism, the field in which Croce's influence had probably been the most pervasive, began to open up to new methods: first, stylistics and semantic criticism, then formalism and structuralism, and finally semiotics, until Croce became something very similar to Marx's *toter Hund* [dead dog].

AN ANTI-CROCEAN AESTHETICS

Pareyson's aesthetics is definitely anti-Crocean. Yet one should not think that Pareyson's opposition to Croce translates into a continual polemic that punctiliously highlights the differences in orientation, as was so often the case for the literature that wished to mark its distance from the most influential philosopher of the first half of the twentieth century. Rather, the contrary is true—Pareyson knew all too well that one cannot overcome a philosophy by remaining attached to the questions that it proposes and by contesting the answers that it gives. The real overcoming occurs when what differs is not only the solutions but also the questions that one considers most relevant. Pareyson's *Estetica* can therefore afford the *nonchalant* gesture of almost never mentioning Croce in the body of the work and limiting itself to some occasional references in the rather few notes that appear at the end of the volume. It is remarkable that only in the preface to the 1988 new edition of his work with Bompiani—that is, in a culturally completely different climate—does Pareyson let himself go to some broader and less reticent consideration on the historical place of his *Teoria della formatività* and its relation to the dominating aesthetics at the time of its first appearance. Pareyson writes:

> Aesthetics is the field within which Croce's predominance has been unopposed the longest. Still in the immediate after-war period, Croce's aesthetics was the only one to which reference

was made in Italy. New needs however were already pressing. First of all, it was urgent to discuss those issues that Crocean censorship had detrimentally deflected from Italy; furthermore, it was necessary to elaborate theories capable of meeting the new needs of the changed situation. Such was the starting point and the ambitious project of the present book, which appeared in subsequent issues of a philosophy journal between 1950 and 1954.

Rather than lingering in one more critique of Croce's aesthetics, this book immediately addressed the topic and proposed, in place of Croce's principles of intuition and expression, an aesthetics of production and formativity. It was time, within art, to stress doing rather than contemplating.[11]

I make use later of the thematic suggestions offered by Pareyson's words. For now, I limit myself to a remark regarding the *tone* of the claim, which is unusually critical—it makes reference to the *censorship* that Croce exercised on orientations different from his own and the *detriment* that derived from it for Italian philosophical studies. These are direct polemical accents that, although probably resonating with Pareyson's attitude when writing the *Estetica*, have not been transposed, as we have already said, into the body of the work, and they cannot be found in those rare writings Pareyson devoted to Croce and his aesthetics. Barring mistakes, such writings can be reduced to the short piece "Significato di una teoria famosa [Meaning of a Famous Theory]" contained in the 1963 *Conversazioni di estetica* [*Conversations on Aesthetics*],[12] the longer and more articulate essay "Il concetto di interpretazione nell'estetica crociana [The Concept of Interpretation in Croce's Aesthetics]" that one can now read in the volume *L'esperienza artistica* [*The Artistic Experience*],[13] and the essay on "Arte e conoscenza [Art and Knowledge]," which was first conceived as the first chapter of the *Estetica* and then was included in the collection *Teoria dell'arte* [*Theory of Art*], published in 1965.[14]

The choice to stay away, in the *Estetica*, from petty polemic and from the confrontation between his own positions and Croce's reveals itself effective: Pareyson's work immediately appears as a rigorous philosophical aesthetics, well structured in its systematicity and therefore capable of presenting itself as an alternative to Croce's because of both its overall layout and its proposed specific doctrines. Unlike many other representatives of post-Crocean aesthetics, Pareyson's philosophical roots were very far from those of the early twentieth-century idealism in its Crocean and Gentilean variations. Pareyson had been educated in

Turin, in a university in which, despite Croce's numerous connections with Piedmont culture,[15] Croce's thought had always remained at the margins. In Turin, Pareyson studied German existentialism, particularly Jaspers, and was working at his own version of Christian personalism.

Let us establish the main points where Pareyson distances himself from Croce's aesthetics. First of all, in my opinion, is Pareyson's rejection of the *theoreticism* of Croce's aesthetics, namely, the idea that art is first and foremost *knowledge*. As is well known, for Croce art is a form of theoretical spirit; for Croce, who in this aspect is a faithful follower of Baumgarten, art is the beginning form of knowledge, the form through which we can know particular objects by elaborating sensible data into *intuitions*. From here comes the famous formulation of art as knowledge of the individual and first step of theoretical spirit. Conversely, for Pareyson art is first of all a *making* [*fare*] and producing: "emphasizing the cognitive character of art . . . has contributed to overlooking its most essential and fundamental aspect, which is that of executing and realizing."[16] In his most well-known saying, Pareyson claims that art is "a making that while making invents its way of making." It is true that, even prior to art, this formulation identifies *formativity* in general, and that through formativity artistic activities regain a relation with knowledge. According to Pareyson, all knowledge has a constructive or creative character (a Christian philosopher, Pareyson carefully avoids the use of the term "creative," yet the translation of formativity into creativity seems to me inevitable if one were to look at the matter without his religious presuppositions). It is also true that in such recognition, favored in my opinion by a shared Kantian suggestion, the distance between Croce and Pareyson weakens. Nevertheless, it is incontrovertible that for Croce art appears as *intuition* of forms, whereas for Pareyson it is *production* of forms.

This first fact immediately has an important consequence: for Croce, the aesthetic experience is, as it were, completely internal to the subject that creates or experiences the artwork, and properly there is nothing external to it; conversely, for Pareyson artistic making always appears as elaboration of an external matter. Art is a making also in the immediate sense that it is a transformation of a given material. For Croce, art coincides with the *internal image*: the artist's intuition-expression happens within the artist's mind and needs to be externalized only so as to be communicated to others. Matter is therefore simply a material support for communication and does not enter the creative process. With a risky move, Croce assimilates even the painter's colors or the sculptor's stones to the status of (alphabetic or musical) notations. For this reason, for the sculptor to pick up brushes or chisel is the same as for the poet to pick up the pen to fix on paper the poem that has already been formulated within the poet's mind.

Pareyson evidently has precisely this theory in mind when, in the opening pages of the *Estetica*, he writes: "The artistic operation cannot be pure formativity if it is not formation of physical material, so that one can say that physical exteriorization is a necessary and constitutive aspect of art and not something inessential and added, as if it pertained only to communication; for there is no work except than as a physical and material object."[17] The choice of the material thus becomes an essential moment of the artistic process and is already loaded with aesthetic meaning. Between the formative intention and its material there is a relation of indissolubility: one does not *employ* or *use* a material; one does not give form to a work "with or through a material; rather, one forms *a* material, and thus one forms the work." This is why materials are not interchangeable and replaceable *ad libitum* [as pleases].

The revaluation of the material and, with it, of the *technical* aspect of art brings Pareyson close to other anti-Crocean positions in the aesthetics of the post–World War II period, such as Dino Formaggio's phenomenological aesthetics, Dorfles, and Della Volpe. Similarly, Pareyson's opposition to Croce's theoreticism resonates with what was written more or less in the same years by Anceschi or Morpurgo-Tagliabue. What is interesting to note, however, is how, through the emphasis on the role of the material, Pareyson opens the way for taking distance from another crucial point in Croce's aesthetics.

Croce had integrated the conception he had presented in the first 1902 *Aesthetics* with an important development, which was proposed first in the conference on "L'intuizione e il carattere lirico dell'arte [Intuition and the Lyrical Character of Art]" and was then addressed systematically in the 1913 *Breviario di estetica* and the 1928 *Aesthetica in nuce*. In these writings by Croce, the content of art is identified with *feeling*, that is, with the affective life of the artist. The intuitive *form* expresses precisely the *feeling* of the creator. Art is always personal expression, but the artist's personality shows itself mainly in the world of feelings that transpires in the content of the artist's works. Eminently content based, in the sense we have described, is also Croce's concrete literary criticism, which for the most part consists in the analysis of feelings and moods described in various works. Conversely, for Pareyson the artwork is *formation of material*, and not *formation of content*. Pareyson does not mean at all to deny that in art spirituality and materiality coincide, that physicality becomes the bearer of meanings. He does want to say, however, that the artist's spiritual world is present in the work not in the role of *object of* expression (Croce's *feeling*) but rather as forming *subject*. The so-called content (the "spiritual world") is nothing else than the *way of forming* a specific material. The artist's personality expresses itself in the way in which that specific artist gives form to his or her own material; it is identical to the artist's *style*. Conceiving of the artist's personality as of content-to-be-formed means considering as "material for combustion" that which is rather "the very principle of flame," the forming energy; it means to consider the inseparability of form and content—a point very important, and with good reason, for idealistic aesthetics—from the perspective of the content, not of the form. This results in the fact that not only can one no longer see the role of the physicality of the work, but one also cannot truly attain that inseparability one presumes to ground.[18] Conversely, identifying style with the way of forming, as Pareyson does, opens the way for two anti-Crocean corollaries of the utmost importance: One, the spirituality that may enter art need no longer be reduced to feelings alone, because intellectual components too may find their expression in the formative attitude; and two, it is no longer mandatory to consider material physicality as alien to the real artistic process, as mere communication because, on the contrary, it is only through physicality that the identity of form and content, namely style, can manifest itself.

The dissatisfactions and needs for innovation characteristic of the scholars active in the postwar period converged on another crucial point of Croce's theory: the fundamental and most notorious theorem of his 1902 *Aesthetics*, namely, *the identity between intuition and expression*. The acknowledgement of such identity had played a fundamental role in the development of Croce's philosophy because it marked the *synthetic* character of intuition and paved the way for analogous coincidences in other fields, for example between volition and action within ethics. The exclusion of all yearnings and dreams that do not find their way into a precise formulation is completely in line with Croce's intransigency toward all projects that remain projects, toward anything that is not strong enough to pass from potentiality to actuality; implicitly, it turns into a moral sanction against those who claim to possess deep contents but not to have the means to express such contents, as well as against a desire that remains such without being capable of self-transformation into concrete action.

In the eyes of the protagonists of the postwar renewal of aesthetics, what was interesting and problematic was not the meaning of the identity of intuition and expression within Croce's theoretical framework but rather its consequential effect on the conception of the work of art and artistic activity. In particular, it becomes increasingly evident that such theorem ends up irremediably contracting the artistic process, the creative process, into an instantaneousness that is not very plausible and ultimately only acknowledges the completed work. The labor that precedes the final form, the whole aspect of the artist's quest, and the entire path of reconsiderations and corrections that characterize painters' and poets' ways of operating are denied or pushed aside in a limbo. Once a French art critic, while going through the rooms of an exhibition, praised a painting to Croce in terms of *"une très belle recherche* [a very beautiful quest; in French in the original]." To him, Croce replied that *"n'est pas une recherche, mais une réussite* [it is not a quest but a success]."[19] It is not by chance that Croce was very quick to make very severe remarks on the critique of authors' variations, for which Gianfranco Contini had offered fundamental examples in his works on Ariosto and on Petrarca's writings in Italian. Through the systematic study of the corrections that authors had brought to their own manuscripts, Contini did not mean to oppose Croceanism frontally so much as articulate its textual approach while procuring for himself a new help in interpretation and a powerful heuristic tool. As he prudently wrote at the beginning of his 1937 essay on Ariosto's *Orlando Furioso*, "there are two ways of considering a poetic work: there is a static way, as it were, that reasons on the poem as on an object or outcome, and in the end ends up with a characterizing description; and there is a dynamic way that sees it as a human work in progress, and tends to represent its dialectical life dramatically. In the poetic work, the former estimates a 'value,' the latter a perennial approximation to a value."[20] Croce immediately released, however, a *trenchant* comment on what he spitefully defined as the "critique of loose leaves," reasserting that the work of art "possesses a completely ideal genesis, which can be drawn from its very presence." Before the author decides "to place his pen on the paper," nothing guarantees, Croce noted, that the elaboration is carried out; or that the first drafts are not simply mnemonic traces, irrelevant from an expressive point of view, so that "in the vary act in which they write them [writers] also know that they do not accept them, and reserve for themselves the right of converting them into something different and opposite."[21]

The identity of intuition and expression already seemed "the mother of not few ills" to Guido Calogero.[22] The need to articulate such identity was quite clear also to Cesare Brandi when, in his *Carmine o della pittura* [*Carmine or On Painting*], he replaced it with the dialectic of the two moments of the *constitution of the object* and the *formulation of an image* between which there is no longer a relation of identification but rather a process relation. Pareyson is the author who certainly contributed the most to developing a *dynamic* conception of the artwork and reclaiming the importance of the artistic process in view of an understanding of the aesthetic experience. Croce considers as meaningless the artist's *trials* on the way to discovering the form; conversely, Pareyson understands well that the "discovery only occurs through a trial, and the completed work is a maturation that presupposes a process of germination and incubation through which the work defines itself in the process of being made through an alternate series of second thoughts, corrections, remakings, choices, erasures, denials, substitutions."[23]

If formativity is constructivism, if it means confronting a task that cannot be carried out by simply subsuming it under a given rule but requires instead that the rule be produced and invented, then the process of finding the rule becomes essential. In the work, what matters is certainly the result, yet the result cannot be grasped by simply considering it as such, in abstraction from the path one has followed in order to find it. "A making that also invents the way of making implies that one proceeds by trials, and the positive outcome of an operation of this kind is, properly speaking, a success [*riuscita*]."[24] To form is essentially *to try*, because I cannot know a priori the rule to apply; rather, I must build it while I proceed. It is not that artists imagine the completed work and then proceed to make it; rather, they "delineate it exactly while they make it," because art's only law is the work's individual rule. The two opposed hypotheses—namely, Croce's, for which the invention completely precedes the execution so that the form preexists the work, and the French philosopher Alain's, for which the invention is completely solved in the execution so that the form only exists once the operation is over—render the artistic process simply impossible to understand, because for the former the execution becomes superfluous and for the latter the invention become unexplainable. One must thus overcome the prejudice according to which the form is in the work only as formed form, and one must become ready to understand how, in art, a real *anticipation* of the future form is at work: "beside existing as formed at the end of the production, the form already acts as forming in the course of such production."[25] From here comes Pareyson's attention for the steps of the artistic process, from the sketch to the draft to the work, and his interest for those antecedents to the completed work that, "once light is cast on them by the work, help greatly to provide and ensure a greater knowledge and penetration of the artistic value." Hence, moreover, Pareyson's constant recommendation to "put the apparent staticity of the final form back into motion" through a *dynamic consideration* of the artwork. The artwork, one should note, may benefit from a *genetic* consideration, that is, from a consideration of the origin of the work (as happens in the case of the critique of variants), but does not coincide with it because in principle it is always possible, given that "the form is the very process that has reached its own completion" and "an understanding of the form is precluded to the one who considers the form *only* in its completeness, as if it were an instantaneous and sudden creation."[26] The perfection of the artwork is a *perficere* [performing], has an operative and poietic nature. Certainly, once it is completed, the form that arises through a rough path that is always at risk of being lost appears as having been made in the only way in which it could and should have been made, and it seems to acquire the internal necessity that belongs to organic products. Artists act consciously; the vicissitudes of their production require a constant critical and thereby intellectual intervention (it is not by chance that among the "big names" of Pareyson's aesthetics is Valéry). And yet the work also seems to develop as if from a seed, to grow of its own life; it is "a living organism . . . endowed with its internal legislation."[27] The preoccupation that guides Pareyson in these developments is clarifying how a single and unrepeatable work may also constitute itself as having an *exemplary* function, offer itself as imitable and generative of stylistic solutions. Here we touch, however, on an issue of tension in Pareyson's systematic construction: his complaint against Romanticism is that Romanticism compromises the understanding of the "tentative" character of formation; yet it is difficult to deny precisely the Romantic provenance (and thus the potential conflict with the theme of the tentative character) of the *organic* conception of the artwork that is equally dear to him, especially through Goethe's mediation.

Pareyson's insistence on the formative process and the dynamic character of the work gives his aesthetics a typical curvature toward the producer rather than the user. I mean to say that Pareyson's work seems to be written while keeping in mind first of all the experience of the art producer, not the art contemplator. With respect to this too, at least in its spirit Pareyson's aesthetics appears not to be distant from Brandi's coeval attempts at retracing the path of artistic creations, from the efforts by the critics of variants to glance into the poet's workshop, and also from Anceschi's predilection for those artists who, also being intellectuals, exercise an intellectual control, as it were, on their own creative faculties. This is a trait of Pareyson's aesthetics that is worth noting for two reasons. First, because the orientation toward the producer is rather rare in the history of aesthetics, which usually chooses the interpreter's viewpoint, as Nietzsche's sarcasms remind us: "Our aesthetics hitherto has been a woman's aesthetics to the extent that only the receivers of art have formulated their experience of 'what is beautiful?' In all philosophy hitherto the artist is lacking."[28] Second, because the aesthetics of a hermeneutic kind, an alternative to Pareyson's hermeneutics, will again give voice mainly to the reception, not to the production of the work.

FORMATIVITY AND INTERPRETATION

Another aspect where Pareyson's aesthetics fulfills needs analogous to those manifested by other coeval theoreticians is his *reevaluation of poetics*. In this instance, too, we find ourselves confronted with a field of inquiry not too dear to Croce, who could have repeated Goethe's admonition "*Bilde, Künstler, rede nicht!* [Make, artist, do not talk!]" and in general tended to identify the entire field of reflection on art with aesthetics. The study of poetics, that is, of the artists' programs and convictions and of the movements they created, is reclaimed as necessary by Banfi, is theorized as being extraordinarily fecund by Anceschi following Banfi, and ends up spreading also to literary critics formed in the Crocean tradition, such as Luigi Russo or Walter Binni. One should note that Croce's little propensity toward the study of poetics can also be read as the other coin of his aversion to contemporary art and especially to avant-garde art, as it is true that especially in twentieth-century art and in avant-garde movements, the *ideas* orienting artistic research, programs, and manifestos become decisive. Symmetrically, in Anceschi the study of poetics is functional to a critical orientation completely favorable to the avant-garde. At least judging on the base of his works, Pareyson does not seem to have a special interest for contemporary art. Perhaps for this reason also, in his work the (albeit theoretically sharp) recognition of the role of poetics seems to be less decisive than in others. Nevertheless, Pareyson's *Estetica* concludes precisely with the legitimacy of poetics, with a final chapter that argues for the difference between philosophical aesthetics and empirical poetics and has a programmatic character: one must distinguish "between aesthetics, which has a philosophical and purely speculative character since it is geared at defining a concept of art, and various poetics, which have a historical and operative character since they arise so as to advance artistic ideals and art programs."[29] For Pareyson, all poetics are legitimate; it is symptomatic though that his preference goes to poetics that translate into concrete works rather than to programmatic poetics: "Indeed a specific poetics has an operative character, but this becomes efficacious only when it becomes operational in a process of formation. Then the poetics embodies itself indissolubly in the work, and coincides with the internal 'poetics' that is its own interior legislation. This suffices to explain why poetics that are fixed in programs anteceding art are generally fruitless, whereas those that 'follow' the already realized art seem to be more fecund, since they ultimately do nothing else than advancing the intrinsic and meaningful exemplarity of such art."[30]

Finally, we must address a last point that, unlike the previous ones, does not bring Pareyson close to the other thinkers of the post-Croce renewal but rather marks Pareyson's greatest originality. I am referring to the role he assigns to *interpretation* within the aesthetic experience. The interpretation of the artwork is thematized in two fundamental chapters (the fifth and the sixth) of his *Estetica* and takes up a relevance at least equal to the other bearing concept in Pareyson's edifice, namely, *formativity*. One could even say that formativity and interpretation are twin notions, or two sides of the same coin. Even interpretation has a "productive and formative" character insofar as, on the consumer's side, it follows up on and retraces the work that has been done by the artist. Interpretation is the form of knowledge that fits all formative processes and eminently the artistic processes. It is active and personal and in it, as in all human activities, receptivity and activity also cannot be disjoined. There is never pure passivity, but neither is there pure creation; the given is always elaborated on, yet it is always necessary. Common opinion accentuates the subjective character of interpretation (my, your interpretation); Pareyson, however, invites us, on the one hand, not to consider the object of interpretation (the forms) as less important than the subjective character and, on the other hand, to speak not of subjectivity as much as of *personality* of interpretation. Interpretation is *knowledge of forms on the person's side*. Formativity has no external guarantees but is rather a constructive search for an individual rule; likewise, interpretation cannot rest on objective rules, but instead consists in a process of ever fallible approximation. The form has a dynamic, mobile character; likewise, "only through a movement can one hope to grasp it, only by setting it back into motion can one force it to disclose its perfection."[31]

Artworks are to be interpreted, that is, *performed*. This holds true for all kinds of work, and not only for those for which we are used to speaking of execution or interpretation, such as musical arts or theater. It is wrong to identify the performance only with the work of *mediation* by the artist or the musical performer because the performance is deciphering, mediation, and realization all together. Even a work that is mediated by a performer must be in some sense re-performed by its consumer. Now, were we to ask why each work demands performance, the only answer would have to be the following: the work must be performed because it is born as performed; it arises as physical reality that is shaped through a process. If the performance is congenital to the work, performing cannot mean adding something to the work as if the work were incomplete; conversely, it means to make the work live in its completeness. The coincidence of work and interpretation must be understood as normative and final; yet it does not exclude the transcendence of the work with respect to its interpretations. Pareyson's position is equally distant from the dogmatism of those who think that there is only *one* valid interpretation and the extremism of those (like Giovanni Gentile and some deconstructionists) who think that the work is reduced to its interpretations. To demand from interpreters a chimeric loyalty is as absurd as searching only for their originality, given that their task is rather *congeniality* and that the work speaks to those who know how to question it by becoming attuned to it. The *judgment* on the work must also be referred back to interpretation because such a judgment is already present in the reading itself, and the evaluation is internal to the very performance: the judgment is identical to the revival and is not subsequent to it; and the difference between reading and critique is a difference in terms of methodological awareness and not a difference of nature. Reading, performance, and judgment end up being substantially identical, for Pareyson. Critical judgment consists, once again, in the confrontation between the work and its intention, which was already at work in the performer's activity.[32]

In this vindication of the centrality of interpretation, once again an anti-Crocean motif is at work. Each author has his or her interests; each theory ends up choosing the problems it cares for the most, thereby relegating the others to the background or answering them in a hasty manner. Now, in general Croce's aesthetics had little or no sensitivity precisely toward those aspects of aesthetic theory which Pareyson is most concerned about—the way in which the consumer revives the artist's work, the nature of critique, the status of performing arts such as music and theater in which one for the most part performs works written by other authors, and the transpositions of a work from one expressive medium to the other, be it a musical transcription or an interlinguistic translation. Croce had moved from the empathic solution in his *Aesthetics* (to judge a work means to relive it, to remake it within oneself) to the logic-oriented solution of the *Breviario* (to criticize a work means to utter the judgment "X is a work of art" or "X is not a work of art"), and had given, with respect to the problems that fascinated Pareyson, one of those final verdicts that solve questions by denying them, one of those "formidable iron gates" of which Luigi Pirandello speaks in his essay *On Humor*. For Croce, on the ground of the theorem of the *individuality* of intuitions-expressions, any work, even any word becomes an unrepeatable monad closed in on its unicity. For this reason, translations, but also musical or theatrical performances, have to be judged as *new* works—this is a solution, as one can see, that solves the problem by denying it at its roots.[33]

In a certain sense, with his theory of interpretation Pareyson accomplishes a distancing from Croceanism by developing an aesthetic theory that displays its most characterizing and problematic core in a set of questions unwelcome or neglected by Croce. At the same time, however, such theory of interpretation opens the way to subsequent developments less in terms of Pareyson's aesthetics than in terms of his entire philosophy, which takes the form of a *hermeneutic ontology* and will address areas different from art.

THE RECEPTION OF PAREYSON'S AESTHETICS

Let me move to some conclusive considerations. I have addressed the topic of the relation of Pareyson's aesthetics to Croce's, thereby defining Pareyson's position with respect to the dominant philosophy in the first part of the last century. By doing this, I have also been able to mark a series of convergences and divergences with the main thinkers within Italian aesthetics in the years following World War II. It seems therefore to be expected that I conclude this overview of Pareyson's role within twentieth-century aesthetic theory with the question of the influences exercised by Pareyson's views on the aesthetics of the second half of the twentieth century and the issue of the audiences that such views were able to captivate in the years after the 1950s.

I address this last issue much more quickly than what I have done with respect to the two previous questions. My impression is, in fact, that the impact of Pareyson's aesthetics on the thought of the second half of the twentieth century is less deep and pervasive than the role for which he was a candidate given his theoretical solidity and the originality of many of his solutions.

I am not at all claiming, of course, that Pareyson did not have, even within aesthetics, disciples and followers. Many of Pareyson's numerous students have continued concerning themselves with aesthetics, and some have acquired a fame far superior than their teacher's, who was always very reticent and discrete. Sergio Givone has developed a philosophy of the tragic, Gianni Vattimo has concerned himself with poetry and ontology, Claudio Vicentini has devoted himself to the aesthetics of theater, and Mario Perniola to contemporary art. Without Pareyson's idea of art as formation of matter and not of content, and its corollary for which the artist's personality can be seen in the way of forming and not in the contents, some of Umberto Eco's first works, including *The Open Work*[34] and *Interpretation and Overinterpretation*,[35] would not have been the same. Eco's essay "Del modo di formare come impegno sulla realtà [On the Way of Forming as Commitment to Reality]," which appeared on *Rinascita* at the beginning of the 1960s, develops Pareysonian motifs when it claims that "the discourse that art carries out is made through the way of forming" or that "the musician is progressive insofar as he or she promotes, at the level of forms, a new way of seeing the world." Later, he will write that "the artist carries out his or her protest within the very structures of his or her work and not by describing suffering miners,"[36] but here one can already recognize Eco's unmistakable style.

Naturally, nearly all of Pareyson's direct students have followed their own lines of inquiry, often ending up very far from their teacher's approach. And, while they moved away, it does not seem that other scholars coming from different traditions followed up on Pareyson's *Estetica*. Briefly, I believe that this happened because of three main reasons:

1. After the mid-1960s, Pareyson himself no longer concerned himself with aesthetics. His interests turned to ontology, ethics, and moral philosophy. The contents of the 1954 *Estetica* were illustrated and resumed many times in the subsequent years, and the theoretical analysis was paired with many and important historiographic explorations; yet, after the collections of essays published in the following ten years, which for the most part gathered previously written texts, there have been no new developments.

2. Starting in the 1960s, within the Italian cultural scenario, philosophical aesthetics has undergone an eclipse and a loss of interest, has been the object of many criticisms and charges of obsolescence, and has been faced with the competition of new disciplines that wished to take its place up to its replacement. Furthermore, the popular fashion of hermeneutics looked for inspiration, rather than to Pareyson, to the various versions on the other side of

the Alps, especially to Gadamer and to Jauss' aesthetics of reception.

3. Pareyson never gave his aesthetics an applied dimension by translating or exemplifying it in art criticism essays. He moved at the level of theory and the history of philosophy. In general, the aesthetic theories that have had greater resonance have always been those that have been able to mark with their influence the tendencies of art criticism and art history, which ensure a wider audience than the one granted by the small philosophical public.

To these substantial reasons one may perhaps add an accessory motif, namely, the very traditional literary form of Pareyson's writings that, in terms of the language they employ, today appear to be affected by a certain dustiness (*absit iniuria verbis* [let injury by words be absent]).

This circumscribed fortune and limits, however, take nothing away from the important function played by Pareyson's aesthetics within the renewal of post–World War II Italian culture. Likewise, they do not affect the solidity and the value of Pareyson's theoretical inquiry within aesthetics. I would even say that they contribute to make us recognize, more than half a century later, the importance of a work that by now deserves being considered a classic within twentieth-century aesthetic theory and one of the few Italian works that, within this field, is destined to last.

—Translated by Silvia Benso

NOTES

1. Luigi Pareyson, *Estetica. Teoria della formatività* (Turin: Edizioni di Filosofia, 1954).

2. Guido Morpurgo Tagliabue, *Il concetto dello stile. Saggio di una fenomenologia dell'arte* (Milan: Fratelli Bocca, 1951).

3. Gillo Dorfles, *Discorso tecnico delle arti* (Pisa: Nistri-Lischi, 1952).

4. Dino Formaggio, *Fenomenologia della tecnica artistica* (Milan: Nuvoletti, 1953).

5. Galvano Della Volpe, *Il verosimile filmico e altri scritti di estetica* (Rome: Edizioni Filmcritica, 1954).

6. Cesare Brandi, *Carmine o della pittura* (Rome: Scialoja, 1945).

7. Guido Calogero, *Estetica. Semantica. Istorica* (Turin: Einaudi, 1947).

8. Gianfranco Contini, "L'influenza culturale di Benedetto Croce," in *Altri esercizi: 1942–1971* (Turin: Einaudi, 1978), 31.

9. Adelchi Baratono, *Il mondo sensibile. Introduzione all'estetica* (Messina-Milan: Principato, 1934).

10. Luciano Anceschi, *Autonomia ed eteronomia dell'arte. Saggio di fenomenologia delle poetiche* (Milan: Sansoni, 1936).

11. Pareyson, "Prefazione," in *Estetica. Teoria della formatività* (Milan: Bompiani, 1988). The rest of the preface of this fourth edition continues identical to the text of the first edition. The second edition of the volume appeared by Zanichelli in 1960 and the third by Sansoni in 1974.

12. Luigi Pareyson, *Conversazioni di estetica* (Milan: Mursia, 1966), 79–86.

13. Luigi Pareyson, *L'esperienza artistica* (Milan: Marzorati, 1974), 259–86.

14. Luigi Pareyson, *Teoria dell'arte* (Milan: Marzorati, 1965). To these more sustained essays one should also add the more occasional (and severe) piece in the 1966 "Nel centenario di Croce [On Croce's Centennial]," now published in Luigi Pareyson, *Prospettive di filosofia contemporanea* (Milan: Mursia, 1993).

15. See on this the proceedings of the conference "Croce in Piemonte," which took place in Turin and Biella in May 2003: *Croce in Piemonte*, ed. C. Allasia (Naples: Editoriale Scientifica, 2006). On Pareyson, see especially ibid., 381–89, where one can find the testimony, between anecdotal and sly, by Carlo Augusto Viano.

16. Luigi Pareyson, *I problemi dell'estetica* (Milan: Marzorati, 1966), 28.

17. Pareyson, *Estetica*, 42.

18. Ibid., 28–40; and Pareyson, *Teoria dell'arte*, 55–79.

19. Benedetto Croce, *Concetti critici inadatti* (1948), now in *Nuove pagine sparse* (Naples: Ricciardi, 1949), vol. I, 200–1.

20. Gianfranco Contini, *Come lavorava l'Ariosto* (1937), now in *Esercizi di lettura* (Turin: Einaudi, 1974), 23.

21. Benedetto Croce, *Illusioni sulla genesi delle opere d'arte documentabile dagli scartafacci degli scrittori* (1947), now in *Nuove pagine sparse*, cit., vol. I, 190–91.

22. Calogero, *Estetica. Semantica. Istorica*, 242.

23. Luigi Pareyson, "Significato di una teoria famosa," in *Conversazioni di estetica*, 79.

24. Pareyson, *Estetica*, 60.

25. Ibid., 75.

26. Ibid., 102, 108, 255; Pareyson, *Teoria dell'arte*, 72.

27. Pareyson, *Teoria dell'arte*, 66.

28. Friedrich Nietzsche, *The Will to Power*, trans. W. Kaufmann and R. J. Hollingdale (New York: Random House, 1968), 429.

29. Pareyson, *Estetica*, 316.

30. Ibid., 316

31. Pareyson, *Teoria dell'arte*, 128.

32. Pareyson, *Estetica*, 226–72; Pareyson, *Teoria dell'arte*, 189–231.

33. It is not by chance that Croce's theories on interpretation, translation, and performance are the aspects of Croce's aesthetics to which Pareyson has devoted the most detailed analysis and critique in his essay *La teoria crociana della interpretazione*.

34. Umberto Eco, *The Open Work*, trans. Anna Cancogni (Cambridge: Harvard University Press, 1989).

35. Umberto Eco, *Interpretation and Overinterpretation* (Cambridge: Cambridge University Press, 1992).

36. Umberto Eco, "Dal gruppo 63 a 'Quindici,'" now in *Il costume di casa* (Milan: Bompiani, 1973), 301.

4

Pareyson vs. Croce

The Novelties of Pareyson's 1954 *Estetica*

Umberto Eco

In this essay, I focus on the so-called second Pareyson, the one who writes the *Estetica. Teoria della formatività* [*Aesthetics: Theory of Formativity*][1] following on the studies on German idealism and existentialism up to the first version of *Esistenza e persona* [*Existence and Person*].[2] The reason is that I have witnessed the birth of the *Estetica* lecture after lecture, and it is a book that has had and still has a fundamental influence on me. Even if I have secularized Pareyson's metaphysics, as I happened to write once, had I not been born with Pareyson's aesthetics, neither could I have concerned myself with the "open" relation between a work of art and its interpreters, with the limits and possibilities of interpretation, with Peirce's doctrine of the interpretant, nor could I have developed my criticisms of deconstructionist theories.

Whereas Pareyson's *Estetica* has exerted such an influence on me, I do not think that one can say the same with respect to Italian culture in general. While obviously met with all due attention within the academic circles, the book has not had the same popular diffusion as Croce's *Breviario di estetica*.[3] Its first paperback edition appeared thirty-four years after the initial publication (I know how pleased Pareyson was that his work would leave the specialized bookcases and instead present itself on the counters by the bookstore entrances).

The reception of Pareyson's *Estetica* has been respectful although not enthusiastic—as it should have been, given that Pareyson was dealing a mortal blow to Crocean aesthetics. This troubled the late idealistic-historicistic *koiné* of the time (from the followers of Giovanni Gentile to the Christian spiritualists to the Marxists up to, of course, the Croceanism of the *stenterelli*)[4] to such an extent that the book was opposed not with polemics but rather with formal deference.

Another reason for such a lukewarm reception is personal and character based. Some may regret that I now bring it up but, [in the case] of a teacher, one should also remember weaknesses and errors, so that one may draw a lesson from these also. Already at a young age Pareyson had acquired an emerging position in the world of academic politics. He was what today one would call *"un barone* [a power broker]," with an enormous influence in terms of nationwide competitions for academic positions. Aware of the power he had, Pareyson tried to handle it with political prudence. I remember that if I suggested that I would review for the *Rivista di estetica* [*Review of Aesthetics*], which he directed, a recently published Italian book, he would say: "No, because the author is a candidate for the next competition, and I do not wish that taking a stand, whether positive or negative, in my journal may appear as an advance judgment."

No matter the philosophical school to which one belonged, the same prudence was of course practiced by anyone who thought of participating one day in a job search for a university position in aesthetics. Respect dictated that Pareyson be reviewed; caution demanded that he not be criticized. Thus it happened that, of the many reviews Pareyson's work received, all of them were overviews void of any polemical remark.

Pareyson tended to ignore, or perhaps he was by character disgusted with, the recognition that thinkers matter only if they provoke a debate and are talked of perhaps even with undue emphasis, so that severe and even unjust criticisms are preferable over silence or, even worse, educated approval. To a reserved man as Pareyson, such debates appeared as loud and vulgar. He was not a character for duels.

I should speak here, however, not of the man but of his work. With respect to that, I limit myself, as I said at the outset, to its relation with Croce's aesthetics.

It is well known that Croce defined art as intuition—an idea in itself not repulsive although limited—had he ever defined in his work the concept of intuition. In the "Conclusion" to his *Aesthetics*, Croce writes, "having defined the nature of the intuitive or expressive knowledge that is the aesthetic or artistic act. . . ."[5] Unfortunately, such a claim is false:

on no page of the *Aesthetics* is there offered a definition of art different from intuition; and yet, there is no definition of intuition that does not refer to the example of art. Croce takes, as it were, the experience of art (the certain, sudden recognition of what art is) as a primitive given from which to start so as to confer on intuition all the (indefinite) features of art. The issue is no different when one moves to formulations such as "lyric intuition,"[6] because one discovers that "lyric" is not a specific difference but a synonym for "intuition." For any fan of the circle, the circularity is perfect: the only intuition is artistic and art is intuition. One should take a look at fulgurating tautologies such as "it seems right and opportune to us to define beauty as successful expression, or better, as expression *tout court*, because when it is not successful an expression is not an expression."[7]

This very vague idea of intuition brought Croce (in the sixth chapter of the *Aesthetics* devoted to theoretical and practical activities) to enunciate the incredible proposition that artistic intuition-expression exhausts itself in internal elaboration, whereas its technical-material externalization (in marble, on canvas, in the emission of vocal sounds) is completely accessory and inessential, only geared to the "conservation and reproduction" of the originary interior flash.[8] How can this be? Are these not the words of the same author who, a hundred pages earlier, had said that "one often hears people claim that they have a lot of important thoughts on their mind but they are not able to express them," whereas "if they really had them, they would express them in many beautiful resounding words"?[9] Croce can, of course, claim that concretizing thoughts into sounds is simply an empirical necessity, a stenographic device, let us say, for future memory, so as to warn Croce himself (or some other judge) that such thoughts really exist. But what could one say about the famous tenor who, one evening, having had the internal intuition of a splendid high note, is booed from the gallery simply because, for the sake of the archives, he has tried to externalize it and his vocal chords have failed him? That he (as Dante says) "knows his trade but has a trembling heart"? The fact is that what Croce says does not correspond to what we know about the practice of other artists, who have drawn sketches after sketches in the quest for the final image, or have hustled with set squares and compasses so as to realize a perfect point of fugue.

Croce's adamantine certainties seemed to be born from his very scarce familiarity with the arts, not only in the sense that he never practiced any, but also in the sense that he must have always been uninterested in what artists do. Croce considers as superficial the observation that "artists create their expressions by painting or sculpting, writing or composing" because artists "in reality never give a stroke without first having seen it with their imagination."[10] If the word "reality" makes sense in Croce's system, in reality all artists never tire of telling us the extent to which the consistency of the material has excited their imagination, and how at times only by rereading their own drafts aloud have poets found, in the aural resonance, the clue that would bring them to alter the rhythm and search for the right word. Yet Croce will claim (in *La poesia*)[11] that poets abhor the empirical externalization of their internal intuition to such an extent that they do not gladly recite their own verses. Were that to be true! But it is statistically false.

In the *Breviario*, the inessentiality of the technique is shown by quoting the case of major painters who use colors that end up altered; in this way though, artistic technique and science of materials end up being confused. Unable to save the *Battaglia di Anghiari*, Leonardo had an admirable painting technique but a miserable chemical knowledge of the materials he was using. I do not know whether Croce ever meditated on the sonnet in which Michelangelo reminds us that "The best of artists hath no thought to show // Which the rough stone in its superfluous shell // Doth not include: to break the marble spell // Is all the hand that serves the brain can do." If Croce read such a sonnet, he forgot about it, and forgot because of preconceived ideas. Here Michelangelo tells us that artists find their intuition-expression by dialoguing with the material, its veins, its lines of development, its possibilities. Out of love of hyperboles, Michelangelo says even more: the statue is already in the marble and the artist does nothing else than take away the surplus that hides it.

Almost as if to be polemical toward Michelangelo, Croce speaks of the "piece of marble that *contains* the 'Moses,'" and of "the piece of painted wood that *contains* the 'Transfiguration'" (italics added). The citation leaves no room for doubts: those which we consider as artworks (and on whose state of ruin, restoration, falsification, or theft we torment ourselves) are mere containers of the sole, unique, true (and by now unattainable) works that consist of their authors' completely internal intuitions.

Unlike Croce, Pareyson had always been very attentive to artists' experiences, so much so that in his *Estetica* there are perhaps more quotations from artists' poetics (from Flaubert to Valéry and Stravinsky) than from philosophical aesthetics. It is to these texts, that is, to artists' poetics, that he refers, and with subtle analysis he explores the dialogical activity through which artists, limiting themselves in front of the obstacle, find their truest freedom. From out of the indistinctness of vague aspirations, artists move in fact to the concrete consideration of the possibilities offered by the material with which they struggle and whose laws they progressively reduce within the frame of an organization that turns them into the laws of the work.

For Pareyson, matter becomes the obstacle on which one exercises one's inventive activity, which dissolves material necessity into the laws of the work. Given this general definition, one of the most original aspects of Pareyson's doctrine consists in his having brought back to the concept of materiality all those various realities that clash and intersect in the world of artistic productions: the complex of "expressive devices," transmissible techniques, codified precepts, the various "traditional "languages," the very tools of art. All this is subsumed under the general category of "materiality," the external reality on which artists work. An ancient rhetorical tradition can be assumed under the same rubric of the marble on which one carves, namely, as the chosen obstacle that becomes suggestion for action. The goal itself to which a functional work is destined must be considered as "material"—that is, a complex of autonomous laws that the artist must know how to interpret and reduce to artistic laws.

An opposition that Adriano Tilgher used to draw between Croce and Valéry comes to mind: "Croce considers poetic activity as something that time after time creates its own measure and rhythm, its law. Valéry asserts that true poetry only comes to light by struggling against the obstacle constituted by traditional metrics and language." Now, according to Pareyson's aesthetics of formativity, through their forming, artists actually invent completely new laws and rhythms. Yet this novelty arises not out of nothing but rather as the free resolution of a set of suggestions that the cultural tradition and the physical world have proposed to the artist in an initial form as resistance and codified passivity.

From what has been said, another point becomes clear in Pareyson's aesthetic theory: artistic production is not the sudden outcome of a not otherwise defined intuition but is rather a *trial*, a proceeding through proposals and drafts, patient interrogations of "materiality." This creative adventure has a point of reference and comparison, though. Artists proceed by trials, but their trials are guided by the work as it will have to be, which orients the productive process in the form of an appeal and intrinsic need for formation: "the trial therefore has an indefinable yet very firm criterion—the presentiment of the accomplishment, the divination of the form."

I think that we have not sufficiently enough read, or reread, these pages of Pareyson's on the production of the work of art as interrogation of that which does not yet exists—pages that by themselves do justice to all commonplaces of idealistic aesthetics. The dynamic and process-based approach to creation implies a similarly trial- and process-based notion of the answer to the completed work, namely, its interpretation. This concept is central in the aesthetics of formativity precisely because it determines the integration between a world of forms endowed with autonomous legality (the world of human forms as well as that of natural forms) and the presence of a human activity that is not only forming but also interpretative. This is so to such an extent that one aspect cannot be disjoined from the other, nor can the concept of form be understood in its entire meaningfulness if one does not question the relation between form and the knowledge of it one may have.

Pareyson's theory of interpretation is perhaps that which, in its time, provoked the greatest resistances in terms of the reception of the aesthetics of formativity because it certainly implied a rather remarkable equation: enjoyment of the work of art, its possible "performance," and specialized critical-interpretative discourse on it are not kinds of activities distinct by intention or method. Rather, they are various aspects of the same interpretative process. They differ as for awareness and intensity of attention, capacity of penetration, greater or less interpretative mastery, but not for their substantial aspects.

To deeply understand the development of this concept, it is not useless to follow it as it has configured itself little by little in Pareyson's thinking precisely with reference to the criticism of Croce's notion of interpretation as it appeared in 1953 in Pareyson's "Il concetto di interpretazione nell'estetica crociana [The Concept of Interpretation in Crocean Aesthetics]."[12]

In this essay, Pareyson examines Croce's opinions with respect to theatrical and musical performances. With respect to the former, Croce thought that the recitation of a drama or the declamation of a poem are new and different works compared with the original. As is the case for translations, here too, after a "first moment" in which the actor or reciter recalls the original work, on the basis of this "antecedent" or "point of reference" a "second moment" unfolds—that is, the real translation, expression of the interpreter's personality and therefore a new work and a "new song." As for musical performances, Croce assimilates them to the recollection that poets have of their own poems; it is not a translation into a new work but rather a *re-creation* of the original work. While this explanation allows for the permanence of the work in its performance, it nevertheless denies any personal contribution by the performer. The musical performance appears as a reevocation carried out along the path of a philological inquiry meant to offer again the *only one* possible face of the work.

Precisely on the ground of Croce's principle of the unity of the arts, first of all Pareyson remarks how the concept of performance must be extended to all arts because performances are also the reading of a page in verses, the correct lightening of a statue, or the representation of a drama. The analogy reveals, of course, some limitations having to do with different behaviors toward different systems of signs and with the distinction between so-called *autographic* and *allographic* arts, that is, between works of art that are entirely present in their physicality (like paintings or statues) and works of arts that need the mediation of a score, like music or literature. To Pareyson, however, all these "appearances" do not seem definitive because *every kind of work requires a performance*—albeit a purely interior one—that makes it live again in the consumer's experience.

Croce thought that the performance of a drama was already a translation, as if the real drama consisted in the written work, and the actor's work were added to it as a provisional mediator; yet this thought rests precisely on the neglect with which Croce gratifies the question of materiality. Conversely, Pareyson observes how, for example in dramas, it is precisely the adoption of theatrical materiality that forces the author to conceive of the written text with constant reference to technical problems of representation, having to foresee gestures, scenes, lights, the relation with the public. Theatrical authors build their texts as a sum of indications for the performance of the real work. By introducing this revaluation of materiality and technique within art, which is a peculiar feature of his theory of formativity, Pareyson reduces the apparent "translation" to being also in this case an act of "performance."

One should add that Croce's concept cannot escape an antinomy: either the performance is a faithful rendition of the work or it is the expression of the performer's personality. In Croce's perspective, the coincidence between unity of work and multiplicity of its performances is not possible. Pareyson remarks how the reason for the antinomy lies precisely in the missed recognition of a plurality of persons dialoguing with the concrete physicality of things. For Croce, "Spirit neither *interprets nor executes* because either it *creates* new works or it *re-evokes* those that it has created."[13] Even in the later developments of his thought, Croce could never free himself of this antinomy. The doctrine of the cosmic character of poetry re-proposes the concept of re-creation, but here too the interpreter's personality, rather than justifying the different interpretations, is absorbed into the universe of the work that is already, in itself, the sum of all its "true" interpretations. Conversely, Pareyson aims at emphasizing the freely active character of the interpreters who confront the work, understand it by discussing it, and by understanding it manifest their own personality.

This conception obviously presupposes a philosophical foundation that, in the abovementioned essay, appears only laterally. As a result, the theory of interpretation that is advanced between the lines and in antithesis to Croce's claims may not appear as completely clear. The perspective changes if one begins to analyze such concepts in light of the *Estetica*, where Pareyson proposes a "gnoseology of interpretation" that, by the way, he had anticipated in some pre-aesthetic writings given that the concept of interpretation was becoming the very ground of his philosophy. Within the perspective of human activities understood as "formative" (in the forms of thinking, morality, or art), the cognitive process itself occurs as a continuous exchange between stimuli that reality offers as "cues" and proposals that persons advance about such cues so as to clarify them into a form.

It is a trial-based process of approximations and returns—neither of mechanical reception of a reality already given once and for all, nor even less of idealistic creation—that, in terms of Pareyson's contemporary proposal of a philosophy of the person, presupposes a "metaphysics of figuration" as guarantee for the objective stability of the cue, but that already foreshadows many current cognitivist approaches.

I would like here to leave aside (and in this sense I said that I was secularizing my teacher's doctrine, which rendered our relationship a bit difficult for a few years) precisely that which for Pareyson is the *conditio sine qua non* of his entire system. For him, the metaphysics of figuration presupposes the presence of a Shaper [*Figuratore*] who has constituted the natural forms precisely as cues for possible interpretations. Conversely, I thought that the entire theory of interpretation could be secularized without a metaphysical recourse to the Shaper, who at best can be postulated as a psychological support for those who embark upon the adventure of interpretation.

The theme I thought should be developed, in light of subsequent discussions, was that of the dialectic between freedom of interpretation and loyalty to the work, because if something was being called into doubt (within the world of literary and artistic theories in general), that was not the existence of a Shaper who constituted the natural forms precisely as spurs for interpretation; what was being called into question was rather the preexistence of all forms to the moment of interpretation.

I recall that when, certainly mindful of Pareyson's theory of interpretation, both in *The Open Work*[14] and in subsequent semiotic works such as *Lector in Fabula* (in English, *The Role of the Reader*),[15] I pushed the moment of interpretation as "cooperation" between work and interpreter, I aroused the diffidence of many supporters of the objectivity of forms. I recall an objection by Lévi-Strauss, according to which "what makes a work a work is not its being open but rather its being closed. A work is an object endowed with precise properties, which is up to analysis to identify, and which can be completely defined on the ground of such properties." In the very years during which Lévi-Strauss uttered such words, however, various and often diverse critical tendencies started to develop, such as the aesthetics of reception of the Konstanz school, Wayne Booth's implied author, Riffaterre's arch-reader, Maria Corti's implicit reader, Iser's *implizite Leser*, and the various followers of the reader-oriented criticism. At first, all of these tendencies were limited to emphasizing the intervention of the interpreter in the realization of the work as such. Little by little, though, they gave way to the idea of a complete autonomy of interpretation, so as to read in an already deconstructionist key Valéry's claim *"il n'y a pas de vrai sens d'un texte* [there is no true meaning of a text]." In many universities in the United States (I am talking of the period between the 1970s and the 1980s), it became politically correct[16] to let students read a text as they wished, with no imposition of a duty of loyalty whatsoever either to the nature of the specific text or to the alleged intentions of its author.

On the wave of Derrida's deconstructionism, which in my opinion was ill interpreted (because Derrida's deconstruction is, if anything, a sort of psychoanalysis of philosophical texts, whereas in the United States it progressively became a theory of reading literary texts), it became then necessary to insist on the other side of the opposition between work and interpretation and to remind [the audience], as I had to do in several occasions, that a title such as *The Open Work* is an oxymoron because that which one wishes to keep open to various interpretations is in the end a work, that is, something that precedes such interpretations. I thus had to title one of my subsequent books *The Limits of Interpretation*,[17] and I did this precisely following up on Pareyson's dialectics between freedom of interpretation and loyalty to the text.

From Pareyson's theory of interpretation I got the idea that, on the one hand, a work of art postulates an interpretative intervention, but, on the other hand, it exhibits formal characteristics such as to stimulate and simultaneously regulate the order of its own interpretations. Or, quoting from Pareyson's *I problemi dell'estetica* [*The Problems of Aesthetics*], I got the idea that "the work resides in its performances as their law and criterion of judgment, that is, the work stimulates all of them, regulates them in their course, approves of them if they are fitting and denounces them if they are failed or arbitrary." To a close analysis, this is nothing other than the reiteration, within aesthetics, of a theoretical principle dominating the whole of Pareyson's thought from the start, namely, the question of *whether* and *that* "a pluralistic yet non-relativistic conception of the truth"[18] is possible—that is, the persuasion that truth is unique even if it can be recognized only through its historical manifestations.

I am, of course, developing freely some Pareysonian suggestions, but as a proof that my interpretation of his *Estetica* is loyal, one should refer to chapter 5, section 11 ("Neither objectivity nor subjectivity of beauty"), chapter 6, section 3 (where he wonders whether a work may have only one correct performance or many), still in chapter 6, section 4 ("Personality of interpretation and infinity of the work as foundations of the variety of performances"), or, again in chapter 6, the fundamental sections that go from 6 ("*Loyalty* and *freedom* of interpretation") to 18.

These ideas still had an influence on me years later in my proposal that, confronted with the unavoidable presence of the form to be interpreted, one may perhaps not always be able to say when an interpretation is better than others, but it is certainly always possible to say, for a sort of Popperian principle of falsification, when the interpretation does not do justice to the interpreted object.

This is also a way of taking a stand with respect to post-Nietzschean degenerations for which there are no facts but only interpretations. There is no interpretation except that of a fact. Pareyson would have said, of a preexisting *cue*.

Now, I have said a lot about the way of approaching a form and the material that precedes it and stimulates its invention. I have not spoken, however, about what should be considered the fundamental point in Pareyson's aesthetics, namely, the concept of form and the fact that his theory is presented as a *theory of formativity*. So as to neither act like those reviewers about whom I spoke at the beginning nor be guilty of prudent "summarization," I would like to address the issue only from the margin, concerning myself with a question that, in Pareyson's *Estetica*, occupies the short section 10, which appears in "The Parts and the Whole," a subchapter of chapter 3 (titled "Completeness of the Work of Art").

In this sense, my discourse presents itself as an attempt at *metamereology* because, while reading an exquisitely mereological section, it tries to consider it as representative of Pareyson's entire system. This is an issue on which I have already written, but to which I return because verifying systems at their margins has always appeared to be very important to me. Let us then consider Pareyson's section 10, which is titled "Essentiality of All Parts: Structure, Fillers, Imperfections."

It is well known that one of Pareyson's central concerns in his *Estetica*, in its polemic against all aesthetics of fragments, is the vindication of the character of totality of the artistic form, and hence the refusal to select, within a work, sporadic moments of poetry as if they were flowers grown amidst the scrub of the simple *structure*. It should not be necessary, yet it is useful to reassert that in those times, and in Italy, the concept of "structure" was something to be avoided. It was a framework, a mechanical device that had nothing to do with the moment of lyrical intuition; at most, it stood in a Hegelian mode as a negative instance, a conceptual residue that could at best serve to make the poetic moments shine as solitary gems. Even if, in the notes to the chapter, Pareyson refers to Luigi Russo as to a timid champion of the "non-extraneousness of structure to art" (and even if Russo recognizes that there is a structure that is not born before poetry, as if it were a skeleton on which then to insert poetical flowers, but that is rather "as it were generated from the interiority of the poetically moved spirit"), Pareyson concludes that such a poetically moved spirit "catches its breath and rest in such doctrinal stations." There is thus an absolution of the structure as a buoy onto which the poetic swimmer can hold; it is good that the structure is there, but only so as to catch one's breath and keep swimming the *crawl* style of lyricity. As if to say that Dante, who could not see, at each and every step, sweet colors of oriental sapphire or Beatrice's smiling eyes, took ample rests by disserting of theology and rambling on the composition of the Heavens.

In any case, by sharply opposing the dichotomy poetry/structure with the totality of the artistic form, Pareyson runs the risk of falling into an organicist rhetoric.

It is one thing to claim that in the completed work (and truly already from the first moment when the cue initiates the formative process), *tout se tient* [everything is connected to everything else]; thus the theory must assert (and the interpretative activity identify) the organic overarching design, the individual rule, the "forming form" that obscurely comes first, directs in its unfolding, and appears as outcome and revelation of the formed form. It is another thing, though, to celebrate such "unitotality of the work" with accents that frankly, forty years later, appear to us as belonging more to a rhetoric of the beautiful than to a phenomenology of forms.

Here is one example of this:

> This dynamic character of the unitotality of the work of art can explain the relations that in it exist between parts and

whole. In the work of art, the parts entertain a double kind of relations: each with the others, and each with the whole. All parts are linked among themselves by an indissoluble unity, so that each is necessary and indispensable and has a determined and irreplaceable location to the point that a lack would dissolve the unity and a variation would bring disorder back. . . . Each part is instituted as such by the whole, which has itself claimed and disposed the parts of which it itself is the outcome; if an alteration of the parts is the dissolution of the unity and the disintegration of the whole, this is so because the whole itself presides the coherence of the parts among themselves and makes them conspire altogether in order to form the whole. In this sense, the relations that the parts have among themselves simply mirror the relation that each part has with the whole—the harmony of the parts forms the whole [*l'intero*] because the totality [*il tutto*] founds their unity.[19]

This sounds too perfect. Here, as elsewhere, Pareyson seems to fall prey to a Pythagorean *raptus*, and some day it might be worthwhile searching beyond Romanticism for some unconfessed sources of his aesthetics—in Renaissance neo-Platonism or in Nicholas of Cusa, not to mention some readings of the mystics, authors with whom Pareyson consorted even if he did not write about them.

How could a theoretician as attentive as Pareyson to the moment of concrete reading of artistic works think in terms of such a strikingly totalizing, holistic experience that is never disturbed by moments of perplexity or dissatisfaction whether on the side of the artists, who, when re-reading, re-seeing, or re-hearing themselves, would wish to correct themselves, or on the side of the interpreters, who would be tempted to correct the artists? Good interpreters, who have penetrated the work, are those who, albeit at the peak of enthusiasm for their authors, once in a while also say "I do not like it" or even "I would have said it better" (and then perhaps out of modesty they remain silent; yet they are impatient). Yet Pareyson is also the first to speak of interpretation as of a performance that is also capable of accentuating, softening, or putting into perspective various aspects of the work and thus, out of loyalty, also of correcting them.

It is precisely after writing the passage I quoted that Pareyson tackles the question of the allegedly dead or "structural" moments, which are essential and not marginal or extraneous so as to redeem the structure and bring it back within the formative project. If "the totality [*il tutto*] is the outcome of the parts united so as to constitute a whole [*l'intero*]," there can be no negligible particular or irrelevant detail. And if, in interpretation, some parts may result as less important than others, this is so because a distribution of functions occurs within the organized form.

Pareyson is not saying—which would mean reading him as if he had written thirty years later or as if he came from different origins—that the *Divine Comedy* is more beautiful because of the theological structure than because of its most celebrated poetic "gems" that conversely represent its accidental moment. Yet he is certainly coming close to saying that the Homeric framework of Joyce's *Ulysses* is as aesthetically important as Molly Bloom's monologue, which could not have the effect it does were it not inserted in that specific framework, so that readers must find, within the monologue, a crowd of intertextual references that necessarily refer such readers to other apparently irrelevant and useless hints that appear in other chapters in the novel.

At this point, Pareyson realizes that he needs to come to terms not only with the structure as framework but also with the twists, weaknesses, patches, coverings, slips, decreases in tension, even misadventures that at times make ugly the alleged harmony and necessity of the structure—indeed, the fillers or wedges [*zeppe*].[20]

"Filler [*zeppa*]" is a clumsy term, like the dysfunction it defines. Phonosymbolically, the Italian word evokes cough, sneeze, regurgitation, and hiccup; semantically, it suggests unsuccessful intrusion, an evident filler. Yet Pareyson, who is an almost aulic writer, does not avoid using such a terminological filler to indicate the aesthetic filler. He does so to speak of the works that appear "unequal and discontinuous," where fillers are seen as supporting points necessary for the well-flowing of the whole, bridges, weldings "in which the artist works with less care, with greater impatience or even with indifference, almost getting rid of them as of passages that, precisely because imposed by the need to move forward, can be left to conventionality without thereby compromising the whole."[21]

Fillers too are thus part of the internal economy of the form, given that the Totality needs them albeit in a subordinate position. Let us speak out of metaphor (because otherwise we risk not realizing to what extent Pareyson's aesthetics calls into question fundamental problems of system organization): let us forget a personified Totality that demands something. What Pareyson is saying is that a filler is an artificial device that enables one part to connect to another; it is an essential joint. If a door needs to open, whether with softness or majesty, it must have a hinge, no matter how mechanical its function is. Poor architects, sick with aestheticism, are annoyed because a door must revolve around a hinge, and redesign the hinge so that it looks "beautiful" while it performs its function; by doing so, the architects' accomplishment is often that the door squeaks, jams, and does not open or opens poorly. Conversely, good architects want the door to open so as to disclose other spaces; thus, they are not bothered by the fact that, having redesigned everything else in the building, when it comes to hinges they have to rely on the eternal wisdom of the ironmonger.

Fillers accept their banality because without the quickness enabled by the banal, a passage would be delayed—a passage that is important for the fate of the work and its interpretation.

Pareyson writes that "with respect to this, the exemplification could be so wide as to embrace almost the entirety of the history of arts."[22] I will try some such examples.

The filler may be a banal beginning, useful so as to attain a sublime end. One night, at three in the morning, standing on the hill of the Infinite in Recanati,[23] where the first words of one of the most beautiful poems of all times are inscribed, I realized that "*Sempre caro mi fu quest'ermo colle* [Always dear to me this solitary hill was]" is a rather banal verse, which could have been written by any minor poet of Romanticism or perhaps of some other period and movement. In poetic language, what should a hill be if not solitary? Yet, without such a banal beginning, the poem would not start; perhaps it had to be banal so that in the end one could perceive the panic feeling of the poetically memorable drift.

I would dare say, albeit out of love for the argument, that a verse such as Dante's "*Nel mezzo del cammin di nostra vita* [In the middle of the path of our life]" has the singsong-like dignity of a filler. Had it not been followed by the rest of the *Divine Comedy*, we would not have given it much importance; perhaps we would have registered it as an idiomatic expression.

I am not identifying the filler with the initial shot. There are some beginnings of Chopin's *Polonaises* that are not at all fillers. Manzoni's "*Quel ramo del lago di Como* [That branch of Como's lake]" is not a filler.[24] Nor is "April is the cruelest month." But if we think of the end of *Romeo and Juliet*, tell me whether it would have not been a better end without the two final sentences: "A glooming peace this morning with it brings; // The sun, for sorrow, will not show his head: // Go hence, to have more talk of these sad things; // Some shall be pardon'd, and some punished: // For never was a story of more woe // Than this of Juliet and her Romeo."

Yet, if Shakespeare decided to conclude with such a moralizing banality, it is because he had to let his audience catch their breath before inducing them to exit peacefully after the slaughter that they had witnessed. It was then good that the filler was there.

It is by arguing how fillers can be redeemed by the whole that Pareyson gradually moves to address mutilations, the action of time, stubs, ruins, fragments, the deteriorations that a work may undergo and despite which we can still reconstruct its internal legality. These Pareysonian pages would not make sense were we not to see the central value of fillers, and the praise of imperfection, because it is only if a work can be enjoyed despite and thanks to its imperfections that it will be able to be enjoyed despite (and perhaps thanks to) its deterioration.

Thus, to counterbalance that sort of Platonic optimism that had brought Pareyson to celebrate form in its adamantine perfection, his remarks on fillers (inspired by concrete reading experiences) bring his phenomenology of art back to much more human dimensions. If, however, we reconsider the issue of fillers in light of Kant's doctrine of reflective judgment, the issue becomes perhaps less marginal than it appears at first sight—both in the sense that fillers cannot be marginal elements in the work, and in the sense that the question of fillers is not so marginal in Pareyson's aesthetics.

Let us revisit Kant's position. The recognition of organicism arises in reflective judgment. The organicism of nature is postulated as an order that must be there in things but that things do not exhibit in themselves: it must be constructed, projected, *as if*. Only because we cannot avoid seeing nature as an organism are we then capable of turning to art with a similar spirit.

Like all reflective and teleological judgments, a judgment of organicism is, however, a hypothesis: nature is tested through some initial schemas and increasingly better subjected to interpretative activity.

The interpretative activity (and this is, for Pareyson, the central point) is *perspectival*. Now, when stating judgments of organicism with respect to the things of nature, we find elements that seem to clash with the postulate of the perfection of the form: fillers indeed, which remain as memories of evolution, elements that do not seem to conspire toward the whole but rather subsist, within a natural body, as memories of a failed attempt. When one studies the form, and then categorizes it, inserting it into the architectonics of kinds and species, these elements are sometimes dropped, left in the shade while the spotlight of interpretative attention moves to floodlight other elements that are considered as central.

We must wonder to what extent this criterion intervenes in the assignation of an internal legality to the work of art. Shaped into its form by the interpretative act that sees it as a completed organism, the work of art denudes itself of apparently inessential aspects that are sacrificed in favor of others; only to a further or parallel interpretation do these aspects take up a more decisive position. The history of Dante interpretations testifies to this—some theological elements of *Paradise* that were considered as fillers by Romantic criticism become fundamental for a critique that has internalized a greater confidence with respect to the medieval cultural universe (a Dante that is reread not only after, let us say, Gilson, but also after Eliot); they become an essential rib in poetic architecture as much as vaults or stained-glass windows are in gothic cathedrals. The perspective of the *cantiche* is overturned, and one discovers that at times Dante is more of a poet when he speaks of the planetary spheres or the glaring of light than when he becomes moved because of Paolo and Francesca's affairs. And when he revaluated the so-called "non-poetical" moments of the work of art, Pareyson had perhaps in mind the essays recently written by his colleague Giovanni Getto on the theological aspects of Dante's poetry.

Fillers survive then as residues of a stage of interpretation, and as such they remain as reserves, ready to assume a different light to a new "reading" in relation to which they will no longer be accidental. They do not intervene simply as prudent correctives to the Platonic or neo-Platonic triumph of the Form in all its metaphysical purity, and as recognition of the material life of *forms*, accepted even as dirty and imperfect. They rather present themselves as something that the interpretation *sets aside*, placing them in reserve as an occasion or latent stimulus for subsequent interpretations. Thus interpretation confirms itself as both free and loyal at the same time, capable of many indulgences so as to rest in the recognition of one form, but also capable of many repentances so as not to let the form rest in the state to which our reading has provisionally taken it.

Were it even the case, reading after reading, that a filler will never and at no price be redeemed (because it truly remains as a testimony of a distraction or a shortcoming), its very presence would remain to testify how and to what extent the interrogation of the work may be capable of being collaborative and *charitable*, may identify a designed design even where such a design was only a sketch, a desire, an intention entrusted as legacy for the infinite work of interpretation.

In conclusion, allow me an illicit reflection—illicit because it betrays my thematic proposal of being concerned only with the 1954 *Estetica*, and illicit because it is only a matter of an illusion, a suspicion, a shadow that has crossed my mind while writing this essay. Ultimately, it is of shadows I would like to speak, shadows as vague as those that are seen on X-rays and are not always interpretable in one single way.

My Pareyson, as I have already said, has been the one from the 1950s and early 1960s. When his hermeneutic period started and his ontology of freedom began to develop, I was theoretically far removed from his concerns, and when, after about fifteen years of cold courtesy, our contacts became stronger in the 1980s and developed into a renewed affection, we did not confront each other deeply on specific philosophical issues.

In 1989, however, when his *Filosofia della libertà* [*Philosophy of Freedom*][25] came out (because in those years I was concerned with hermetic doctrines and therefore also with gnosticism, and amused myself with the kabbalah by consorting with my friend Moshe Idel),[26] I could not avoid noticing an analogy—and this happened not because Pareyson at a certain point made some reflections on an initial *berehsit* in the Torah.

The fact is that at the end of such a short text by Pareyson, the idea was sketched out, which was then developed in *Ontologia della libertà* [*Ontology of Freedom*],[27] of "an upsetting and perturbing element—evil in God," that is to say, the idea of a godhead that in some way experiences the negative, overcomes it but does not get rid of it, and preserves, as it were, the trace of it, its mark, shadow, "a sort of darkening of its own brightness."

In the idea of a divine evil I had then identified a gnostic root, and I do not recall how Pareyson had exactly reacted to my insinuation. I think he did not affirm it but did not deny it either.[28] More than by the gnostic root, however, I had been intrigued by the kabbalistic root, which I had not mentioned to him.

I am thinking not so much of the idea that the Torah is one but that its legitimate interpretations are infinite throughout the centuries as much as the kabbalistic set of problems concerning the nature and origin of evil; in other words, the cosmic evil that derives from a dialectic internal to the process of emanation. In some versions of kabbalistic mysticism, evil is seen as the product of the refusal of an organic process and is compared to residues of bad blood, to the scum that remains after gold has been refined, to wine sediments. Finally, in Lurianic Kabbala, the act of creation implies a withdrawal, a contraction of God within himself, the *tzimtzum*; in the moment of creative expansion, because of a complex phenomenon called the *shattering of the vessels*, the light of emanation is, as it were, fragmented, and through the debris of the vessels that used to contain it, it generates the dark forms of the *qelippot*, source of rough materiality.

I do not mean to say either that Pareyson practiced a reading of kabbalist authors—which would not surprise me because, among his unexpected readings, once I heard him quote from a very rarely known, occult mystic, Saint-Martin—or that the traces of "God's past," as is said in *Ontologia della libertà*, of such a possibility that has been certainly tamed but is "always available" and we can always rediscover and re-actualize, have something to do with the *qelippot*.

I am simply struck by the suspicion that if in Pareyson's ontology there is something that in the divine nature remains as trace or residue of an ancient error, invisible because redeemed by the whole form of God's positivity, then we must reconsider the figure and function of fillers within the formed form of the artwork. As if, which is not a negligible hypothesis, the artistic form hid, within its apparent perfection, the image of the gnawing that deeply affects the Shaper of all forms; as if, in those few pages on fillers, Pareyson echoed or anticipated other ontological preoccupations.

Except that artistic fillers cannot be a source of pain (unless one practices an obtuse aesthetics of fragments). Perhaps for this reason, the metaphysics of formativity succeeded in eliminating from the aesthetic perspective the suffering that the later Pareyson confronted up to his end, in philosophy as well as in life.

—Translated by Silvia Benso

NOTES

1. Luigi Pareyson, *Estetica. Teoria della formatività* (Turin: Edizioni di Filosofia, 1954).
2. Luigi Pareyson, *Esistenza e persona* (Turin: Taylor, 1950).
3. Benedetto Croce, *Breviario di estetica* (Naples: Laterza, 1913).
4. Stenterello is a masked character of the *commedia dell'arte* and is traditionally very poor and generally very hungry.
5. Benedetto Croce, *Estetica come scienza dell'espressione e linguistica generale* (Milan: Sandron, 1902), 176.
6. Croce, *Breviario di estetica*, 1.
7. Ibid., 101.
8. Ibid., 123.
9. Ibid., 13.
10. Ibid., 130.
11. Benedetto Croce, *La poesia* (Milan: Adelphi, 1994). The volume, on which Croce worked between 1934 and 1935, was first published in 1936 [trans. note].
12. Luigi Pareyson, "Il concetto di interpretazione nell'estetica crociana," *Rivista di filosofia* 44, no. 3 (1953).

13. Ibid.
14. Umberto Eco, *The Open Work*, trans. Anna Cancogni (Cambridge: Harvard University Press, 1989).
15. Umberto Eco, *The Role of the Reader: Explorations in the Semiotics of Texts* (Bloomington: Indiana University Press, 1979).
16. In English in the original Italian text [trans. note].
17. Umberto Eco, *The Limits of Interpretation* (Bloomington: Indiana University Press, 1991).
18. Luigi Pareyson, "Dal personalismo esistenziale all'ontologia della libertà," in *Esistenza e persona* (Genoa: Il Melangolo, 1985), 9–38.
19. Pareyson, *Estetica*, 107.
20. Many times I have wondered whether, for the notion of "*zeppa* [filler]," Pareyson was inspired by some previous discussion. It is well known how poor in notes the *Estetica* is, and the references are often general. On this specific issue, I have found no quotation or reference. Taking a deconstructionist license, I observe that dictionaries provide, as an example of a "*zeppa*," also the "*cuneo* [wedge]," and I decide that I am going to see, in the choice of this technical term, an unconscious tribute to Pareyson's own native province, precisely the province of Cuneo.
21. Pareyson, *Estetica*, 111.
22. Ibid., 112.
23. Eco is here referring to a famous poem by Italian poet Giacomo Leopardi titled precisely "The Infinite" [trans. note].
24. Eco is here referring to the opening sentence of Alessandro Manzoni, *I Promessi Sposi/The Betrothed*, trans. Bruce Penman (London: Penguin, 1972).
25. Luigi Pareyson, *Filosofia della libertà* (Genoa: Il Melangolo, 1989).
26. Moshe Idel is a professor at the Hebrew University in Jerusalem and a renowned scholar of Jewish thought. He received the Israel Prize for Jewish Thought in 1999, the Emmet Prize in 2002, and has been a member of the Israeli Academy since 2006 [trans. note].
27. Luigi Pareyson, *Ontologia della libertà. Il male e la sofferenza* (Turin: Einaudi, 1995).
28. So as to provoke him, I had then written a false sacred hymn by Manzoni devoted to Gnosis, now in *Il mio secondo diario minimo* (Milan: Bompiani, 1992). Had I done so twenty years earlier, the Master would have been scandalized, but by now the Friend had learnt to accept my desecrating trips.

5

On Pareyson's Interpretation of Kant's Third Critique

Massimo Cacciari

OPUS PHILOSOPHICUM MAXIME

The most important contribution of Pareyson's *L'estetica di Kant* [*Kant's Aesthetics*],[1] which was published for the first time in 1949 and in its definitive edition in 1984, lies in its sharp affirmation of the *systematic* character of Kant's Third Critique. There is of course no overall inquiry into Kant's philosophy (at least within "continental" hermeneutics) that does not remark on the significance of the *Critique of the Faculty of Judgment* as the "discovery" of precisely a faculty that seems to "be added" to those of knowing and desiring and that enables the mediation or "move" between their principles. Pareyson's perspective distances itself completely from such a traditional approach. For Pareyson, the Third Critique has a systematic relevance not insofar as it is the mere "completion" of the inquiry into the faculties of the soul but rather because the analysis of judgment plays a fundamental function in the *construction* of the entire critical philosophy. "System" does not in fact mean a more or less coherent aggregation of parts; rather, it refers to an organic totality in which each element mirrors, from a particular viewpoint, the whole, and in which each part takes up again and unfolds the overall problematic. Now, the boldness of such a task does not escape Pareyson because the *Critique of Judgment* resolutely begins by positing the irreducibility of the foundational principles of judgment to the principles of the intellect on the one hand, and to those of practical reason on the other. Will it not be a violation of the text or of Kant's intentions to claim that *the problem* of aesthetic or reflecting judgment emerges from within critical philosophy itself, that it is imposed by the constitution of the very intellectual and practical spheres? It is neither simply a matter of the need to *show* the transcendental character of such form of judgment (which is in itself a difficult task) nor, on such a base, of the possibility of the passage (*Übergang*) from the constitutive character of the intellectual-determining judgment (capable of *legislating* nature) to the principle (*freedom*) that makes it possible to conceive of an action in view of an *unconditioned* end. Well beyond this, the matter is rather that of reconsidering constitution and meaning of the other faculties in light of the results of the analysis of the faculty of judgment. No extrinsic mediation, no bridge could ever join banks that remain opposite by their very nature. The dimensions of the soul can form an organic totality only insofar as each of them turns out to be immanent in the others.

And yet, by posing the question in these terms, do we not perhaps set out on a path "prohibited" by Kant? Do we not end up assuming a romantic perspective in reading the *Critique of Judgment*? At times this seems precisely the perspective explicitly advanced by Pareyson, and there is no doubt that his interpretation situates the Third Critique within the field of Romantic and idealistic aesthetics. At the same time, however, it seems to me that Pareyson highlights its *theoretical* relevance precisely in the sense I have just indicated: the *Critique of Judgment* carries out an unavoidable function in terms of clarifying the structure of critical philosophy and is not at all a sort of "first step" beyond its limits. This means that the transcendental principle of reflecting judgment, the *agon* that it represents with respect to the "immeasurable gulf" (*unübersehbare Kluft*) between the concepts of nature and freedom, may be *operative* within the realms of the intellect and of practical reason. Briefly stated, only if the form of reflecting judgment turns out to be "determining" in terms of explaining the concrete constitution of the other faculties can one consider the systematic demand that moves the entire *Critique of Judgment* to be satisfied. This demand is therefore completely irreducible to a mere need, to an unfulfillable nostalgia, or to the form of an empty "ought" (*Sollen*).

Pareyson insists on showing that the principle that grounds the possibility of the "judgment" (*Mittelglied*) between the "kingdoms" of necessity and freedom can have nothing objective, that it remains purely thinkable, that the move occurs only within the subject. The nexus (which will never be a synthesis or conciliation) can be grounded only in the subject-that-thinks, in Kant's sense of thinking (*Denken*). Yet finding and founding such a nexus is *necessary* so as to "save" the system. This means: without the thought of such a nexus, it is not possible to consider the fundamental domains of pure and practical reason as completely "systematized" either. If the *Critique of Judgment* is to be considered, as it is by Pareyson, an *opus philosophicum maxime* [a philosophical work in the highest degree] and not simply, as it has been done for the most part, the foundation of an aesthetics or of aesthetics *tout court* as a particular "modern" discipline, it is not possible to proceed along a different path; and this path is infinitely more complex than a mere broadening of the critical horizon.

SHARED DRAMA

There is no doubt that the 1790 *Vorrede* and *Einleitung*, which were written at the conclusion of the work, greatly reveal the need to justify the transcendental, neither empirical nor pedagogical, character of the inquiry into the faculty of judgment rather than the problematization that such an inquiry entails with respect to the entire realm of critical philosophy. Kant is essentially keen on showing how the aesthetic judgment's "claim to validity for everyone" is *grounded* on the universal condition of judgment as reflecting judgment. This condition is not made to operate in the structure of the determining judgment in any way except extrinsically in the claim that the unification of principles, the "agreement" (*Einstimmung*) of nature with the faculty of knowing, represents *an unsuppressible need* of the intellect itself. Kant had already gone beyond the expression of such a "need of the intellect" (*Verstandesbedürfnis*) in the so-called *Erste Einleitung*, whose manuscript was found by Dilthey in 1889. Such "Introduction" is of such theoretical depth that its first editors titled it *Über die Philosophie überhaupt*. It is strange that Pareyson does not make explicit reference to this extraordinary essay, which supports precisely the fundamental angle of his own interpretation.

In this *Über die Philosophie*, the faculty of judgment can determine neither the concepts of the intellect nor the ideas of reason. Nevertheless, it does not limit itself at all to *thinking* the things of nature "insofar as [nature] regulates itself according to our judgment"; that is, it does not limit itself to thinking some "purposiveness" (*Zweckmässigkeit*) of nature (nature as a product of art-*techne*). Rather, it reveals the ineliminable immanence of the principle of finality within the very movement of the legislative intellect. With an anachronism that I believe is justified, we could say that the analysis of reflecting judgment ends up showing the *anthropic* nature of the concrete functioning of the intellect itself. The connection of experience to nature in conformity with laws confronts us with the disquieting (*unheimlich!*) multiplicity and heterogeneity of its forms. In its concrete *operari* [functioning], the intellect is forced to presume that they belong to a *system of nature*. The principle of finality is therefore a *maxim* that one cannot ignore in the very concreteness of scientific processes. The increasing connection of experiences that it generates is not dispersed in the *labyrinth* of various particular laws because the intellect produces all of them and *thinks* in the direction of their unity. It is the intellect that must think of nature as of a *logical system!* Reflecting judgment here reveals its proper function, its authentic goal: "to regard nature a priori as having in its diversity the quality of a logical system under empirical laws" (*die Natur a priori als qualifiziert zu einem logischen System ihrer Mannigfaltigkeit unter empirischen Gesetzen anzusehen*) (*KU* 20: 214).

Within this general theoretical perspective, Pareyson can abandon "the analytical division of faculties," or show their inconsistency, and grasp their unifying sense while at the same time preserving their distinction. There is neither juxtaposition among them nor any extrinsic nexus among their principles; rather, there is involvement of all in a shared *drama*. Pareyson thus shows the merely functional character of the distinction among the various forms of pleasure, between pure and impure aesthetic judgment, between the dimension of taste and the "figure" of the genius, and the reciprocal implication of aesthetic judgment and value or moral judgment. These are critical acquisitions that will characterize all subsequent inquiries into the *Critique of Judgment*.

IMAGINATION AND ITS MOST DISQUIETING *FACIES*

The real knot to be solved for a systematic interpretation of the Third Critique concerns its relation with the *Critique of Pure Reason* with respect to the meaning and function of the *imagination*. One should restrain the evocative power of the term and bring it back, first of all, to the context of problems of transcendental schematism. The inquiry should not "precipitate" to the treatment of the specific form of expansion (*Erweiterung*) of the imagination produced by pleasure of the sublime; rather, the very imagination that animates the *Geist* of the genius should be considered in light of the theory contained in the First Critique. Here imagination is called to found the relation, the adequation, between the multiple of sensibility, which is given to the soul by intuition (transcendental aesthetics), and the *concept*. Such a founding (without which there is no *science*) is, however, made possible by the fact that imagination already operates *a synthesis in general* at the level of multiplicity, of sensible experience. The synthesis that defines the concept is not possible except on the ground of the former. Imagining means placing a given multiplicity into *one* image. The concept is the *comprehension* of something that has already been synthetized, and it never deals with mere im-mediacy. In other words, by imagining, the soul "opens itself up"; its first gaze is imagination. The concept is not a "leap" to another kind; rather, it is prepared ever since the originary "opening" of experience.

The crucial function of the imagination is not limited to this first level. The transcendental schema is the representation that mediates sensibility and intellect. Here too does the faculty of the imagination (*Einbildungskraft*) operate. In the first stage, the image assumes a particular, determined value; it is the spontaneous product of the soul in its opening up to an entity. In the scheme, what is instead expressed is the image in its universal value. The scheme is the image that the intellect produces so as to unify the sensible multiple. Yet it is the same faculty that makes the two syntheses possible! This faculty is not a faculty of the intellect as such; yet the intellect utilizes it, and it cannot do otherwise, in order to reach the concept and apply the concept to the phenomenon. The intellect works through the imagination, but the imagination is not at all one of its products. The faculty of imagination is *presupposed* for the work of the concept. The operation of schematism is founded on imagination as on "an art concealed in the depths of the human soul" (*verborgene Kunst in den tiefen der menschlichen Seele*) (*KrV* A 141/B 181). It is so hidden that it can never be disclosed. The same words occur in the First and Third Critiques: the principle of the faculty of judgment, grounded on imagination, lies perhaps "in the supra-sensible substance of humankind" (*in das übersinnliche Substanz der Menschheit*). The nature of imagination loves to hide. . . .

Both the concept and the ideas are *mediated* out of sensibility through imagination, and this always occurs a priori. Imagination does not work through mechanical association of the data of intuition, it does not proceed by "reproducing" them. The schema is as a priori as the concept; it is an expression of the spontaneous-productive power of the soul. The schema displays the transcendental possibility possessed by the subject in itself to apply the categories to the sensible. Analogously, in the *Critique of Judgment* the ideas of reason display themselves in the faculty of imagination as *in themselves* turned toward the sensible. There are no "abstract" ideas; all ideas accompany and "embody" themselves in an image; all concepts "temporalize" themselves through the schema.

In imagination, Pareyson grasps the constitutive and systematic nexus among the three Critiques. In illuminating it and indicating it as *the* problem for any subsequent inquiry, he provides an essential contribution for understanding this crucial period of European philosophy. After Pareyson, it is impossible to speak of imagination in the *Critique of Judgment* in a "subjectivistic" sense; it is impossible not to connect it theoretically to the problem of schematism. There is, of course, expansion (*Erweiterung*) in the move from the First to the Third Critique, but this is so not so much in the sense of development and broadening as much as, essentially, in the sense of problematizing. In the *Critique of Judgment*, imagination appears in its most disquieting *facies* [aspect], as a "striving to progress to the Infinite" (*bestreben zum Fortschritt ins Unendliche*)," as a "claim" (*Anspruch*) to the Whole. We could say that this is the other face of imagination that had recognized itself within the limits of the intellect. In the First Critique, imagination brings concepts back, time after time, to the *necessity* of their empirical use. In the *Critique of Judgment*, the imagination "launches" any spatiotemporally defined intuition toward the exhibition of that which transcends it. Imagination would be inconceivable if it were not also able to reach its own boundaries and therefore imagine the unimaginable, and moreover assert precisely the "prohibition" of images as the climax of the idea of the sublime. What matters is that the distinction, which has to be held firm in place, between imagination as articulation of the nexus appearance-concepts and imagination as necessary tension toward the sensible exhibition of ideas is a distinction that occurs *in the unity* of imagination (*Einbildungskraft*). Such a faculty can therefore only be studied within the unity of the *system*.

How problematic this unity is; how schematism and imagination remain the crux of transcendental philosophy—these are questions that cannot be taken up here. Reading the pages of the *Opus Postumum* will suffice to understand how open such questions remain for Kant, to the point that they concern the entire "destiny" of subsequent philosophy. Pareyson approaches the *Critique of Judgment* within the context of his studies on romanticism and idealism exactly because he is aware of this. The *Critique of Judgment* is by no means a pre-romantic "manifesto"; yet there is no doubt that the romantic cannot be understood philosophically apart from the background of the Third Critique, and precisely as alleged "emancipation" of imagination from its systematic hinging on the limits of pure reason. The productivity of imagination "pretends" to free itself from the necessity of schematizing and thus presents itself precisely as *conciliation* of sensible and suprasensible, as *supreme organ* of reason. Never, though, in Kant, could nexuses, systematic relations, and analogies give rise to unities that overcome or eliminate distinctions. To the *limits* of the intellect there correspond the *limits* of the genial-imaginative *Geist* analyzed in the *Critique of Judgment*. The systematic nexus is established among domains of the soul that are all, in themselves, *finite*. In its aesthetic *facies* [aspect], the imagination's ability to schematize without concept does not represent an overcoming of the imagination that is operative in the transcendental schematism precisely because such a faculty must be considered in its deepest unity—and this unity critically assumes within itself the limits of intellectual knowing *and* of reflecting judgment.

FEELING AND JUDGMENT

The imagination, as the faculty of schematism, is essential to understanding the meaning of the *Critique of Judgment* in another way as well. In its first fundamental stage, imagining-schematizing shows how there is no impression that is simply immediate; how intuition is already in itself a "gathering" multiplicity; and how the *legein-logos*, as it were, in its most originary meaning appears as already immanent in sensible intuiting. This is exactly the problem that in the Third Critique appears in its entire theoretical relevance: in aesthetic experience, what is at stake is certainly judgment, but a judgment that is however simultaneously *feeling* [sentimento] *or expression of a feeling*. This means to claim that the subject is endowed with forms of judgment that coalesce with receptivity itself, that the universality of judgment, under certain conditions and within definite limits, does not contradict at all the "passivity" of sensing [*sentire*] but rather is connatural to it. In other words, the *Critique of Judgment* shows that *it is impossible to conceive of pure passivity or im-mediate receptivity*. Knowing coalesces with sensing as thought does with language.

The theme of feeling-taste (*Gefühl-Geschmack*) opens to the consideration of the ontological connection between sensing and judging, to the idea of an originary connection between feeling and judgment. More originary than any distinction between determining judgment and reflecting judgment is the "form" according to which [*per cui*] feeling judges and judgment "feels" the thing, on this-or-that side of any rational schema of a goal, of all practical finality. It is impossible to feel anything without, at the same time, thinking-judging it. A sentiment of pleasure or displeasure, of joy or pain that does not entail, at the same time, wondering about its "reason" is impossible.

I think that Pareyson's interpretation is geared toward valorizing these aspects of the *Critique of Judgment* rather than those that will prove central in romantic philosophical aesthetics. Pareyson is correct, of course, to emphasize the truly epochal role played by the concepts of *Genie* and *Geist* in subsequent artistic and philosophical culture. Yet their meaning will change radically in comparison to the *Critique of Judgment*. Here they do not at all represent a real overcoming of the gap (*Kluft*) between sensible and suprasensible, between necessity and freedom. The Genius is nothing else than the faculty of imagination when grasped at its limit, at its extreme. Such a faculty indicates nothing else than the ability of the soul to sensualize (*versinnlichen*) ideas. The conceptual nonrepresentability of such ideas remains indubitable. Imagination does not limit itself to imagining the unity of the sensible of intuition and then the schema of the intellect; it also imagines the contents of freedom. Neither of its dimensions overcomes the other. Yet, precisely in their play, we discover all the power of imagination and how the subject's ability to image, to put-in-an-image belongs to its ontological reality—it is nothing accidental or psychological. *Geist* is an organ of imagination as much as the schematizing imagination is. The work that the Genius produces does not determine any law; nor does it conceptualize the ideas of reason or teleologically appear as the goal of a process that implies nature and reflection. Likewise, the schema on its hand has nothing to do with sensualizing (*versinnlichen*) ideas of reason. Between the various levels of imagination there is no possibility of value hierarchy or *reductio ad unum* [reduction to one]. There is only systematic understanding of their co-belonging.

Precisely this co-belonging, this *free* play (and yet, like any play that can be read transcendentally, it can only be played on the basis of its own laws) raises a question of an overall theoretical order. In the *Critique of Judgment*, the idea is postulated that the faculty of judgment implies an *aesthetic* dimension—that is, the idea of the unsuppressibility of the aesthetic moment within the form of judgment. This moment is grasped in its *singularity* because the validity of the aesthetic judgment, in its concrete expression, remains absolutely subjective. This moment is not overcome, is not resolved in the creativity of the *Genie-Geist*. Neither is it comprehended within the overall meaning and destiny of the development of the arts, as in Hegel. The aesthetic judgment in its singularity belongs to the concrete constitution of every experience and refers any expression of thought back to its connection with the conditions of receptivity, feeling, *pathos*. There would be no schema of the intellect if imagination had not *beforehand* operated a synthesis of the multiple, a synthesis immanent in intuition itself; likewise, there is no aesthetic judgment without the "hit" that the subject receives from a beautiful or sublime appearance. The two moments explain each other and together open up to the problem of passivity or receptivity *within* the spontaneity and productivity of reason.

HEIDEGGER, NIETZSCHE, LEOPARDI, AND SCHELLING

At this point it become perhaps possible to grasp the connection that is in place between Pareyson's reading of Kant and his "discovery" of Schelling—the Schelling of positive philosophy. The very singularity of beings, which in its manifestation is an "abyss" for reason, is the "wonder," the *thauma* from which there originates the aesthetic judgment, absolutely singular and yet transcendental in its form. The imagination imagines nothing else than the presence of the thing—and it is such presence, in its singularity, that turns out to be nonrepresentable, exactly like the idea of reason. Aesthetic judgment manifests this foundational character of judging in general: in turning to the thing without any finality whatsoever, either conceptual or practical, it reveals that all acts of thought are originally "thrown" into the self-giving of beings, which are not its product and on which it cannot exercise any domination.

To better illustrate these relations, Pareyson could have utilized the fundamental interpretation of the *Critique of Judgment* offered by Heidegger in his *Nietzsche* (in which Schelling's lesson is very present). The "first move" of the Third Critique, which consists in affirming the a-theoretical character of aesthetic contemplation, that is, its "disinterest," means the opposite of indifference; and, we would add at this point, also the opposite of indifference for the meaning of the determining judgment. The mere representation (*blosse Vorstellung*) of the thing, accompanied by pleasure, manifests the thing precisely in its unavailability to any form of being possessed or used. It liberates it from being named "*utilitas*" [usefulness]; at the same time, it reveals it as the *thauma* [wonder] toward which all thinking is necessarily and originally "thrown." It is only in this way that the thing comes to light as the abyss of reason. In the contemplation of the thing, its abyssal provenance is revealed. That is, we *imagine* such provenance precisely in aesthetic or reflecting judgment; we reach the point of rendering sensible, of turning into the "object" of feeling that dimension of the entity that must remain absolutely inaccessible to the intellect as well as to reason. In the beautiful and explicitly in the sublime, the subject a-theoretically commemorates the *thauma* (wonder), the disquieting being-beyond the *phenomenon* of the entity—that is, the *phainomenon* is, ultimately, the appearing of such being-beyond. The subject discovers itself to be itself sublime not because it subsumes the sublime under its forms, thereby possessing it, but because it comes to *feel* the sublime, and therefore it renders it sensible (one should not forget that etymologically in the word *Gefühl* there resonates the tone of fear, of trembling).

Heidegger correctly criticizes Nietzsche's fundamental misunderstanding of Kant and of the *Critique of Judgment*. Nietzsche was hindered also because of the influence of Schopenhauer's interpretation of "disinterest" and in general because of his own negative preconception of idealism. One could, however, affirm that it is precisely Nietzsche who, with his vision of artistic making, comes closer than Heidegger to those fundamental ideas of the *Critique of Judgment* that we have tried to highlight. Art as expression of the *power of feeling*, art as *love for the senses* insofar as they manifest themselves as *intelligence*, art as ability to represent sensations *exactly*—these ideas that pervade Nietzsche's entire body of work have a relevance much greater than only for the "aesthetic" sphere or a "philosophy of art." They imply the fundamental tenet of the *Critique of Judgment*, namely, that every form is born from the imagination, which is ontologically connected to feeling, feeling the thing in its inaccessible singularity.

The connection that operates everywhere in Nietzsche between art and life can no longer be interpreted in a vitalistic register. The *physical vigor* emanating from the work of art (versus the "dried-up type of the scholar") and the beautiful as a "powerful stimulant for life" do not contradict at all the power of the form, and therefore of *customs*. Art is *affirmation*; but what is affirmed in it is the tragic thrownness of all forms into the art (*Kunst*) that is hidden in the depths of the soul, namely, imagination, on which we have no power, the same way in which we have no power over simple willing. In the productivity and spontaneity of artistic making, imagination is revealed as *source* of the life of being in all its expressions, theoretical and non-theoretical. Nietzsche's revaluation of Kant's *Critique of Judgment* in an anti-idealistic (and anti-decadent) sense could have consisted of what we have just stated.

This perspective had already been traveled by the "thinking poet" whom Nietzsche loved so much, Giacomo Leopardi. Against all ideas of art as supreme organ of the conciliation between sensible and suprasensible (conciliation that can only express itself as fiction, and never be real) and as overcoming of the limits of the intellect (Leopardi understands well that this "overcoming" can only mean a super-intellectualization of the artistic dimension, and this is a move that could bring him very close to Hegel's aesthetics), Leopardi asserts, in a Nietzschean manner, that art, as the "friend of the senses," aims at arousing the *pleasure* that is *the* goal of all living beings. The feeling of pleasure is the product of imagination as the faculty of sensualizing, making sensible (*versinnlichen*) the ideas. In a Kantian manner, this sensualization, however, has no theoretical-cognitive relevance. The more the power of the intellect imposes itself, the less does the power of the imagination—the cost of this is that we lose the goal of life, namely, pleasure, and we are condemned "to dying of truth" (Nietzsche). This is the tragic connection through which Leopardi seems to join the themes of the *Critique of Judgment*, projecting them in the direction of Nietzsche.

The "becoming true" of this historical-critical perspective could be founded on that part of the *Critique of Judgment* that Pareyson has been among the first to valorize. I mean the *intersubjectivity* constitutive of the aesthetic judgment. The forms of the imagination are founded on primary imagination; likewise, the possibility of communication is grounded on *Gemeinsinn* [common sense]. All intellectual communication, that is, the communicability of all forms of knowledge, presupposes the nondeterminate and nondeterminable agreement of feeling. We might even ask whether this is "a principle higher than reason itself" (Kant); yet it is nothing else than the explication of the originary character of imagination (*Einbildungskraft*). It is the possibility of the free play of all our faculties in a sensible representation; it is such common sensing/feeling that founds the idea of *community*. The community of pure intellect or pure reason cannot be thought. But neither could their specific communicability be realized if it were not because of the originary power of sensualizing (*versinnlichen*), which is thematized in aesthetic judgment. Thus its paradoxical character is clarified: its being singular-subjective and, at the same time, its claiming to universal consensus. Precisely because of its "free" singularity, it expresses the ought (*Sollen*) of a *common life*. The "aesthetic community," of which one speaks with respect to Kant, is simply the foundational value of feeling and imagination with respect to and in all acts of thinking. The ground, however, is such precisely because in it all "ground" disappears. Again, is this Kant read from Schelling's perspective? And how could it be different for Pareyson?

—Translated by Silvia Benso

NOTE

1. Luigi Pareyson, *L'estetica di Kant* (Milan: Mursia, 1984).

6

Pareyson's Aesthetics as Hermeneutics of Art

Federico Vercellone

BEYOND BENEDETTO CROCE AND THE PHILOSOPHY OF ART

Luigi Pareyson's extensive confrontation with aesthetics concerns especially the first stage of his philosophy, even if one could say that Pareyson never abandoned art as a continuous point of interest of his theoretical reflection.

If one wanted to summarize the trajectory of Pareyson's thought within aesthetics, one could describe it, albeit with some degree of ambiguity, as a move from a hermeneutics of art to a hermeneutics of myth. The consideration of the literary tradition always remained central in Pareyson's thinking, though, especially with reference to some great authors and novelists, first of all, Dostoevsky.

In any event, Pareyson's aesthetics anticipates, with extreme lucidity and well in advance, what later will become a European phenomenon, namely, the end of the period, which started with German Romanticism, of aesthetics as philosophy of art, as specific delimitation of a wider metaphysical orientation that is universal not only because of its meaning but also because of its latitude, of its encompassing and omni-comprehensive features.[1] This occurs in Pareyson through his proposal, in *Estetica. Teoria della formatività* [*Aesthetics: Theory of Formativity*],[2] of an aesthetic model that is alien to the traditional structure of the philosophy of art and instead places aesthetics in a very close connection with hermeneutics. This is the really distinct, original, and innovative standpoint from which to grasp the meaning of Pareyson's reflection within the contemporary scenario and especially the relevance of such a significant work as his *Estetica*. Pareyson's aesthetics calls into question the classic structure, of Romantic and Hegelian making, of nineteenth- and twentieth-century aesthetics that under close analysis persists until Adorno. The reason why Pareyson's aesthetic theory can accomplish such a meaningful move is that it thematizes the relation between aesthetics and hermeneutics.

Pareyson's *Estetica*, which was published by various presses, from Istituto di Filosofia to Sansoni to Bompiani, appeared in print in 1954 but underwent various revised editions until the last one, in 1988.[3] The interest in aesthetics remained the central focus in Pareyson's thinking for about twenty years, from after World War II until the mid-1960s.[4] After that time, Pareyson increasingly turned toward ethical and religious themes.

At the center of Pareyson's aesthetics is the idea of *formativity*. As he states from the start, in the background of his position is the teaching of Augusto Guzzo. For Guzzo, human life is to be understood as an "invention of forms."[5] Formativity is a concept that does not pertain only to the aesthetic sphere; rather, it concerns spiritual life in its complexity. We are thus confronted with a theory that studies formativity within the whole spiritual life and indicates, within all human operations, the formative feature that makes such operations be simultaneously a kind of production and of invention. In other words, each operation "makes" while inventing "the way of making"; that is, it succeeds in "realizing" or actualizing only by proceeding by trials toward its success and thus producing works that are "forms."[6]

For Pareyson, art thus derives from the development of a formativity that pervades all human activities. A sort of *nisus formativus* [formative drive] permeates nature itself. What emerges here is an accentuation of Goethe's influence, which by Pareyson's own admission is absolutely central to this stage of his thought (such an influence will diminish in the later Pareyson also in relation to a changed cultural climate, to a changed thinking environment that does not deem to seek its center in a morphological perspective).[7] Within this framework, the centrality of the morphological perspective, for the most part shared also by Schelling in his "philosophy of identity" (another reference figure for Pareyson at this time), widens the spectrum of artistic meanings in the direction of nature and *poiesis* and thus enables a shift in the traditional focus of aesthetic considerations. Pareyson's position already implies a critique of the notion of an autonomous aesthetic consciousness, a critique that takes form and configuration well ahead of Hans-Georg Gadamer's similar criticism. Moreover, Pareyson takes his reader in a different direction than Gadamer: he leads the reader in the direction of a critique of aesthetic consciousness that does not principally concern the question of its relation with historical consciousness, as is the case in *Truth and Method*.[8] On this path, whose prelude is Goethe, art precedes historical consciousness and exhibits its own autonomy as an originary, almost primal event. For Pareyson in the *Estetica*, art derives "from the intentional and programmatic accentuation of an activity that is present in all human activities and that accompanies, even constitutes, any manifestation of human industriousness."[9] In the same vein, Pareyson continues: "What we properly name 'art' is 'formativity,' that is, a 'making' that while it makes invents 'its way of making': production that is simultaneously and indissolubly invention. All aspects of human industriousness, from the simplest to the most complex, have an ineliminable and essential feature of formativity."[10] This claim constitutes the premise to recognize and underline the absolutely philosophical character of aesthetics. The exquisitely philosophical nature of this discipline prevents the characterization of aesthetics as "second" philosophy in comparison to the consideration of ground to which "first" philosophy would instead be devoted, according to the classical tradition that has dominated the philosophy of art.

With respect to this point, Pareyson asserts that, "first of all, aesthetics is not a part of philosophy but the whole philosophy that is focused on the questions of beauty and art; secondly, the concrete questions of aesthetics do not cease being philosophical by virtue of their being particular. . . . Rather, one could say that aesthetics is a happy example of the meeting point of the two ways of philosophical reflection, namely, the way upward, which draws universal results from the meditation on concrete experience, and the way downward, which uses such universal results to interpret experience and solve its problems."[11]

The viewpoint that Pareyson is here unfolding—and it is one of the main tenets of his thought—is anti-Hegelian even before being anti-Crocean. In some aspects, it recalls the position of Giovanni Gentile, for whom art "is always a moment or aspect of the fulfilled actual synthesis of Spirit,"[12] constantly overcoming itself and reemerging in the framework of a cyclical proceeding.

Formativity and therefore art constitute some anthropological and ontological constants that do not depend on any kind of historical maturation. From this perspective, following Pareyson yet certainly somewhat pushing his thought in a direction left unaddressed by him, one could even claim that the autonomy of art rests on the evolution of living beings and precedes the properly cultural development of the human species.[13] In any event and leaving aside this extemporaneous consideration, Pareyson continually stresses the feature of "making" that belongs to artistic creation. His reference to the artist's awareness opposes, following Paul Valéry,[14] the Platonic motif of the artist's inspiration and conversely emphasizes the extent to which the artwork is, as it were, its own guide in its pursuit of its formative goal.

Considerations of this kind of course relativize the notion of aesthetic consciousness as a necessary factor in the identification of artistic objects. With Pareyson, we are beyond the "death of art" and the notion of *l'art pour l'art* that constitutes the necessary premise thereof. For Hegel, the historical maturation of the spiritual content brings art to a necessary decline and death, at least in terms of art's ability to constitute the climax of a certain culture. Conversely, Pareyson leads us to look at things in a profoundly different manner. As already indicated earlier, for Pareyson art is the specification of a more universal "formativity" that is in itself independent from historical, or historico-metaphysical, variables.

On the ground of this approach, Pareyson finds himself in the position to elaborate a concept of dynamic form that allows him to come into direct contact with the indeterminacy of the form. This presages the notion of an "open work" later developed by Umberto Eco.[15] This intuition of Pareyson's is absolutely fundamental because it draws him near to contemporary art and allows him to build an aesthetics that cannot be mistaken for some variety of poetics. His aesthetics thus is neither partisan nor sectarian and yet it works without the major categorial invariants that characterize classic aesthetics. Instead of such traditional categorial invariables, Pareyson's aesthetics insists on the process of work formation and on the articulation of the rule that presides over such a work. This aesthetics proposes the work and the process of its formation ahead of all categorial features. It orients itself toward the work as its epicenter and does so with a remarkable awareness of the relevance of aesthetics as the discipline structuring the philosophical reflection on art.

In this context, it is perhaps helpful to recall that the critical attitude toward Benedetto Croce, an attitude that values the dynamism of form, is prepared by Lionello Venturi, a great art historian who, like Pareyson, is also an anti-fascist.[16] In any event, it is Pareyson's dynamic conception of form that enables him to articulate his confrontation with Croce. The rejection of the immediate, non–process-based identity of the relation between intuition and expression will be, as already mentioned, the step that enables Pareyson to engage a conversation with contemporary art.

If we now move to Croce, we may want to recall that for him, any real intuition, that is, any successful intuition, is expression. Between the two there is complete correspondence. In his 1902 *Estetica*, Croce claims that "every real intuition or representation is, at the same time, expression. That which is not objectified in an expression is neither intuition nor expression but sensation and naturalness. Spirit only intuits when making, shaping, expressing. Those who separate intuition from expression are never ever able to join them again."[17]

In this context, the move is in a direction that exalts formal success and, with formal success, beauty that cannot be distinguished from success. Croce emphasizes this a few paragraphs after the abovementioned quotation. With this, we approach one of the crucial issues not only in Croce's 1902 *Estetica* but in his entire reflection on this topic. He writes: "In the aesthetic act, expressive activity is not added to the fact of impressions; on the contrary, impressions are elaborated and formed by expressive activity. They reappear in expression, as it were, like water that is put through a filter and that, on the other side of the filter, reappears both as the same and different. The aesthetic act is therefore form and nothing else than form."[18]

We are here confronted with a work of transferal that leaves no residues. The beautiful has to be understood as successful expression and the ugly as unsuccessful expression. In this work of transferal of intuition into expression, which is the source of lyricism by means of feeling, there is a complete absence of all process elements, of all dynamic components in the process of structuring or forming the work of art. Pareyson's criticism of Croce, whether explicit or implicit, is to be placed within this context. His conception of dynamic form allows Pareyson to advance beyond Croce on several accounts. First, Pareyson is able to value the path toward the form itself in its various stages, which therefore become themselves meaningful. Second, on this path, elements that Croce had excluded, such as cues, materials, and techniques, become important when evaluating a work of art. On this ground, there occurs also an implicit opening toward the possibility of a critique of variants. Third, on the ground of a dynamic conception of form, the connection of form and interpretation becomes also possible. Thus, and fourth, one can recognize the intrinsic rather than extrinsic meaning of factors such as execution or performance, reception, critique, historicity, and even the patina (as in Brandi) for the consideration of the work of art. This enables Pareyson to advance the idea of an aesthetic of production without underestimating all the features that have to do with what one can broadly name "the fruition" of the work of art. The consideration and the importance of the productive moment are mitigated by the motifs of interpretation and reception in the context of an extremely balanced and pondered theoretical construct.

Crucial for Pareyson is the element of invention, of trial through which the work of art is made. Pareyson repeatedly underlines that formal invention has a character of experiment and research. As he writes,

> It is evident that success presupposes a making that must also be invention of the way of making. Whatever the work to be made, the way of making it is not known ahead of time and with evidence; rather, one must discover and find it, and only after one has discovered and found it will one clearly realize that that was precisely the way in which the work had to be done. In order to discover and find how one must make it, one must proceed by trials, that is, by figuring and inventing various possibilities [. . .] until one finally arrives at the discovery of the only one possibility that the operation itself required at that point in order to be finished and successful. Once discovered, that possibility reveals itself as the one that one knew one had to find.
>
> To form is essentially to try because forming consists of inventiveness capable of figuring multiple possibilities and at the same time of finding among them the only good one, the one that is necessary for successfulness. Trials extend to the entire spiritual life, and affect all areas of human laboriousness. This confirms that their domain is the same as the domain of formativity because all spiritual life is formativity. Certainly this destiny of human beings, the fact of not being able to operate except than by proceeding by trials, is the mark of human misery and greatness at the same time—human beings cannot find without searching, and they cannot search except that by making attempts; yet in trying they figure and invent so that what they *find* is what they have, truly, *invented*.[19]

From this perspective, unlike Croce, Pareyson accepts entering what we could call "the artist's workshop." He accepts the recognition that practice, cues, and even improvisation are central elements in the consideration and evaluation of a work of art. Pareyson can also emphasize that matter and technique should not be understood separately from the work; rather, they are integral parts of its formation. Without naming it explicitly, Pareyson takes thus part in a debate started a few years earlier in 1951 by the art historian Giulio Carlo Argan with his work *Walter Gropius e la Bauhaus*.[20]

ART AND INTERPRETATION

As the outcome of a path that is open and yet predisposed by a law that is itself intrinsic in the becoming and making of the work, art is indissolubly tied to interpretation. Art is tied to interpretation on the side of both the artist who creates it and the interpreter who enjoys it.

Interpretation occurs insofar as its object is a form and its subject is a person. Constitutive of the human being as person is a kind of knowledge that is given through interpretation. It is a "multiple and infinite" knowledge.[21]

Interpretation is grounded on a dynamic consideration of the form, which confronts itself with the work of art in its mobile morphological unity. What this consideration, simultaneously hermeneutic and morphological, of the work of art prefigures is the notion of the hermeneutic circle, which will be articulated in a different context by Hans-Georg Gadamer in *Truth and Method*. In a passage that refers to mutilated works but that can be expanded to the whole of aesthetic theory, Pareyson claims that "it is true that the whole can only be grasped by grasping its parts, because the whole is manifested through their connection. Yet this tie that binds the parts is not external to any of them; rather, it is the irradiation of each part from the whole, so that the deep intention of the one who explores the parts so as to grasp the whole is to see the whole that is present in each part, requires each of them, and connects all of them together. . . . The issue is that of finding the form through a dynamic consideration, which grasps the whole while it reclaims its own parts and sees the parts while it responds to the appeal of the forming form."[22]

It is the operative effectiveness of the form, which presides over the self-structuring of the work, that guides interpretation and puts the artist in contact with the consumer [*fruitore*], thereby making both of them participants in a single creative process.[23] What we have here is an interpretation (and this constitutes a fundamental intuition that deeply differentiates Pareyson from Gadamer) that conjoins artist and consumer and thus activity and passivity.[24] In this context, the relation between subject and object of interpretation escapes all possibilities of objectification on either side: "The known is a form and the knower is a person."[25]

The burden, and as it were the "historical" responsibility of interpretation, does not lie exclusively in its *Wirkungsgeschichte*, in the "history of effects"; rather, it concerns also its realization and successfulness. In this context there emerges the interpreter's responsibility that, joined with the primacy of personhood, impresses an ethical mark on the act of interpretation. On this ground, aesthetic cognition assumes a universal meaning. Knowledge as a whole, and not only knowledge of the work of art, is now to be understood as "non-disjoinable synthesis of activity and passivity" and thus as "interpretation."[26] Interpretation, in which what is at stake is not only the understanding but also the successfulness of the work, is continuously subject to the risk of failure. This is a risk that constitutes (and this would be entirely unacceptable for Croce) a motive of the realization itself of the work deriving from a process of self-interpretation of its own forming form.

Furthermore, Pareyson claims that any kind of knowledge that does not have an objectifying character, that does not derive from an epistemological attitude "that defines and constructs its object," has an interpretative nature. This kind of knowledge is constantly exposed, as said above, to the risk of not being successful, that is, of encountering the double limitation "of incomprehension and incomprehensibility."[27] Precisely here, however, is the richness of interpretative knowledge, which works in such a way that the form is regarded "in a very determinate perspective that casts light on it in a determinate manner," while "in the unmistakable determinacy of form, aspects and perspectives are infinite."[28] From here emerge both the possibility and the necessity of "infinite possible interpretations,"[29] so that knowledge is characterized by an inexhaustible richness that originates from the encounter between interpreter and interpreted form.[30] The work thus actualizes itself also in the course of the interpretative process that involves, as we have seen, both the artist and the interpreter, who is also a participant in the creative process.

Pareyson introduces the idea that "regarding things as 'persons' entails the impossibility of reducing persons to 'things,'"[31] and thus he accentuates the ethical aspect inherent in his aesthetic viewpoint. This aspect is in conformity with the perspective of ontological personalism Pareyson espouses especially in his earlier years. Pareyson also adds that one cannot know things except by "personifying" them, thereby restoring them to their life and independence.[32]

Within this framework, Pareyson offers many remarkable suggestions having to do with an analysis of the act of reading understood as an act of participation in the rule constitutive of the work. Years later, this Pareysonian orientation, perhaps derived from Valéry,[33] finds additional important developments in Wolfgang Iser's aesthetics of reception. Thinking about the act of reading, Iser emphasizes the character of indeterminacy of the literary text.[34] For Pareyson, perhaps with a Schlegelean resonance, to read means "to master the work itself rendering it present and lively, that is, *making* its effect work."[35] Additionally, the work of art always requires its execution or performance, which constitutes an essential element of it. The execution/interpretation in fact warrants that the multiplicity and infinity of the work do not contradict but rather legitimate and strengthen the identity of the work. In this context, historical or cultural distance does not constitute an obstacle to the understanding of the work, according to the perspective that is developed otherwise by Gadamer in *Truth and Method* through the notion of the "fusion of horizons." There can be no historical or cultural distance capable of annihilating the content, the relevance of the work, the possibility of enjoying and actualizing it. This possibility of interpretation should not be utilized *ad libitum* [at liberty] but rather should constantly be exercised within the watchful bind dictated by the forming form that is at work in the work.

The account of the further maturation of an aesthetic thinking that renders Pareyson one of the most fecund figures in the realm of the aesthetics of the second half of the twentieth century is not a matter that can be taken up here. Although with different accentuations than at its beginning, this maturation occurred through the elaboration of a hermeneutic theory that turns Pareyson into one of the masters of contemporary hermeneutics; it also occurred through the proposal of a "tragic thought" that finds in a novelist-philosopher such as Dostoevsky one of its fundamental figures of reference. There is no doubt, however, that the turn in the direction of "tragic thought" interrupts the morphological unity of Pareyson's thinking and introduces instead an unbridgeable hiatus between ground and its consequences, between forming form and formed form. The happy harmony and unity that Pareyson had admired in Goethe's position and in Schelling's philosophy of identity is interrupted in his elaboration of "tragic thought." What is attained instead is a less confident and more embittered philosophy that no longer admits of elements of continuity between the invisible ground and the forms of the visible.

—Translated by Silvia Benso

NOTES

1. With respect to the idea of the end of aesthetics as philosophy of art, allow me to refer to Federico Vercellone, *Oltre la bellezza* (Bologna: Il Mulino, 2008); English translation by Sarah De Sanctis, *Beyond Beauty* (Albany: State University of New York Press, 2017). For an excellent overview of Italian aesthetics in the last century, see Paolo D'Angelo, *L'estetica italiana del Novecento* (Rome-Bari: Laterza, 2007).

2. Luigi Pareyson, *Estetica. Teoria della formatività* (Turin: Istituto di Filosofia, 1954).

3. Luigi Pareyson, *Estetica. Teoria della formatività* (Milan: Bompiani, 1988).

4. For what concerns the sequence of Pareyson's lecture courses and his historiographic and theoretical production within the field of aesthetics, see Francesco Tomatis, *Pareyson: Vita, filosofia, bibliografia* (Brescia: Morcelliana, 2003), 69–71.

5. Pareyson, "Prefazione," *Estetica*, 7.

6. Ibid., 8.

7. This is what Pareyson remarks, several years afterward, in the notes published under the title "La natura tra estetica e ontologia," in his *Essere, libertà, ambiguità* (Milan: Mursia, 1998), 112–13: "When I was young I was fascinated by this conception/fervent Goethian many years many courses./Yet I perceived that something was missing, because it did not take into account the fact that human activities are tentative, and that the artist's operation is an adventure whose outcome one does not know, and the work begins to exist only once it has been made. . . . I derived a theory while intending to remain faithful to Goethe's spirit . . . but I had to give it an extremely subtle development, and this cost me a search for constant recalibrations so as to keep things in balance and not let one part predominate." The courses on Goethe and Schelling are now part of Luigi Pareyson, *Estetica dell'idealismo tedesco III: Goethe e Schelling*, ed. M. Ravera (Milan: Mursia, 2003).

8. Hans-Georg Gadamer, *Truth and Method*, trans. Joel Weinsheimer and Donald G. Marshall (New York: Continuum, 1975).

9. Pareyson, *Estetica*, 18.

10. Ibid., 18.

11. Ibid., 15.

12. Giovanni Gentile, *La filosofia dell'arte*, in *Opere* (Florence: Sansoni, 1950), vol. 8, 194.

13. This is what is suggested by Winfried Menninghaus, *Wozu Kunst? Ästhetik nach Darwin* (Frankfurt: Suhrkamp, 2011).

14. See Luigi Pareyson, "L'estetica di Paul Valéry," in *Problemi dell' estetica II: Storia*, ed. M. Ravera (Milan: Mursia, 2000), 38–40.

15. See Umberto Eco, *The Open Work*, trans. Anna Cancogni (Cambridge: Harvard University Press, 1989).

16. See the 1926 work by Lionello Venturi, *Il gusto dei primitivi* (Turin: Einaudi, 1972). On the relation between Venturi and Croce, see Federico Vercellone, "Forma ed estetismo: La Torino di Gobetti e di Lionello Venturi," in *Morfologie del Moderno* (Genoa: Marietti, 2006), 177–91.

17. Benedetto Croce, *Estetica*, ed. Giuseppe Galasso (Milan: Adelphi, 1990), 12.

18. Ibid., 31.

19. Pareyson, *Estetica*, 60–61.

20. Giulio Carlo Argan, *Walter Gropius e la Bauhaus* (Turin: Einaudi, 1951). See Pareyson, *Estetica*, 134–36.

21. Pareyson, *Estetica*, 186.

22. Ibid., 113.

23. Ibid., 141.

24. See also Pareyson, *Estetica*, 180–81.

25. Ibid., 180.

26. Ibid., 182.

27. Ibid., 186.

28. Ibid., 187.

29. Ibid., 187.

30. Ibid., 188–89.

31. Ibid., 208.

32. Ibid., 208.

33. See Pareyson, "L'estetica di Paul Valéry," 25.

34. See Wolfgang Iser, *The Implied Reader: Patterns of Communication in Prose Fiction from Bunyan to Beckett* (Baltimore: Johns Hopkins University Press, 1978) and *The Act of Reading: A Theory of Aesthetic Response* (Baltimore: Johns Hopkins University Press, 1980).

35. Pareyson, *Estetica*, 223.

7

The Unfamiliarity of Kindredness
Toward a Hermeneutics of Community

Robert T. Valgenti

This essay arises from a commitment to pursue a hermeneutics of non-violence and a desire to continue thoughts I began in a reflection on the concept of tradition in hermeneutics some years ago. These thoughts are not solely, however, a return to ideas left undeveloped, but their continuation through a philosophy of interpretation that articulates understanding and transformation within acts of recognition and communion rather than in violent ruptures of continuity. More than ever, we are compelled to ask how communities can become more inclusive, develop a sensitivity to alterity, and undermine the violence of identity politics. Yet on what grounds can such a community be built if it is to offer something other than the empty promise of abstract equality or the false hope of real revolution? The hermeneutics of Luigi Pareyson, and specifically his reflections on aesthetics, offer some clues for building a community in light of the issues of tradition, identity, and inclusiveness.

The problem of a hermeneutics of community (one that sees any basis for a community as a matter of interpretation) begins in the shadow of tradition and amidst the typical critiques of a certain brand of hermeneutics that relies on continuity rather than on rupture. On this count, Pareyson is close to Hans-Georg Gadamer, despite their rather different methodological approaches to the study of hermeneutics. Any hermeneutics of community must first reckon with one of the traditions of hermeneutics itself, one that is voiced in Heidegger's famous epigraph in *Being and Time* and that depicts hermeneutics as a conflict of interpretations, a final struggle over Being, rather than as dialogue and conversation.[1] This tradition of conflict is the one to which Pareyson seems to be responding. Early in *Truth and Interpretation*, Pareyson examines the concept of tradition within the context of historical values. Tradition, as opposed to mere historical endurance, is what liberates every interpretation from the pitfalls of historicism and relativism through an engagement with life's transformative and self-determining power. Tradition flows from neither the object of history nor the subject of perception, but stands forth from within the flow of history and worldviews, "in the same way that a work of art, far from dissolving in a plurality of arbitrary actions, remains identical to itself in the act that consigns it to always newer interpretations that collect and render it, identifying itself with it."[2] A work of art endures, one could say, because it resists any reduction to objective history or to subjective points of view, and in fact constitutes itself through that very resistance. And yet it is a resistance shaped not by difference, but rather through similarity and kinship. The creative and innovative singularity of art is therefore the figure through which Pareyson articulates its very exemplarity as the site of tradition and, more importantly, of kindredness [*congenialità*] among all human interpreters. My contention is that this kindredness—one that takes shape through formative acts of creation—constitutes the basis for a hermeneutics of community, one that articulates a shared origin through acts of interpretation.

FROM AESTHETIC EXEMPLARS TO KINDREDNESS

A survey of Pareyson's aesthetic theory will not only help to trace the development of his concept of kindredness; more importantly, it will reveal how Pareyson's aesthetics of formativity could provide the theoretical basis for a community of kindred individuals. Pareyson's interest in this sort of theoretical foundation dates back to his early courses on aesthetics, delivered at the University of Torino from 1945 to 1946.[3] In the attempt to distance himself from the idealist philosophies of Croce and Gentile, Pareyson uncovers rich resources in the proto-hermeneutic thinking of Giambattista Vico, particularly in Vico's theorization of artistic production within a tradition. Pareyson notes that in a Vichian perspective, imitation is much more than the mere practice of copying.

In the best circumstances, "the act of imitation is at the same time an act of invention, as one cannot invent without imitating, and the same imitating is the manifestation of an inventive capacity."[4] Inventing implies a certain knowledge of reality, the ability to recognize the situation and to place one's creation into conversation with it. Ingenuity or intelligence is likewise the faculty of gathering similarities and yet also of inventing the new—an active process such that imitation is rediscovery and invention.[5]

At this early stage, Pareyson has yet to formulate what he later develops into the dialectic of kindredness and exemplarity found in *Truth and Interpretation*; yet, even in this early form, Pareyson understands that any invention of the truly new—whether a unique work of art, or even a new moment of understanding—requires some form of continuity. Even when a work is challenging and originates within an unfamiliar context, a successful aesthetic understanding requires the recognition of elements that persist within this novel figure, no matter how transformed their state might be. One motive behind Pareyson's position involves his persistent efforts to rescue the singularity of the individual interpreter from idealism and historicism, whether that individual is the artist or the audience. This motive is evident in his lecture titles and the trajectory of his questioning: How does the singularity of the person emerge from the continuity of tradition and the influence of existing works? What is recognized in the interpretative act of creation and understanding that distinguishes them from mere imitation and reiteration? Such questions indicate that in these early lectures Pareyson might already be thinking about a reformulation of *truth* in a hermeneutic key—whether in a work of art or in any human endeavor. Truth is not associated with any work's or thing's essence or with the quality of any individual judgment. Truth is what emerges through and only ever within an interpretation—it is how a work, or an interpretation, articulates its uniqueness and singularity. It is the articulation of a work's life, its kindredness with all processes that resist reduction to a subject or an object. One cannot help but remember how Vico, in this same work cited here by Pareyson, invokes the ancient adage *verum esse ipsum factum*—truth is what is made. For certain, truth is not something invented out of nothing. The truth of the work of art has something, it seems, to do with its fluid multiplicity of formulations, something to do with this multiplicity as a kindred attribute among all interpretations: their shared creative force or "con-geniality."

In the years that follow these early lectures, Pareyson develops a complete theory of the work of art that is published in 1954 under the title *Estetica. Teoria della formatività*.[6] Pareyson's *Estetica* explores the manner in which aesthetic forms and production serve as exemplars for the plurality of modes in which humans exist and understand their world. Aesthetic truth, as with all truth in Pareyson's thinking, is articulated through acts of interpretation that, because of their singularity, always bear a certain risk and responsibility. Interpretation, as an active choice or "attempt" [*tentativo*], navigates the space between thought and deed, philosophy and experience, in such a way that truth emerges through a creative act that simultaneously reflects the context in which it unfolds. The tension between a shared universal act of creation and the particular lived context for that creative act thus unfolds as a hermeneutic "play" whereby the process of artistic formation and evaluation continually slips away from any simple expression of genius or reduction to a set of specific techniques. And even though art operates in Pareyson's aesthetics as an exemplar for all understanding, it would be incorrect to claim that this ubiquity of interpretation leads to a general aestheticization of experience. Art is able to distinguish its unique character as a purely formative activity precisely because experience itself entails a deeply aesthetic element. Or, to state it otherwise, the recognition of alterity relies, somewhat paradoxically, on the presence of a shared and kindred element. There is a kindredness within all artistic production and evaluation that not only distinguishes it from other human activities, but simultaneously uncovers the common element in every human endeavor.

This kindred element is *formativity*: a type of doing that, during the course of doing, invents the way of doing. Any completed work, as "formed form" [*la forma formata*], is the realization of the process of forming such that the end product is not some formed thing, but rather a form that accomplishes its intrinsic and self-imposed end: "In short, the working [*l'operare*], the activity that it specifies for itself, always involves that process of production and invention that constitutes the forming, and all works, as results, are forms endowed with independence and exemplarity."[7] The exemplarity of any human production is found not in its unique characteristics, but in the formative process through which that uniqueness and singularity are attained. Moreover, all formative activity can be understood as "aesthetic," and therefore worthy of contemplation, because it achieves its uniqueness through this shared process. All human activity is therefore, at its root, formative, and thus born from infinite interpretative possibilities while still bound to the finitude of an individual choice. Art, morality, and philosophy, as formative activities, all share in an autonomy that drives the formative process. What gives art, as a specific form of human activity, its exemplarity in relation to all other human endeavors is thus its ability to release that formativity from any particular ends other than the formative process itself. Pareyson is not simply making the case for "art for art's sake," but instead pointing out how the kindred element in all human activities can, through art, bring itself to the forefront of human attention and effort.

In the chapter of *Estetica* dedicated to the "exemplarity" of the work of art, Pareyson introduces his dialectic of exemplarity and kindredness. The dialectical relation between incommensurable opposites is a common feature in Pareyson's thinking, and the general effect of this trope captures the productivity of opposing forces within the play of any work or interpretation. The dialectical movement is neither temporal nor conceptual, but indicative of the simultaneity of these two ideas within any interpretation, and therefore in this context, within any work of art. And rather than find synthesis in a final moment, the dialectical tension instead points back to a shared origin. The exemplarity and singularity of the source—in this case the work of art itself as formed form—along with the unique character of the inspirations taken from it, are choices made possible through the recognition of a profound kindredness, choices "which are at the same time the consequence and the confirmation, the manifestation and the support, that the recourse to a shared source is already the index of an affinity, which is deepened yet more in the degree to which the derived forms appear among them."[8] This connection to the *choice* of the interpreter—one who creates new works of art, or even one who merely seeks to understand a given work in a new way—is for Pareyson an indicator that a work is not only the source of criteria for judgment, but also serves as the inspiration for new and profound successes. Building upon the connection between imitation and creation, the choice of the interpreter to recognize an inherent similarity underscores the one pole of *kindredness*; on the other hand, the *exemplarity* of the artistic form consists not in its ability to close off possibilities after it is recognized by the interpreter, but in its capacity to stimulate new forms and to regulate their development. It is in this manner that Pareyson endeavors to explain how an artist can develop her craft in a way that is inimitably personal and yet need not make recourse to romantic notions of artistic genius.

Nonetheless, if not by artistic fiat or creative force of will, how is it possible that transformation occurs in art and in life—namely, that new ways of being emerge without a violent overturning of the old? Pareyson's student Gianni Vattimo, who is rather adamant about his desire to resist the metaphysical residues of his teacher's work, interprets Western thinking as the history of nihilism in order to arrive at a philosophy of non-violence. But, as critics have justly noted, this reliance on the arguably historicistic narrative of the "weakening of Being" is all too reductive, if not hypocritical, given Vattimo's resistance to meta-narratives. Could an ethics of nonviolence arise from sources neither concerned with nor resistant to the refrain of metaphysical violence? An answer—and one that might ultimately stretch beyond the limits of aesthetics—can be found in Pareyson's understanding of the way that new and original works of art nonetheless remain comprehensible and even edifying.

As Pareyson voices it, a particularly profound and successful work of art is able to "open up paths for new artists to follow by opening up a previously indicated way and at the same time by carrying an irreplaceable contribution that is truly original."[9] The shared quality of any work of art, its universality as *a* formed form, indicates that all such works are governed by individual and singular rules of formation. The commonality shared by all works of art is their uniqueness.[10] It is a universal verified in its singularity, a universal that is not the reflection of a shared content, but that comes to be through each unique constitution. This universality is for Pareyson the necessary condition for any and all unique work. Moreover, Pareyson holds that there are two aspects to this universality. The first is *valuative*: its ability to be recognized in any case [*onniriconoscibilità*], the value of its singularity that is tied to the fact that it can be recognized and judged as a work of art by all those who view it. The second is *performative*: the work of art appears exemplary from this point of view, paradigmatic as a norm in the act of formation that guides its own living process of formation.

A work of art is thus exemplary because it is complete and unrepeatable—in its completeness, it points (indirectly) to the universal form of its being guided by a rule of its own formation, and in its inimitability, it points back to the unique personality of *any* artistic formation. Both are consciously held together in a new act of formation by another artist or interpreter. Artistic imitation is therefore creative because of its *kindredness*: the type of originality that is open to "recognizing, indeed soliciting, the influence of preexisting activities and works; far from being eliminated, diminished, or compromised, this originality is reinforced in its proper intention and confirmed in its proper direction."[11] In this way, Pareyson suggests not only that an act of imitation might contain a creative and originary moment, but also that some level of imitation might be the only way that originality happens, namely, that the difference between imitator and inventor has nothing to do with a protected or even sacred notion of originality. In fact, "these cases in which production and imitation play back and forth without the one ever vanishing into the other are proof that originality and imitation are not always mutually exclusive and that imitation can be the way through which originality manages not only to appear but to undertake its activity."[12] The exemplary character of an original work of art thus "operates only within an act that recognizes, which is certainly an act of choice . . . [and] whether it is kindredness that justifies the choice or the choice that institutes kindredness, these two terms are always inseparably conjoined."[13] An imitative performance can be exemplary through an act of consent, through a choice that recognizes an intimate kindredness with the source of its inspiration and thus orients the new performance. The singularity of any work of art demands that its imitation also institute and develop *its own* singularity or personality through that imitative act—through the recognition of a shared origin in a plurality of possibilities—if it wishes to share the formative quality of art.

Pareyson is clear that mere imitation and emulation are nothing more than that—poor copies of a model set up as the norm. Continuity in style and spirit certainly does not ensure originality and, all too often, is what undermines it. Nonetheless, if one wishes to explain how artistic creativity is possible, one must have some recourse to imitation, some connection to the exemplarity of works that have come before. The exemplarity of any work of art, its singular status and inimitable presence, can be recognized only through an act of consent because the work itself does not and cannot confer its exemplarity. Any new exemplary work must, like all works of art, follow its own formative norm that is put to work by the personality of the artist. Thus, "to take a work as a model does not mean constituting or creating its exemplarity, almost as if imitation were a pure act of originality, lacking the support of any prior reality, but means to interpret the work to the point of drawing out and making active its intrinsic exemplarity, even if that is possible only through a new and original performance"[14]—that is, by repeating the conditions for its singularity. One knows that the artist is not simply applying normative rules to create a work of art when the model or inspiration is considered in its dynamic (and thus plural) qualities and, furthermore, when the originality of the new formation is one marked by its kindredness with the model within an inheritance of possibilities.

Within the context of the interpretation of a work of art, Pareyson explains that while the encounter with a work requires that we listen to it and attenuate our own personal view, this does not mean that the personality of the interpreter is an impediment to understanding its meaning: "Understanding, therefore, presupposes kindredness, penetration is the reward for sympathy, discovery happens as syntonization, revelation responds to spiritual affinity: that explains the difficulty and the failures of interpretation, when diverse spiritualities produce unkindred and incompatible situations and provoke antipathy and indifference."[15] But these are not insuperable obstacles, as humans are adaptable and plastic; as interpreters, whether readers or performers or critics, individuals can take on the views and attitudes of others by "exploiting the kindredness already available and trying to institute it when it is lacking."[16] On the one hand, one needs to know how to listen for artists who share a certain spiritual kindredness, as this is already some proof of a connection; on the other hand, the ability to adapt and transform springs from that exercise of alterity which underscores the incomplete nature of our own perspective and draws us out of our myopia. The encounter with the other and its exemplarity and inimitability is nonetheless "an 'exercise of kindredness' that, sustained by the imagination, *searches and invents and produces* the most revelatory points of view, indeed *it makes* an adequate organ of penetration of the entire person of the interpreter. Thus it happens that the reader not only learns from the kindred work to be assured in one's own taste, but even to form a new taste, and receive from the work the suggestion to transform, enrich and refine one's own spirituality."[17]

ART AND THE TIMES

In the years leading up to the publication of *Truth and Interpretation*, Pareyson's later contributions to his aesthetic theory[18] further elaborate features of the dialectic of exemplarity and kindredness. In the opening chapter of the work, titled "Theoreticians of the substitute" [*I teorici dell'Ersatz*], Pareyson states that the close ties between art and society warrant a new aesthetic theory that reflects the rapid changes in society and technology, and that it no longer makes sense to speak of the absolute nature of the work of art, as it would be tied to the historical time in which it was born. The work of art carries with it neither universality nor eternality, but is nonetheless recognizable and lasting only to the degree to which it can reflect its time and the place that gives rise to it. Art is present in all aspects of life, and its origins within choice and recognition render any historicistic explanation of its relevance incomplete. The extension of aesthetic understanding to all other spheres of human life does not devalue the specificity and dignity of art, but recognizes the human root of art, namely, the fact that "art penetrates completely human life, feeding and nourishing it from the inside; and the presence of art in life does not mean burdening art with human efforts to the point of reducing it to the pursuit of enjoyment or usefulness, but to see it operating with the complexity of its artistic and extra-artistic functions on the fullness of human experience—as solicitation and nourishment, as stimulus and guide, as example and model."[19]

Pareyson, however, does not want to confuse any of the artistry in human life with art proper. Art is what provides the model and exemplar; artistry is what can recognize and develop it through tradition—it is the ability one has to recognize and participate in, to interpret and create, through formative activity. Artistry must be present in humanity for true art to develop and, moreover, to be recognized through a connection of kindredness. And once true art does emerge, it grants life a normativity and exemplarity such that "the 'continuity' that persists among all 'artistic' manifestations does not at all contradict the qualitative distinction between what is artistic and what is true art, indeed because this distinction requires in a precise way that continuity, granting it an irreversible direction and guaranteeing its 'ascendant' character."[20] Pareyson's fear, particularly in the years leading up to 1968, is that the emerging culture industry will replace the dignity of art with mere technique, flattening any distinction between the two and producing, at the level of society, what in philosophical terms Pareyson refers to as the technicization of thinking reduced to its mere instrumentality and historicistic expression.

But has Pareyson merely traded the vitality of tradition for traditionalism? One could easily argue that Pareyson risks slipping back into an idealist conception of art based in an authenticity or genius somehow untouched by the vicissitudes of modern culture. Even though Pareyson attempts to find the singularity of art (as compared to artistry) within its unique and historical expression, such an expression is not, however, reduced to the effects of the present culture. In these essays on aesthetics, the singularity of artistic expression unfolds through a dialectic of tradition and innovation.

Tradition and innovation are bound by a profound solidarity, one that can be explained on the basis of two conditions: the exemplary character of the result and the spiritual affinity between it and its sustainers—what has already been identified as exemplarity and kindredness. These two conditions, in their confluence whenever a work is executed or an interpretation formulated, explain how a tradition begins and persists, and in their divergence explain how a tradition falls into crisis and dies.[21] The confluence of the two is not, however, limited to grand expressions of artistic genius, or even to the radical departures from tradition one might recognize in a great many works of the twentieth century. Pareyson's attention here is drawn to *habit*—not merely the routines any society or its individual members develop through respect for cultural norms, but in this case even the artistic habits that permeate the shared spaces of modern mass media. Habit is not a passive forgetting of innovation and exemplarity; it is a product of a reserve of energy, one that perpetuates the same impetus of innovation and thus is always connected to the orginary act of creation. When art is perpetuated through its repetition in a tradition, it is not simply a matter of normative imitation. It participates in that same creative, formative element as long as it meets the criteria essential to any interpretation, first and foremost among them the unrepeatability of any personal formulation of truth.

Tradition properly construed is therefore the active taking up and recognition of exemplarity and originality: "The natural result of innovation is tradition,"[22] as it is its prolonging in action, with exemplarity as its foundation and the recognition of kindredness as its impetus for continuation. Thus, "[t]he fecundity of the form consists in being not so much the archetype of a series of imitations, but rather as the progenitor of the work of art's dynasty."[23]

Kindredness is the fertile environment in which this exemplarity can flourish, as "exemplarity is effective only if it happens within an act of *personal agreement* which as personal is in turn original and innovative."[24] The personality of the act/choice of consent is what provides another source of originality in the tradition ensuing from any given exemplar: "Originality can produce originality only on grounds favorable to a kindred and like spirit, because exemplarity is the result of a choice and an elective affinity, and the continuation is a new and original production."[25] The artist takes on the internal rhythm of tradition by following the original work through an act of choice and kindredness. "Tradition, therefore, in the very act that determines it as the will to conservation and perpetuation, is born as a reality destined to innovate and transform."[26] And "when the solidarity between exemplarity and kindredness is interrupted, innovation is no longer possible except as rupture."[27] Exemplarity then rules from the outside and withdraws into the notion of the "classic," which is outside of taste and the living times, as those are always in flux. The dialectical exercise of conservation and innovation therefore cedes its ground to the dilemma of repetition and rupture, to a mere conflict of interpretations and perspectives unable to find a common ground. To put it in another way, innovation ceases within the realm of form and merely becomes an exercise in content: whether the blind preservation of dated content or the dogmatic imposition of novel content. There is no exemplar, and thus no kindredness, because the work is reduced to its own time and lacks the formative element that allows its recognition outside of its own situation. Rather than ask "how is art performed?," one can only ask "is this art?" and thus commence the unending conflict of interpretations.

THE KINDRED RETURNS IN THE OTHER

To consider Pareyson's 1971 work *Truth and Interpretation* with the dialectic of kindredness and exemplarity in mind underscores the manner in which he understands hermeneutics as a way to challenge relativism. While a relativistic understanding of truth would either treat the work of art as an ineffable source about which interpretations are made or reduce the work of art and the weight of its truth to its presence—a mere expression of its own time or of an artist's will—a "revelatory" interpretation of the work of art demands (rather than happens to be) a plurality of formulations because of its focus on "form" rather than "content." In this case, the relations between varying works or interpretations are constituted neither by antagonism nor by indifference, but rather coexist in a community of qualitative differences, all of which derive their ground from the creative formativity of any work of art. Such works and interpretations—whether they exist in art, philosophy, or other realms of human action—are, in the language of *Truth and Interpretation*, at one and the same time *expressions* of history and *revelations* of being. What keeps such interpretations from being locked in their own historical moments—from being reduced to their present, even when understood historically and carried out of the past into one's own present—is illustrated in Pareyson's understanding of tradition as originary, as the site of a genesis. Through interpretation, "the past is delivered from its mere temporality and recovered in a more originary manner," in its possibility as the condition for any and all traditions.[28] The past is in this case never simply repeated, and rather than simply exalt the specific (and thus unrelatable) content of discreet historical forms, it indicates the "conditions of such a loyalty and transmission"[29] by pointing to a shared and common element—the kindredness of all formative acts.

The one who bears the conditions of such creative acts—the artist, for certain, but also more broadly the actions of any individual interpreter—is from Pareyson's earliest works captured in the figure of "the person" [*la persona*].[30] And while it is clear that for Pareyson any and all interpretations bear the unmistakable fingerprint of the person's singular perspective on the world, it also would not be incorrect to claim that the emphasis on the person in Pareyson's thinking points, paradoxically, away from the ontological primacy of any individual person and toward a recognition of a shared community of interpreters and interpretations: "Only when truth is possessed in one of its formulations"—as an interpretation—"can one understand that truth is present also in a different formulation."[31] In contrast to the purported objectivity of historical science or even an objective criterion in aesthetics or ethics, the possibility of understanding through an interpretation occurs "solely through empathy, kindredness, and elective affinity."[32] The ontological weight of any interpretation in Pareyson's hermeneutics relies upon these conditions, upon "the unifying and diffusive force of truth, namely, on that unicity and universality of the true which becomes valuable within every single formulation as the appeal to freedom rather than the conformity to evidence, as the demand for communion and dialogue rather than as a respect for habitual conventions."[33] An interpretation, which for Pareyson is always "of the truth," institutes, rather than merely reflects, represents, or reproduces, a community of "kindred persons."

Pareyson's condemnation of art and artistry as a mere expression of the times is mirrored, albeit with a slightly different emphasis, in the second section of *Truth and Interpretation* where he critiques ideology as a poor substitute for philosophy. In the latter segments of this critique, Pareyson points to the ontological weight of revelatory thought as the essential feature of dialogue and the conversation of ideas among diverse viewpoints. This notion has an important role to play within revelatory thought, and more importantly, within the use of dialogue as a means for overcoming the impasse of relativism as the conflict of singularly incommensurable viewpoints. Thus, despite the emphasis on kindredness and imitation, difference has a role to play:

> In order for there to be dialogue, two things are needed: truth and alterity. That, yet again, is possible only through the concept of interpretation because on the one hand, interpretation is by its nature multiple and infinite, since there is never interpretation without plurality or without alterity, and on the other hand, interpretation is always the interpretation of truth, and of the truth, there is nothing but interpretation, given the infinite and inexhaustible character of truth. In order for there to be dialogue, neither sympathy nor ideas are enough, because sympathy tends to dissolve in generic benevolence, in itself incapable of grounding respect for the person, and ideas may be mere historical products devoid of truth and thus incapable of establishing a common plane of understanding. Dialogue requires what I have elsewhere called

a real "exercise of alterity," as well as the presence of truth in the plurality of interpretation.[34]

Knowledge of the other through the exercise of alterity is never complete and remains open—one needs to find the balance between the other's historical substance and the other's possibility for freedom. This point is likely never attained, but it is nonetheless continually sought after through a succession of interpretations: thus "the knowledge of others has all the characteristics of *interpretation*, that is, of a knowledge in which subject and object are both individuals and in which the object reveals itself according to the measure in which the subject expresses itself, and of a knowledge that attains its scope if not with the risk of failure, and that, far from being unique and definitive, cannot present itself other than as the result of a continual exertion of revision and deepening."[35] More than just knowledge of an individual, this *solidarity* "contains together the *duty* of judging and being judged in the name of the universal, the *need* and the *right* of being understood by others, and a solicitation to be modified according to a mutual *call* to the laws of universal reason."[36] Perhaps here is where one finds that tradition of tradition within philosophical hermeneutics—not as the reference to a dogmatic past or unbearable inheritance, but as the *shared condition* for alterity and the plurality of viewpoints. Alterity and plurality are therefore possible on the basis of that common element within human existence.

This latter element, as the companion to the exercise of alterity, is thus the exercise of kindredness or, in other terms, the recognition of truth as the source of plurality and alterity, the understanding that, as in the case of art, the distinctive alterity of any interpretation requires a grounding in a shared interpretative element. The recognition and choice for kindredness reveals infinite interpretability (which is also its infinite reformulability), the basis for any understanding, or, in other words, truth. And such a truth is revealed in an act of understanding precisely because it exposes the condition of possibility for any and all understanding. This shared origin grounds Pareyson's challenge to relativism; but could it, construed more broadly as a basis for communities of interpreters, also ground a democratic politics capable of resisting the violence so often associated with metaphysics?

A COMMUNITY OF TASTE?

If one pulls together the elements of this conceptual development in Pareyson's thinking—from questions of originality and imitation in the work of art to broader issues of interpretation and its role in the cultural and political life of communities—what emerges is, albeit incompletely, a pathway toward a hermeneutics of community where kindredness drives, rather than inhibits, the inclusiveness of ever transforming interpretations.

On the one hand, Pareyson shows that imitation can be invention, and thus what matters within the aesthetic model is that any invention or original creation is, likewise, grounded upon a kindred or shared condition of being a formative act: the recognition of kindredness—by the creator, but also by the audience—is a choice and granting of consent that reveals the ontological weight of any interpretation. Recognition announces what sort of thing the work is and places its existential weight within a communal event, rather than within the genius of the artist or the mystery of the work itself. Art—within the realm of taste, and thus within the realm of formed perspective that resists reduction to nature or essence—not only provides the exemplar of this formative form, but also is understood as exemplary only because all human endeavors share in some degree of artistry: in other terms, they all have *formativity* as their kindred element. With a new sense of what is shared, tradition can now be understood as the recognition and carrying forward, through innovation, of that kindred element. Moreover, this notion of tradition, rather than alienate and exclude, has the potential to provide a nonviolent basis for inclusive communities of understanding, ones that resist the unending conflict of interpretations and the scourge of relativism.

Here we find ourselves perched on the edge of what appears to be a transcendental investigation, an uncovering of conditions of possibility for a hermeneutics of community. Even the casual reader of Pareyson's philosophy might balk here, as there seems to be little to validate such an interpretation, and others (notably Vattimo) certainly have not exploited this element within Pareyson's hermeneutics. It is strange territory, so let me briefly mention some points of reference so that we might better orient ourselves in our thinking.

Perhaps one major point of reference should be the events of 1968, as Pareyson's *Truth and Interpretation* is undoubtedly a response, albeit a conservative one, to what he perceived as the end of certain (favored) cultural and political traditions and the emergence of new (problematic) practices conducive to widespread consumerism. Two divergent paths emanating from these events (with both appealing to a version of nihilism) can be traced in the ways that Gianni Vattimo and Roberto Esposito have articulated the foundations for community: the former through the interpretation of metaphysics as a history of nihilism, and the latter through a biopolitical critique of essentialistic conceptions of identity and community. Pareyson offers another alternative. Rather than stake the origin or basis of community on a historical "weakening of Being" or a "nothing in common,"[37] Pareyson lays claim to a certain absence, an origin that resists essentialization and presencing by always formulating itself through what it is not—an alterity conceived through the kindredness of the formative process. An alterity that carries Nietzschean overtones (ones not read as Vattimo reads them) in the key of becoming "who one truly is" in a manner that never escapes its past and, in fact, flows from it through ever newer interpretations. Contrary to another product of 1968—Jacques Rancière—who conceives of art and its political, democratic force as a form of dissensus, Pareyson reminds us that the recognition of the kindred element in art and in human activity is instead a form of *consensus*.

But to what do we give our consent? What is it that we recognize in each other—in our works and judgments, institutions and creative endeavors—and, most importantly, in our political relations? Perhaps in the end Pareyson's insistence on the exemplarity of art as an ontological paradigm can lead us to a renewed and revised interest in taste. Not simply the tried and true traditions of artistic taste (wrapped up so often in modes of exclusion), but first and foremost in the democratic challenges that accompany the realm of gustatory taste. We all have a right to our own taste—*de gustibus non est disputandum*—and thus a right to our own creativity . . . and perhaps this could be the basis for a democratic, nonviolent community of dialogue in which taste is recognized through its shared form (and formativity) rather than its exclusive content. Where biology is connected to culture, and the demands to be fed (and thus live) are never removed from the claims to be unique (and thus to thrive). A shared community of taste can reject the consumerist mantra to "have it your way" precisely because the recognition of such a community denies the atomizing politics of neoliberalism. In other words, taste provides the origin and demand for a community, rather than a conflict of interpretations. This is so not because the interpretations are incommensurable, but because the incommensurability of individual taste is the shared origin, the kindred element, of all interpretations. Incommensurability is not the result, but the originary demand that solicits from us the risk and responsibility of interpretation.

NOTES

1. This chapter is, in many respects, a continuation and deepening of a line of thinking I pursued in "The Tradition of Tradition in Hermeneutics," in

Consequences of Hermeneutics, ed. Jeff Malpas and Santiago Zabala (Evanston, IL: Northwestern University Press, 2010).

2. Luigi Pareyson, *Truth and Interpretation* (Albany: State University of New York Press, 2014), 42.

3. The lecture courses, along with later material, can be found in volume 10 of Pareyson's complete works: Luigi Pareyson, *Problemi dell'estetica I. Teoria* (Milano: Mursia, 2009), 11–87.

4. Ibid., 43.

5. Ibid., 47. Here Pareyson is drawing from Giambattista Vico, *On the Most Ancient Wisdom of the Italians*.

6. Luigi Pareyson, *Estetica. Teoria della formatività* (Florence: Bompiani, 1954).

7. Ibid., 19.

8. Ibid., 130.

9. Ibid., 140.

10. This idea—of art's uniqueness or "unicity"—is not restricted to art for Pareyson, even though art is the exemplar for all articulations of truth. Even philosophies find common ground in their ability to be unique. See Luigi Pareyson, "The Unity of Philosophy," *Cross Currents* IV, no. 1 (1953): 57–69.

11. Pareyson, *Estetica*, 143.

12. Ibid.

13. Ibid., 143–44.

14. Ibid., 144–45.

15. Ibid., 243.

16. Ibid., 244.

17. Ibid., 244–45.

18. Luigi Pareyson, *Conversazioni di estetica* (Milan: Mursia, 1966).

19. Ibid., 9.

20. Ibid., 11.

21. Ibid., 25.

22. Ibid., 26.

23. Ibid., 27. This is also a moment to recall "the absent origin" at the root of any inheritance. Is there a way that any new formulation in the continuation of a tradition is, in essence, a claim to the right of inheritance, a deduction in the Kantian sense, whereby one carries on the exemplary spirit of the "original" that is nowhere to be found as an actual work—we have only our interpretations of it. . . .

24. Pareyson, *Conversazioni di estetica*, 27.

25. Ibid., 28.

26. Ibid.

27. Ibid., 30.

28. Ibid., 41.

29. Ibid., 41.

30. The notion of "the person" is central to Pareyson's thought as early as 1948 and is part of a position he describes as "ontological personalism." See Luigi Pareyson, *Esistenza e persona* (Genoa: Il Melangolo, 1985).

31. Pareyson, *Truth and Interpretation*, 74.

32. Ibid. Compare this with what Pareyson states in *Estetica* about kindredness and interpretation (243).

33. Ibid.

34. Pareyson, *Truth and Interpretation*, 148.

35. Pareyson, *Esistenza e persona*, 211.

36. Ibid., 212.

37. I am thinking, respectively, of Vattimo's reading of Western metaphysics as *pensiero debole*, and Roberto Esposito's understanding of the basis for community in his work *Communitas*. See Gianni Vattimo, *Weak Thought*, trans. Peter Carravetta (Albany: State University of New York Press, 2013) and Roberto Esposito, *Communitas*, trans. Timothy Campbell (Stanford, CA: Stanford University Press, 2009).

8

Truth as the Origin (Rather Than Goal) of Inquiry

Lauren Swayne Barthold

INTRODUCTION

Every human relation, whether it is knowing or acting, the understanding of art or interpersonal relations, historical knowledge or philosophical reflection, always has an interpretative character. This would not occur if interpretation were not in itself originary: It qualifies that relation with Being in which the very being of humanity resides; in it, the primigenial solidarity of human being with the truth is realized.[1]

If the first sentence of this quotation indicates Pareyson's broad hermeneutic commitments, insofar as he esteems the ubiquity of the interpretative experience, its final clause distinguishes his own brand that defines interpretation as the human expression, indeed revelation, of our fundamental relation with Being and truth. This chapter is an effort to understand the meaning of this claim and to demonstrate its significance for contemporary discussions of truth. I explore how his general hermeneutic approach, which defines truth in terms of human "being" rather than human "doings" (that is, formulating beliefs and propositions), gains traction from his more specific claim about human being's origin in truth as the condition for freedom.

Traditional Anglo-American philosophical analyses of truth have been directed at inquiring into what sorts of things truth applies to. Some of the following have been put forth as truth bearers: propositions or sentences (as proposed by correspondence theories), systems or languages (as proposed by the coherence theory), reason or verification (as proposed by pragmatism), and mind (as proposed by identity theory). Another approach asserts that there is nothing to which the term "truth" can adequately apply without resulting in redundancy and/or meaninglessness (deflationary accounts). Because Pareyson neither defines truth in terms of what sort of particular human activity it is a property of (e.g., beliefs, propositions) nor rejects truth as a meaningful concept, his theory of truth does not fit into any of the mainstream ways of classifying truth. In other words, the four categories of traditional accounts of truth, namely, "deflationism, intrinsicism, and the two forms of relationalism, coherentism, and correspondence,"[2] are not adequate to describe Pareyson's account of truth.

I submit that the reason for this incommensurability is Pareyson's refusal to take up the standard trope for truth, namely, as the goal or aim of inquiry. Instead, he insists that truth is fundamentally our starting point, our origin. Accordingly, if truth is not our goal, then it does not make sense to attempt to articulate a method or criteria that secure it. However, Pareyson goes further than claiming that efforts to establish a method prove vain: he insists that denying our origin in truth leads to domination and oppression. In other words, the significance of his approach that defines truth as our origin is found in its implication for human freedom. Thus in spite of the fact that his is neither a theory about the property of propositions nor a defense of the assertion that "there simply isn't anything which truth in general, *is*,"[3] this chapter argues that he does offer a viable account of truth that demonstrates its relevance for human existence.

Yet, in defending the relevance of Pareyson's *hermeneutic*, rather than epistemic, approach to truth, I argue that he goes further than either Heidegger or Gadamer, whose own important work on truth also could be characterized as demonstrating that truth is fundamentally a condition of human being not a property of human doing. Pareyson's hermeneutic emphasis certainly recalls Heidegger's rejection of traditional analyses of truth that have attempted to expand and clarify what Aristotle meant when he declared: "to say of what is that it is, and of what is not that it is not, is true" (*Metaphysics* 1011b25). Both Pareyson and Heidegger affirm that analyzing truth merely in terms of the human activity of utterance is reductive. However, in spite of the fact that Pareyson's account of truth follows this general Heideggerian gesture, one must attend to how Pareyson himself is explicit about his differences from Heidegger. As we shall see, Pareyson rejects Heidegger's defense of ineffability and instead defines truth as the free expression of humanity's original relation with Being.

In defending truth as present in human existence-as-interpretation, Pareyson, like Gadamer, rejects attempts to define truth in terms of its criteria. Gadamer stresses that we arrive too late if the aim of our pursuit of truth is to know what we should believe: "In the event of understanding we are drawn into an event of truth and arrive, as it were, too late, if we want to know what we are supposed to believe."[4] But if there is no criterion for truth then how can we discern truth from falsehood? One of the supposed desired effects of articulating what truth is a property of is to provide criteria that then allow one to know if a given proposition is true. Pareyson mentions that he is often asked how to distinguish philosophical from ideological thoughts (TI 115). His brief reply comes: "this very question is not philosophical" (TI 115). Yet, unlike another twentieth-century philosopher,[5] namely Richard Rorty, Pareyson offers this reply not to change the subject but to invite us to think more deeply about truth by rephrasing the question. By denying the philosophical nature of such a question, Pareyson is remarking on how such a question is reductive and serves to instrumentalize reason. For example, Pareyson explains that to ask for definitions of philosophy and ideology in order to be able to distinguish between the two implies that the respective definitions themselves serve as criteria (TI 116). The assumption is that a definition of philosophy provides the necessary and sufficient conditions that function as criteria; what does not meet these conditions is rejected as philosophy—hence the normative implication of such a definition. However, Pareyson does not want to dispense with definitions and distinctions altogether; in *Truth and Interpretation* he himself gives definitions of both philosophy and ideology. Yet he offers his definition of truth not to provide a method, that is, path, to secure our arrival at truth but to invite us to practice freedom. As we shall see, Pareyson's explicit concern with the way in which ideology-as-the-opposite-of-truth impedes existential freedom is a move that takes him beyond Gadamer's own efforts to expose the limitations of method as found in his antisubjective account of truth-as-event.[6]

This chapter argues that what is at stake in Pareyson's explication of truth, then, is not only its rejection of the instrumentalization of human reason as a means to achieve truth-as-end, but also its promotion of human freedom. If our only interest is to inquire: "What do all true propositions share?,"⁷ then we reduce truth to its criterion for measuring human doings, and we miss something more fundamental about truth and human existence. For Pareyson, this "something more" that emerges from articulating a more radical account of truth is its ability to promote human freedom. To unpack and demonstrate the significance of Pareyson's change of metaphor regarding truth and its connection to freedom, I focus on Pareyson's comments in *Truth and Interpretation* regarding truth's relation to interpretation, Being, and ideology.

UNITY OF TRUTH AND INTERPRETATION

For Pareyson, there is a fundamental unity of truth and interpretation. Pareyson speaks of truth as that which "appears," is "revealed," or is "formulated," and he maintains that all revelations, appearances, and formulations of the truth are always and only expressed through interpretation (TI 53–54). In this sense it is not that we arrive at truth, as traditional accounts imply; rather, truth arrives through us via interpretation (TI 54–55). By describing the way in which truth "entrusts itself" to each interpretation, he wants to emphasize how interpretation possesses truth. However, even this way of putting it might misleadingly suggest that truth is a property of interpretation. But Pareyson insists: "as *interpretation*, the formulation of truth *is truth itself*" (TI 56). Pareyson does not mean that every single interpretation is always true; he does not claim that interpretation is identical to truth. Rather, his point is that truth can only ever express itself through interpretation. Whenever truth appears, is revealed, or is formulated, it is always via interpretation. Here Pareyson sounds close to Gadamer, who maintained that "being that can be understood is language."⁸ For Gadamer, language or interpretation (which is necessarily always linguistic) just is the human expression of Being, which nonetheless always remains in excess of what can be said.

If truth and interpretation are "at one and the same time truth itself," then it does not make sense to articulate a criterion for truth that would allow one to judge the truthfulness of the interpretation (TI 62). For, if one cannot access truth apart from interpretation, then there can be no measurement of the interpretation (TI 63). To measure something is to be able to stand apart from that object and apply a separate object of measurement to it. The ruler-as-object is separate from the line to be measured, for example. But Pareyson rejects the need for a criterion of truth external to itself, and maintains that truth "is *index sui* [the mark of itself]" (TI 116). Truth can never be an object external to interpretation because interpretation is the fundamental expression of humans who are already in truth. Accordingly, if truth is not human-independent then it cannot properly be described as "objective." Nor is it "subjective"—for although it must always and only be expressed personally, it must also be expressed historically in a way that transcends any single individual (TI 133–34). Thus Pareyson's account of truth places it not only beyond realism and deflationism but also "beyond objectivism and subjectivism/relativism."[9] But what justifies Pareyson's claims about the unity of truth and interpretation and that truth is the mark of itself?

UNITY OF TRUTH AND BEING

Truth is fundamentally neither metaphysical nor epistemological but hermeneutical, having to do with the ontology and existence of persons (TI 62), not a property of propositions. Truth concerns our very being, indeed our relation to Being, rather than objective knowledge claims or Being itself.[10] Pareyson describes our "relation with Being and the truth that human beings are, and that human beings live" (TI 180). He tells us: "Truth is more present *in* thought as source and origin than present *to* thought as an object to be discovered" (TI 63). But what does it mean that truth is source and origin and what warrants him making such a claim? If we reside originarily in Being, and it is that relation that both gives us our being as well as gives rise to truth, then truth reflects our source. Before we are interpreting specific objects like texts, we are in a relation with Being that is truth-ful. Interpretation is the expression of this relation as we attempt to understand the world and through which truth is subsequently revealed. Truth is revealed in that expression of humanity that occurs in interpretation, an interpretation that fully acknowledges our fundamental relation with Being. But what is the significance of insisting on a relation between Being and truth?

For Pareyson, the significance of Being lies in its inexhaustibility that invites finite humans to remain open to further understanding, interpretation, and dialogue. He writes:

> if I have emphasized the ulteriority of Being and the unobjectifiability of truth, I have done it not so as to assert its ineffability, but so as to affirm its inexhaustibility, that is, its ability to reside in the world without identifying itself with it

> but always holding itself in reserve, to confer itself to every formulation without ever being exhausted in it, and to enter into discourse only to radiate outward new meanings of it. (TI 100)

I understand his move to connect up truth to the inexhaustibility of Being as indicating that there is a reflection, or image, of that inexhaustibility in human being's own nature: namely, in the human capacity to keep on saying, questioning, creating, dialoguing, deciding, and, in a word, revealing. The image of Being is manifest in human beings as they endeavor to articulate its inexhaustibility via interpretation. Pareyson insists that truth is always revelatory (of the inexhaustibility of Being) as opposed to only expressive (a purely subjective or objective articulation). When Pareyson maintains that "that which is not gathered as inexhaustible cannot be truth" (TI 101), he is explaining why we both feel a need to, and should, keep on inquiring. There is a reason humans have for speaking of truth; it signifies that there is something more than what any single individual or theory can espouse. If Being stands for what is inexhaustible, then truth is the articulation via interpretation of human being's assumption of inexhaustibility. Where such an assumption is refused, namely, where one believes one has asserted *the objective* truth, an interpretation is not in truth.

Pareyson's emphasis on inexhaustibility opposes Heidegger's claim about the ineffability of being and humanity's subsequent need to remain silent.[11] Pareyson wants to show that interpretation, though limited, is not contradictory to Being and truth so long as one acknowledges that one's interpretation must remain open to further scrutiny. To defend the unity of truth and Being is to remind humans, and thus philosophy, of our limits while at the same time resisting efforts of totalization that lead to silence:

> A philosophy which knew the whole truth would no longer be philosophy: it would be *sophia* without further qualification. No longer would it be that *human sophia* which is proper to the finite: it would be a higher-than-human knowledge, and would both transcend the condition of man and stop all inquiry. Actually the whole truth does not offer itself to man in the form of a possession achieved and definitively conquered. It is rather present as exigency and norm; as exigency exciting man to search for *the* truth, as norm acting as judge of *the* truths such inquiry attains.[12]

Truth as the Origin (Rather Than Goal) or Inquiry   129

As scions of the inexhaustible, we are driven to keep interpreting what is beyond, what remains always as other. When we fulfill this particular exigency of human existence, our interpretations reveal truth. Denying this inexhaustibility creates staid silence of the one who has either allegedly already spoken "the truth" or who fears making any utterance that remains incomplete. Some may protest, however, that when Pareyson speaks in the above quotation about the "norm" of truth he is doing exactly what he warned against previously, namely, suggesting a criterion that allows us to discern whether or not we have arrived at the truth. Is he not advocating a norm that allows us to know when we have arrived at this truth we are "searching" for? To save Pareyson from charges of inconsistency and to preserve the meaning of his claim that truth is our origin, let us approach his statement from a different angle.

Pareyson goes on to clarify that there is a "need for truth that motivates every thinking mind which has become conscious and reflective."[13] If a need is an expression of what one desires and lacks, then how are we to make sense of his insistence that we both need truth and originate in truth? The answer lies in admitting that our erotic relation to truth cannot be reduced to the need to possess fully truth-as-an-object. There are different ways in which "need" can be understood. One can *need* correct directions in order to arrive at one's destination—this is the picture of truth on traditional accounts. But one's *need* can also be directed toward what one in one sense already possesses yet in another sense has not yet fully experienced. To say that a child needs a parent's love is not to say that that child does not already have that parent's love. (It is this sense that students often express when they dispute Diotima's definition of love as the desire for what one does not possess: "But you can still love your boy/girlfriend even when you have him/her," they protest.) The sense of need referred to here expresses incompleteness and hence the inexhaustibility of what one already experiences. One has something (parental love, friendship) but still needs to experience it continually through time, which means that as finite beings, humans can never possess it completely. After all, Diotima's riveting tale instructs us that the human ability to possess the good forever does not mean we possess the good-as-object. As beyond being, the good-as-idea is not an object we can ever possess and fully "make our own." Rather, she illustrates how the erotic nature of humans, indicative of our very becoming, finds fulfillment through the cultivation of virtues in others. In this way, paradoxically, our becoming-ness gets us the immortality we want! To return to the above example: what would it mean for a child to claim that she fully possesses her parent's love? In saying that one wants more love, one is not saying that experiencing more love is like possessing an object, which will terminate the desire: one desires a cup of coffee, consumes it, and desires it no longer. Parental love, like truth (and the good), must keep on being expressed and experienced, and hence desired. On this picture, it makes no sense to ask for a criterion that will allow one to know when one has fully possessed enough love, truth, or good. To demand a criterion in this instance is to have misunderstood the experience of love, taking it as a finite object able to be possessed. Love, like truth and the good for Plato, are infinite, beyond being, yet, as the aim of our *eros*, they remain relevant for human finitude—and it is in this sense that I read Pareyson's reference to the "norm" of truth.

Thus in warning us away from objectifying truth, Pareyson endeavors to spell out the existential consequence of thinking that truth is an object that one can possess, where possession signifies that one no longer needs (to pursue) it. I find his point similar to one made by Socrates when, at the end of his dialogue with Cratylus, he chastens Cratylus for his excessive confidence and certainty in his own conclusion. Socrates instructs: "It's certainly possible that things are that way, Cratylus, but it is also possible that they are not. So you must investigate them courageously and thoroughly and not accept anything easily" (*Cratylus* 440c–d). This warning by Socrates to summon courage to query one's own comfortable conclusions indicates the significance of Pareyson's account of truth that departs from traditional ones. For believing that truth is that at which we must arrive privileges stasis over movement and thus encourages overconfidence in our belief that we have indeed arrived—that is, that the criterion of indubitability has been met and that we can rest assured. Where truth is taken as the goal of inquiry, the continual effort to interpret is derided. (And where the aim is absolute certainty and correctness, the obsession with defining criteria becomes paramount in order to avoid the "Cartesian angst" over whether one has really have arrived or not.) But what if we really have not attained indubitability? The danger Socrates and Pareyson warn of is that deeming a belief indubitable prohibits one from continuing to search and to journey onward. Similarly, Socrates's insistence that hypothesizing is the best that humans can achieve is instructive for understanding Pareyson's emphasis on truth as a starting place that privileges the ongoing quest. We posit (that is, hypothesize) what we believe and think to be the case but must always remain open to the possibility that we could be wrong. And such hypothesizing is another way of describing interpretation: as humans we cannot but help hypothesize about, that is, interpret, make assumptions about, our existence, in order to give it meaning. Both

Pareyson and Socrates remain dubious about claiming that one has investigated enough and thus can, as Cratylus assumes, retire peacefully by oneself in the country with the truth in hand. For both Socrates and Pareyson, the opposite of truth is not a false belief per se but an occlusion of further exploration and openness to the other. Pareyson takes this existential conclusion a step further by demonstrating how a solipsistic approach to truth results in ideology.[14]

TRUTH VERSUS IDEOLOGY

For Pareyson, the opposite of truth is not false propositions but ideology, which he defines as "thought" or "action without truth, which is technics" (TI 85). "Technics" or "technical reason" is "an empty and superficial rationality . . . , not only in the sense of being capable of projecting and verifying an action to the degree that it can control and correct itself, but above all in the sense that it enslaves itself to action in the very act of promoting and guiding it . . ." (TI 85). Below I explore further the significance of his claim that the lack of truth is fundamentally manifest in technical reason rather than in propositions. But in the meantime I want to address the question of what it might mean to think without truth if truth is characteristic of our fundamental relation with Being. To think without truth means denying our primordial relationship with truth and Being. Pareyson argues that when we forget this relationship or actively deny it, we end up with reductive rationalization, instrumentalized reason, and technologization, all of which result in impoverished experience (TI 180) and domination characteristic of ideology. When we forget our starting place in truth, we lose our freedom by becoming enslaved to means-end reasoning that aims only at efficiency (TI 152). As a consequence, we forsake the ability to think or decide for ourselves. Hence ideology is understood as a mode of thought that indeed "enslaves" us by "forcing" us to think in a certain way.

To illustrate Pareyson's point about ideology curtailing our freedom, we could consider one of the first recorded accounts of how claims to truth and objectivity can be used as a means of domination. Gorgias argued that if Helen of Troy had been persuaded by "reason" to leave her home, she would have been just as impotent as if she had been carried away by force. One is not free to refuse the claims of reason. Pareyson would seem to agree with Gorgias's point about the forcefulness of certain "truths" and for that reason strives to remind us that there is more to truth than "rationality." When rationality is used to compel in such a way that it shuts down further thinking, and hence fundamentally opposes the ongoing nature of interpretation, it functions as a type of ideology. Ideology, then, stands directly opposed to interpretation. As Robert Valgenti explains in his introduction to *Truth and Interpretation*: "Ideology expresses the necessity of the given, but unlike philosophy, does not possess the critical freedom to interpret that given" (TI xxxv). When a proposition is declared true, there is nothing more to be said; further interpretation and conversation are occluded. To avoid ideology, it is not enough to summon reason alone, as Hannah Arendt proves in her discussion of the way in which the banality of evil can go hand-in-hand with calculative reason. Pareyson insists that the antidote to the evils of ideology is the realization of our origin in truth (TI 129).

What does such truth, freed from instrumental reason and technique, look like? Pareyson writes:

> As unobjectifiable, truth demands freedom and decision because it is not a matter of re-cognizing a definite object, but of determining a presence without figure, which confronts us with the responsibility of personally formulating truth. Furthermore, the revelation of truth, by implying the courage to give truth one's own formulation, and thus assuming the character more of a testimony than of discovery, coincides with the decision for Being, that is, it coincides with the exercise of that radical and deep freedom. . . . (TI 92)

Truth is not a weapon to compel others to submit but an invitation to decide and testify for oneself in freedom. Rather than objectifying oneself or another, truth requires recognition of freedom: for oneself as well as for another. Asserting truth as calculative rationality denies human relation with Being and as a result forecloses the affirmation of human *being*. What compels such a reductive attitude? In an Augustinian moment, Pareyson warns that it is the very condition of freedom, namely, the inexhaustibility of truth (TI 64), that permits us to choose alienation in the first place. Only freedom permits the human choice for alienation. He explains:

> The true "alienation" is the individual's separation from Being and the splitting of the originary nexus of person and truth, the ontological closure and the relinquishment of interpretation: In their freedom, human beings reject Being and renounce truth. In such a way, on the one hand, they

identify themselves with their own situation and are reduced to merely historical products, and thus they replace their own freedom with their own "reification"; on the other hand individuals make themselves incapable of turning their own situation into an opening to Being and a pathway to truth, and replace interpretation, which is the profound essence of thought, with abstraction. . . . (TI 97)

This quotation changes the debate away from defining criteria for how to assess an isolated statement as true or false to the realm of human existence that recalls our more fundamental way of Being. Philosophy that directs itself only to the truth of statements becomes ideology masquerading as philosophy and by promoting abstraction alienates us from the truth of Being found in practical existence. The real worry in missing truth is not that we end up with epistemological error but with an existential loss of freedom.

CONCLUSION: THE SIGNIFICANCE OF PAREYSON'S HERMENEUTIC ACCOUNT OF TRUTH

I have been emphasizing that a key motif in Pareyson's account of truth distinguishing it from traditional approaches is the way he defines truth as our starting place rather than as an end to be reached. I would now like to defend the significance of his account by taking a closer look at how his call to "recover the origin" (TI 195) of our belonging to Being and truth promotes existential freedom. What does such freedom look like, and how is it connected to truth?

If all human being in the world is marked by interpretation—as the epigraph to this chapter iterates—then we should understand the imperative of freedom as directed at interpretation in its most general sense, that is, in our interactions with other human beings. Specifically for Pareyson, freedom occurs where humans "recognize infinite *other* possible formulations and the demand for a continual conversation with them. . . . [For] only such a *free opening of dialogue* constitutes a relation adequate to the order and nature of interpretation" (TI 68, 69, italics original). Our origin in truth becomes a source of freedom for humans insofar as it provides "the stimulus for an unending revelation" (TI 66), which for Pareyson takes the form of inclusive and continual dialogue. Dialogue is one form free interpretation takes. Pareyson explains the connection:

> To grasp does not mean to be able to enunciate it in a complete and definitive explication, which would rather imply that one has not really grasped it at all. Conversely it means to begin a discourse that continually regerminates from its own source, that incessantly reproblematizes its own questions, that always alludes to something other and more than that which it states explicitly. (TI 140)

If the excess and inexhaustibility of Being are best expressed by encouraging a free and open dialogue,[15] then Pareyson's account of truth proves relevant for thinking about and explaining various forms of social oppressions that result from a lack of such freedom. For example, claims to know the truth, which prevent further inquiry and dialogue and thus force others to agree, lead to oppressive silencing. Such claims can occur on the political, juridical, institutional, or individual level. Ideologically infested media wars, legal decisions taken out of the hands of the community, policies handed down from administrators where questioners are dealt with punitively, and the implicit wielding of one's privilege are all examples of silencing that curtail freedom. Oppression occurs when some group or individual acts to prevent others from joining in the dialogue or from offering new interpretations.[16] An example of such oppression can be seen when an institution functions solely according to its internal logic—that is, ideology in the sense quoted above—whereby "reason" "enslaves itself to action in the very act of promoting and guiding it, or even in the sense that [technics] dissolves into action as is identified with it" (TI 85). In such an instance, where an institution (or group or individual) refuses to consider new interpretations, we could say it is enslaved to a particular "truth." As a consequence of that enslavement, others are dominated through the practice of exclusion. The operating assumption is: conform to "logic" or leave. Insisting that one's truth is universal leads to the exclusion of those who are deemed "untruthful." If freedom, according to Pareyson, is the rejection of the possibility of totality (TI 143), then to practice freedom means constantly exposing and working to undermine practices that aim at or assume totalization.

Some forms of totalizing are quite subtle. For instance, a proposition that is true in one context of rules may work to oppress when wielded as a weapon to silence those who inhabit different meaning-contexts. When one assumes universal truth for one's statement, one forecloses the openness needed for an interpretive stance toward the world that invites dialogue among a plurality of individuals and perspectives. I read Pareyson as maintaining that the objectification and reification of truth that permits one to claim total or final access to a "truth" curtails practices of freedom. In other words, where the aim is to possess truth-as-object, and if one comes to believe one possesses it, then one no longer perceives a need to be open to another and one might easily feel justified in any tactics that exclude the "other-as-untruthful." Certainty in one's own beliefs denies a fundamental experience of human existence, namely, our shared fallibility. Pareyson insists that

> the human formulation of the true always contains the possibility of error and that the human practice of the good always presupposes the possibility of evil. This fact belongs to that situation of *insecuritas*, precariousness, and risk that comprises the essentially tragic nature of the human condition, which realizes the positive only within an act that contains the constant and effective possibility of the negative, to the point that the suppression of the possibility of evil would not be possible if not as the suppression of freedom itself, that is, as the suppression of the unique source through which human beings are capable of realizing the good and being worthy of praise . . . Human nature is ambiguous in itself, able to hide the good under the appearance of evil and to camouflage evil with the features of good, and indeed to mix good and evil in the motivations of the very same act, which is therefore neither less good than evil nor less evil than good, according to the point of view. (TI 125)

Recognizing our fallibility means refusing clear delineations between good and evil, truth and falsity. Insisting one knows the truth is not simply a matter of epistemic arrogance; such a claim denies the humanity of another being by forbidding her voice at the table. I read Pareyson as demonstrating that when philosophy becomes preoccupied with focusing on truth solely as that which is a property of human activity, like the formulations of propositions or beliefs, our very human existence becomes threatened by a reductionism that promotes false dichotomies between good versus evil and truth versus falsity. Such false and rigid dichotomies make us forget our finitude and fear facing the inexhaustible; we consequently disdain openness. For falsehood is not just the inability to measure up to a predetermined standard, as the correspondence theory of truth proposes. Rather, falsehood is the perversion of truth, which Pareyson describes as "obfuscation and oblivion, forgetting and abandonment of truth, distancing from it and the loathing of it"

(TI 127). Falsehood is not just incorrect seeing but, as we have seen, manifests itself as an ideology that asserts the certitude of one's belief. As an antidote against such a narrow conception of truth, Pareyson bids us acknowledge the inexhaustibility of Being in order to encourage us to engage a dialogue wherein a plurality of expressions of truth arise. It is in this sense that I understand the practical relevance of Pareyson's claim that the expression of truth invites participation and freedom for all. Thus the solution cannot be to secure a more explicit criterion that works to exclude by fixing the boundaries, but to practice freedom, which requires "personal commitment, deliberate struggle, and knowing resolve, all of which lead to conquest and victory only through constant risk for failure and defeat" (TI 128). Such a struggle is the existential form interpretation takes.

Pareysons's efforts are directed at exposing the inadequacy of reductionism and instrumentalism in their various forms—both theoretical and social—insofar as their fundamental ideologies curtail human freedom. Keeping in mind the fact that Pareyson's writing offers both a critique and extension of existential philosophy, we could read him as attempting to critique all philosophies where the "person is negated by necessity" (TI xxii). While his theory does not fit into any of the standard classifications of truth, he nonetheless defends the relevance of truth for humans as a way to promote existential freedom. As Pareyson reminds us, "human freedom appears possible only as the site of truth" (TI 117). For Pareyson, to reduce or deflate truth is to reduce or deflate human existence. Thus his assertion that humans are originarily connected with truth via Being is a summons to reflect on a richer conception of truth, one that cannot be captured in terms of the most efficient means-end reasoning or propositional logic. Describing truth as fundamentally connected with Being is his attempt to explain the significance of interpretation and its connection to human freedom. Accruing isolated truths, ensuring our utterances maintain the property "true," is not what humans fundamentally crave. For filling our minds with "true" beliefs can never get us what we really want: namely, freedom to interpret, freedom to truly be.

NOTES

1. Luigi Pareyson, *Truth and Interpretation*, translated and with an introduction by Robert T. Valgenti (Albany: State University of New York Press, 2013), 47. Hereafter parenthetically referred to as TI.

2. Simon Blackburn and Keith Simmons, eds., *Truth* (New York: Oxford University Press, 1999), 207.

3. Crispin Wright, "Truth: A Traditional Debate," in Blackburn and Simmons, *Truth*, 205.

4. Hans-Georg Gadamer, *Truth and Method*, trans. Joel Weinsheimer and Donald G. Marshall (New York: Crossroad, 1992), 490.

5. See Richard Rorty, *Philosophy and the Mirror of Nature* (Princeton: Princeton University Press, 1979), chapters 7 and 8.

6. Although I do not have the space here to further develop a comparison between Gadamer and Pareyson on truth, I note that in my own work on Gadamer I have argued that we can find two specific criteria for truth therein: change and solidarity; see Lauren Swayne Barthold, "True Identities: From Performativity to Festival," *Hypatia* 29, no. 4 (Fall 2014): 808–823. My reading of Gadamer that portrays him as inviting an openness toward continual change and gesturing toward the importance of solidarity born of dialogue for human understanding ends up making Gadamer's account of truth seem quite friendly with Pareyson's more explicit existential and sociopolitical account. Thus the difference I am most comfortable asserting between Gadamer's and Pareyson's accounts of truths is one of emphasis and explicitness.

7. Blackburn and Simmons, *Truth*, 1.

8. Gadamer, *Truth and Method*, 474.

9. Richard J. Bernstein, *Beyond Objectivism and Relativism* (Philadelphia: University of Pennsylvania Press, 1983).

10. Luigi Pareyson, *Existence, Interpretation, Freedom: Selected Writings*, ed. Paolo Diego Bubbio (Aurora, CO: The Davies Group Publishing, 2009), 230.

11. Pareyson writes of wanting "to push [Heidegger's work] beyond the *impasse* of negative ontology into which he has unfortunately and hopelessly forced it. The fact that truth eludes complete explication should not force one to consider it as ineffable . . ." (TI 100; see also TI 143).

12. Luigi Pareyson, "The Unity of Philosophy," *Cross Currents* 4 (1953): 66.

13. Ibid., 66.

14. Pareyson's proximity to Plato can also be seen by considering the following selection from the *Cratylus*, which expresses a key theme in Pareyson's account of truth, namely, the commitment that there is something more to truth than as a property of human utterances. Socrates explains to Hermogenes:

> "*Aletheia*" ("truth") is like these other [names] in being compressed, for the divine motion of being is called "*aletheia*" because "*aletheia*" is a compressed form of the phrase "a wandering that is divine" (*ale theia*). "*Pseudos*" ("falsehood") is the opposite of this motion, so that once again, what is restrained or compelled to be inactive is reviled by the name-giver, and likened to people asleep (*katheudousi*)—but the meaning of the name is concealed by the addition of "*ps*." "*On*" ("being") or "*ousia*" ("being") says the same as "*aletheia*" once an

"*i*" is added, since it signifies going (*ion*). "*Ouk on*" ("not being"),
in turn, is "*ouk ion*" ("not going"). (421b)

Here Socrates highlights a similarity between truth and Being in terms of their ongoing and infinite nature. Inactivity, stasis, is referred to as *pseudos*; truth and Being require wandering, motion. Similarly, Pareyson's emphasis on the interrelatedness among Being, interpretation, and truth reveals that what is required for truth is not cessation, arrival, but constant movement marked by openness toward the inexhaustible. Truth is revealed in the process of movement; it is not a property of a static entity.

15. Pareyson, "The Unity of Philosophy," 67.
16. For an excellent discussion of the way in which oppression can function epistemically, see Miranda Fricker, *Epistemic Injustice* (New York: Oxford University Press, 2007).

9

The "I" Beyond the Subject/Object Opposition

Pareyson's Conception of the Self between Hegel and Heidegger

Paolo Diego Bubbio

There is an aspect of Luigi Pareyson's thought that has received little critical attention to date: the place that his distinctive conception of the "I" occupies in the history of post-Heideggerian philosophy. Quite naturally, his notion of "person" (*persona*), which sits at the core of his philosophy, has received a significant amount of attention; however, it has not been considered in a broader historical and theoretical context, with the consequence that Pareyson's importance has often been underestimated, especially in the Anglophone world.

In this chapter, I contend that Pareyson's conception of the "I" represents a distinctive, original, and fruitful solution to the problem of the overcoming of both subjectivism and objectivism. By "subjectivism," I mean the philosophical tenet that the nature of reality, as related to a given consciousness, is dependent on that consciousness—a position that was typical of modern philosophy from Descartes's "prioritization of the 'cogito'" onwards, and that is paradoxically related with "the attempt at a purely 'objective' understanding of the world"[1]—that is, objectivism.

Pareyson was in a unique position to appreciate this complex and fundamental issue, and to advance a possible solution. The uniqueness of his position derives, I maintain, from a deep understanding of issues and problems of the German idealist tradition (which, as suggested by Beiser, can be considered in its entirety as a "struggle against subjectivism")[2] on the one hand, and from a critical proximity with existentialism in general, and Heidegger in particular, on the other.

I devote the first section of the chapter to Pareyson's complex relation to Hegel, focusing especially on the notion of the "I," and the second section to Heidegger, showing that Pareyson had a deep understanding of Heidegger's achievements but also of his limits. The choice of Hegel and Heidegger is far from obvious, and it might be objected that, if the goal is to explore the way in which Pareyson's dialogue with German idealism and existentialism informs his conception of the "I," then Fichte, Schelling, and Jaspers respectively would be more appropriate choices, as those were the thinkers whom Pareyson considered a constant source of inspiration for his philosophical work. There is no doubt that Pareyson's relation to Hegel and Heidegger was much more critical (especially with the former); and yet I contend that, precisely because of this critical distance, it is in the context of his dialogue with these thinkers that it is possible to identify Pareyson's innovative conception of the "I" that overcomes (or at least attempts to overcome) both subjectivism and objectivism. In fact, in the conclusion, I suggest that Pareyson effectively pioneers a fruitful philosophical strategy to formulate a new paradigm of the self beyond the subject/object opposition.

HEGEL

Pareyson always maintained—as a statement made in the context of a 1977 interview makes perfectly clear—that his interest in classic German idealism was not primarily historical but rather due to a "nexus" connecting those very high manifestations of speculative thought with contemporary problems.[3] The importance of Hegel within and beyond that tradition was not a subject of dispute for Pareyson. In the 1988 Naples Lectures, he claimed that he had always considered Hegel's philosophy "the center of contemporary philosophy"—although he suddenly added that he considered "its dissolution more important than its continuation."[4]

In the development of the German idealist movement, Hegel occupies a critical position, as he sought to establish a conception of the "I" based on the *unity* of subject and object (rather than on their opposition, as it was traditional in Cartesian and post-Cartesian metaphysics) while at the same time demanding that this unity have objective validity.⁵ This revolutionary move was connected with Hegel's critique of the Cartesian idea of the immediacy of the self, which inevitably led to the subjectivism of which even other German idealists, such as Fichte, were not immune. In Fichte's system, in fact, the "I" is presented as absolutely immediate: historical determination is completely absent from Fichte's model of the "I," which is also why Fichte's infinite strife (*Streben*) produces, in Hegel's view, an "unsatisfied I." The only object that, for Hegel, can satisfy the "I" is *another* "I," another self-consciousness.⁶ Therefore, in Hegel's view, the "I" must be thought of as a "mediated and achieved identity, which is realised through the process that Hegel calls 'World-history.'"⁷ In other words, both the "I" and its perspectives on the world (philosophies) are historical products.

Pareyson has an excellent understanding of the fact that Hegel's philosophy represents the fulfillment of that process initiated by Kant, which, on the one hand, sanctions "the end of objective philosophy" (the old pre-Kantian metaphysics), and, on the other "defines a new objectivity of philosophy."⁸ Hegel, in other words, understands that the fact that philosophies are historical realities, which are related to the situation of their own time and to the needs of their own age, does not at all imply the relativistic and skeptic conclusion that they are therefore merely changeable opinions, determined by their historical environment and destined to mutual destruction. In fact, Pareyson argues, the claim that no philosophy has the right to present itself as the unique custodian of truth does not mean that the sequence of philosophical perspectives is vain or ineffectual. Not only does the variety of philosophies not undermine the possibility and the existence of philosophy, but it is also its essential and necessary condition.⁹ "Despite the difficulties and the disadvantages of his conclusions," Pareyson claims (and we are soon going to consider what these "difficulties and disadvantages" are, according to him), Hegel had grasped as few other philosophers had the idea of philosophy as "*confilosofia*" ("philosophizing-with"), that is, as that realm of truth to which everyone brings a contribution.¹⁰ Hegel wants to affirm at the same time both the historicity *and* the truth of philosophies—that is, both their historical conditionality and their speculative value. This is, Pareyson argues, one of the most genuine and valuable aspects of Hegel's thought. Unfortunately, Pareyson deplores, this aspect was also subsequently downplayed, and instead what was emphasized was the affirmation that the multiplicity of philosophies and their being historically determined can be appreciated only from an external point of view, which is—in Pareyson's view—either the Hegelian "God's eye-view" (the "absolute philosophy that contemplates and includes the totality of philosophies," according to Pareyson's definition) or—once this has been assumed unreachable—a nonphilosophical standpoint, like that of the sciences.[11]

Pareyson agrees with Hegel's struggle against that form of subjectivism that, from the consideration of the multiplicity of the self's perspectives on the world (philosophies) as historical products, draws the consequence of their ineffectiveness. This was one of the dangers that Hegel identified in the Romantic movement—a preoccupation that was also shared by Kierkegaard so that on this point, at least, the two philosophical opponents, Hegel and Kierkegaard, are in perfect agreement. This is, Pareyson reminds us, the danger of "aestheticism": namely, the "exaggeration of the individual, the most subjective and capricious whit," which "forgets any supra-individual element."[12] However, for Kierkegaard (and Pareyson seems to agree), "aestheticism" is only *one* of the two dangers that philosophy faces, the other being precisely the Hegelian "panlogism": Hegel sees that "the center of reality is dialectical," and that everything is "contrast conflict contradiction, living contradiction";[13] but then he dissolves the individual in the absolute reason that "resolves everything in itself."[14] As Pareyson claims, Hegel "sees well" but "thinks poorly."[15]

To charge Hegel of "panlogism" was quite common, especially in the existentialist circles of the twentieth century. Without devaluing Pareyson's critique of Hegel in any way, it is however possible, I suggest, to unpack this generic charge by identifying at least two (important) aspects of that critique that should be more appropriately regarded as directed against particular evolutions (or, it might be argued, *involutions*) of Hegel's thought, rather than against Hegel's philosophy itself.

First, Pareyson claims that the "catastrophic" error of Hegel[16] (or even Hegel's *only* error[17]) was the confusion of eternal and divine history with temporal and human history—which, in Pareyson's view, has the consequence of generating a dialectics of necessity rather than a dialectics of freedom. This claim, however, should be evaluated in the context of the Italian philosophical scene within which Pareyson had received his philosophical education, a scene that was heavily influenced by the neo-idealism of Giovanni Gentile. Italian neo-idealism, in fact, presents some distinctive characteristics (which extend to the other important figure of that movement, Benedetto Croce) that distinguish it from other forms of neo-idealism, such as the Anglo-American neo-idealism of thinkers such as Bradley and Royce. Italian neo-idealism is still concerned (like classical idealism) with the identity of the finite and the infinite, but it aims at reaching that identity *positively*, that is, by showing the presence and reality of the infinite within the very structure of the finite, in its intrinsic and necessary rationality.[18] Specifically, Gentile's version of neo-idealism, also called "actualism," contends that the object of thought (be it nature, God, one's own self, or someone else's self) has no reality outside the *act* of thought that thinks that object and, by thinking it, posits it.[19] As a result, Gentile's actualism regards history as a "tendentially linear process" aimed at a progressive achievement of immanence as the true dimension of Spirit.[20] Pareyson considered Italian neo-idealism in general, and Gentile's actualism in particular, as "the last great attempt to re-affirm rationalism in its most coherent and definitive form" by "resolving dialectically any irrationalist motive in philosophy qua self-consciousness."[21] Pareyson also remarks, however, that Gentile's actualism has somehow "prepared that climate in which speculative themes subsequently recognized as existentialist could germinate"[22] because of Gentile's emphasis on the question of the place of individuality in the universality of Spirit.

It is not possible here to engage in a discussion of the influences of Gentile's actualism on Pareyson's early philosophy, and the extent to which Gentile's thought had an impact even on Pareyson's mature thought. The following remark will, therefore, suffice for the present purposes. On the one hand, it is true that in the first half of the twentieth century, Gentile's actualism effectively provides an entry point for German existentialism into the Italian philosophical scene; on the other hand, precisely because Pareyson (among others) used that entry point, he inevitably ended up, to some extent, reading Hegel through Gentile's eyes with the consequence that the Hegel whom Pareyson criticizes is somehow a "Gentilian" Hegel. As a result, while Pareyson acknowledges Hegel's attempt to overcome the alternative between subjectivism and objectivism and grasps the concrete dimension of Hegel's idealism (two aspects of Hegel's thought that were maintained and indeed strengthened by Gentile), he also implicitly attributes to Hegel a linear conception of history seen as a process of progressive and actual identification between the finite and the infinite in which the individual is eventually and *necessarily* resolved in an abstract and "purely conceptual" process. This conception though comes from Gentile's conception of Hegel rather than from Hegel himself.[23] As an implication, Pareyson tends to downplay (and even ignore) other important dimensions of Hegel's philosophy that were neglected in Gentile's actualism, such as the emphasis on recognition and the attempt to realize a concrete "idealistic" objectivity that does not dissolve in the subjectivity of the act (I come back to this point in the final section).

This leads us to the *second* aspect of Pareyson's critique of Hegel, which, I suggest, should be more appropriately regarded as directed against a particular development of Hegel's thought rather than against Hegel's philosophy itself: that is, the charge that Hegel intended to "resolve reality into pure thought, and turn the philosopher's thought into absolute reason itself."[24] The point is: What is "absolute reason"? Here, it seems to me, either one interprets the notion of "absolute reason" in a *relational* way, relying on the notion of recognition and emphasizing the intersubjective dimension of it, or one is driven to reduce the infinite to a mere projection of the finite. The latter is effectively Feuerbach's philosophical strategy. Feuerbach deprives the finite of every relational dimension, anthropomorphizes the ideal aspects of Hegel's philosophy, and eventually reduces the rational to the real and the real to what is sensibly perceivable. Thus, when Pareyson criticizes Hegel for resolving reality into the subject, it is mostly because, it might be argued, Pareyson already has in mind the nonrelational alternative that from the dissolution of Hegel's thought leads to Feuerbach—a philosophical perspective that dissolves the nonsensible into mere subjectivity.

In Pareyson's view, Feuerbach represents only one of the two alternatives emerging from the dissolution of Hegel's idealism, the other being Kierkegaard's existential philosophy. Kierkegaard's "subjective reflection," Pareyson maintains, is "based on an intimate relation of subject and object according to which the subject grasps the object through an act of appropriation in which it is affirmed as subject, and truth ceases being objective and indifferent precisely because knowledge is personal and existentially engaged with truth."[25] In this kind of knowing, Pareyson adds, "what disappears is objectivity, that is, that indifference of truth and that impersonality of knowledge that are connected with the separation of subject and object."[26] In other words, both Feuerbach and Kierkegaard build on the Hegelian overcoming of the opposition between subject and object; the Hegelian solution, though, that is, the mediated, or idealistic, subjectivity, was perceived by both of them as too ambiguous. Thus, Feuerbach—"the objective thinker"—solves that ambiguity by absolutizing the (human) subject and treating any relationality with the nonsensible as a mere projection of subjectivity; Kierkegaard—"the subjective thinker"—sees (more appropriately, in Pareyson's view) that a true overcoming of the opposition between subject and object can only be realized by a thought that starts from the human being's concrete existence and does not renounce the relationality with the nonsensible. This is, in a nutshell, the origin of existentialism. Hence Pareyson's claim that existentialism "still deals with Hegel, either directly or indirectly, but always within a Hegelism in dissolution, and therefore it is always anti-Hegelian and Hegelian at the same time, always in the middle of a crisis, between the conclusion and the new beginning."[27]

For Pareyson, as Maurizio Pagano poignantly puts it, Hegel has the merit of having overcome the static opposition between subject and object, but that overcoming is "articulated according to the dialectical movement, which moves from a setting that is still universal, impersonal, and unable to place thought in that degree of full engagement with the existential experience Pareyson is aiming at."[28] This is the reason why Pareyson sees Kierkegaard so favorably. The "subjective thinker," Pareyson argues, is such not in the sense of *romantic* subjectivism (which "exalts whim and clouds faith"), but insofar as such a thinker inseparably maintains and preserves, together with "the most alert and accurate reflection" (which is the legacy of Hegel and German idealism in general), also "the most real and concrete existence." "Subjective thought"—Pareyson concludes—"consists therefore in a 'double reflection': on the one hand, it is about thinking without forgetting to exist, on the other hand, it is about existing without thereby ceasing to think. That way, true thought and authentic existence are both realized, because thought oblivious of existence is not true thought."[29] When Pareyson praises the overcoming of Hegelian thought into an "existential and subjective thought, which consists in a reflection strictly combined with existence,"[30] he is clearly referring not exclusively to Kierkegaard's thought in its specific and historical dimension, but rather to that kind of philosophy that had in Kierkegaard its pioneer—existentialism. Pareyson is somehow already thinking of Heidegger.

HEIDEGGER

Hegel wanted to overcome the opposition between subject and object while at the same time maintaining that the unity between subject and object has some (idealistic) "objectivity"—which is not, of course, the objectivity of pre-Kantian metaphysics but a mediated (idealistic) objectivity. Symmetrically, it might be argued, Heidegger wanted to overcome the opposition between subject and object while maintaining that the unity between subject and object has some (existential) subjectivity. This subjectivity is not, however, the traditional Cartesian subjectivity, which is the reason why Heidegger even coined the word *Subjektität* ("subjectity" or "subjectness")[31] as an alternative to *Subjektivität* (subjectivity) to avoid any reference to subjectivism (in contrast to objectivism) and its apparent restriction of the subject to the mental and the "I."

As early as in the 1925 lecture notes later published under the title *History of the Concept of Time*, Heidegger proclaims the rejection of an approach according to which "the 'I' is given without the world." Even a formulation such as "first an I is given with my being-in-the world" is, however, "false," remarks Heidegger.[32] The point is that the "with" already expresses an externality that runs the risk of pushing the self back into the metaphysical definition of the self typical of the Cartesian *cogito* and of modern philosophy in general. As Christopher Fynsk states, "Heidegger seeks to unseat this subject from its central position as *subjectum*, but does not renounce all effort to situate or position the subject or self; he situates it elsewhere—in the 'there' of Da-sein—and describes the condition of possibility for Dasein's assumption of a position or stance in terms of the structure of Dasein's Being as care."[33] The labyrinthine concept of "care," which of course cannot be addressed here, is, among other things, meant to capture the inextricable and originary relation of Dasein with the world.

Pareyson has a great understanding of Heidegger's project and of what is at stake in it. He writes:

> For Heidegger, human beings are not defined by their own being-in-the world, if with that claim one means (as Sartre does) that existence precedes essence (which is merely a polished way of saying that human beings are such as they are made by the circumstances). The world is not the totality of things and circumstances in which human beings would find themselves immersed and by which they would be determined in their historicity. The world as organized totality of things and circumstances is there only because there is an organizing perspective, that is, the human being. But this in turn does not mean that the world is a creation of the human being, a projection of the human being as a knowing subject: nothing could be further from Heidegger than this kind of idealistic subjectivism. [. . .] if the human being is in the world, this is because the human being is originarily in a relation with Being.[34]

Well aware of the centrality of Heidegger's notion of *Geworfenheit* ("thrownness"), Pareyson develops his own notion of *situazione* ("situation"). Initially introduced by Pareyson as "the novel contribution of existentialism,"[35] and as such conceived as a notion shared with other thinkers such as Jaspers and Heidegger, Pareyson's notion of situation gradually assumes distinctive characters: "My situation is my concreteness, my configuration, or, to use Marcel's word, my 'incarnation': without it, I, as a single person, would not exist."[36] As the reference to Gabriel

Marcel's use of the notion of "incarnation" indicates, Pareyson emphasizes the concreteness of the notion of situation: "Only in the *essential relation* between myself and the situation am I really myself: unique, incarnated, placed, singularized, concrete."[37] The situation is conceived as the relationship of the human being with the world as it limits and conditions, grounds and determines human possibilities. As such, the notion of situation clearly anticipates Pareyson's later theory of interpretation.

What makes Pareyson's theory of interpretation very distinctive—a theory that, one should not forget, was developed not by relying on other philosophies such as those of Gadamer and Ricoeur but independently of them and, to some extent, even anticipating them—is, in my view, his emphasis on the notion of the "I" as *personal* perspective,[38] as something that he does not see as an obstacle to the overcoming of subjectivism and objectivism but rather as a *condition* for that overcoming. Pareyson writes: "Ultimately, every person conducts a monologue, imprisoned in his or her own situation, and is faced with no other alternative than to understand his or her limitations with greater depth and clarity."[39] This lack of alternatives, however, can become a possibility, that is, a philosophical strategy: understanding limitations allows human beings to grasp the empty abstraction of the subject/object opposition and, at the same time, realize that the problem of truth is not merely gnoseological and epistemological but, more fundamentally, metaphysical. In a 1977 interview, Pareyson addresses this issue with admirable clarity:

> It must be understood that, with the concept of interpretation, subjectivism is definitively overcome. In fact, it can be said that the concept of interpretation arises precisely to eliminate subjectivism, and to rid the path of the opposition between subjectivism and objectivism forever. The basic terms are no longer "subject" and "object," and so it is no longer possible to require an "objective" principle, otherwise one would relapse into "subjectivism," and it is no longer possible to call the personal appropriation of truth "subjective." The problem of truth is not so much a "gnoseological" problem, soluble in terms of knowing subject and known object, but rather a problem which is, so to speak, "metaphysical," concerning the roots of human beings in Being, that is, the ontological character of the originary union of person and truth.[40]

On the issue of truth being a metaphysical problem prior to being an epistemological one, Pareyson is basically echoing the Heidegger of *The*

Fundamental Concept of Metaphysics.[41] Heidegger's fundamental lesson, as Pareyson sees it, is that if I am a personal perspective on the world, then the "I" is not conceivable without the world, and the world is not conceivable without the "I." If this is true, though, then the entire old metaphysics grounded on the subject/object distinction is no longer tenable. Gianni Vattimo writes: "If one recognizes, with Heidegger, that our experience of the world is always an interpretation (that is, an encounter in which, as Pareyson writes, 'the matter reveals itself to the extent that the person expresses him or herself') and not a passive mirroring where the subject annihilates itself in order to reflect the object more adequately, then one must speak of being too in terms that no longer belong to the metaphysical tradition."[42] Pareyson's theory of interpretation is therefore conceived as overcoming both "subjectivism with all its arbitrariness, and impersonalism with all its abstractedness."[43]

If, on the one hand, Pareyson takes Heidegger's lesson to be necessary, on the other hand, he is also critical of some aspects of Heidegger's philosophy. As early as in his "Esistenzialismo 1941," Pareyson remarks that in Heidegger, "phenomenological researches and transcendentalist preoccupations not only freeze [*raggelano*] the dramatic nature of existence but also constitute it in a purely formal sphere."[44] Pareyson is critical of Heidegger's philosophical project that aims at identifying the a priori structures of existence because such a philosophy runs the risk of turning existence into an abstract notion, which is precisely what Pareyson wants to avoid.[45] Later on in his *Studi*, Pareyson addresses the connection between *Jemeinigkeit* ("mineness," the Heideggerian principle of individuation) and *Geworfenheit* ("thrownness"), and notices that because of the way in which this connection is established by Heidegger, *Geworfenheit* too is conceived existentially and hence structurally. It is thus not clear how the *Da*, which is anonymous, can become *individualized* and *personalized*: "The existential [*Existenzial*] does not succeed in the explanation of the existentiell [*existenziell*]: neither the inauthentic nor—even less—the authentic one." Where is the *person* in Heidegger's philosophy? Someone might object that Heidegger's notion of person could coincide with the self-identity in which the relation with Being is "circularly clarified." Pareyson would counter-object, though, that a person conceived in such a way is "merely formal, a structure of empty, and not concrete, relations, in which the activity of an initiative that reacts in *this* way to *this* situation is missing." As Pareyson concludes, "the doctrine of existentiality jeopardizes the possibility of thinking the individual [*il singolo*] and the person philosophically."[46]

In Pareyson's view, this is a serious shortcoming, both practically and theoretically. *Practically*, because if the person cannot be thought of philosophically, then a proper ethics cannot be developed[47]—we are left with a "solitary self." *Theoretically*, because, according to Pareyson, only a form of ontological personalism can properly address the relation between the human subject and Being. The impossibility of thinking the notion of person leads Heidegger to a "negative ontology," according to which the truth is ineffable. This generates the risk of a new subjectivism in the worst sense of the term, that is, a conception according to which "the multiplicity of perspectives is reduced to the multiplicity of existences."[48] As Pareyson claims in *Truth and Interpretation*, those who want to take Heidegger's discourse "beyond the *impasse* of negative ontology into which he has inconveniently and uselessly forced it"[49] should affirm, against Heidegger, that the truth is not ineffable, but inexhaustible [*inesauribile*]. "The word is the inadequate site of truth only if one understands it rationalistically as a total explication; but, if one takes stock of its infinite capacity, it appears rather as the most appropriate site for welcoming truth and preserving it as inexhaustible."[50]

The theory of the inexhaustibility of truth is absolutely central to Pareyson's hermeneutics (and here one should recall Pareyson's brilliant claim that "there is nothing but interpretation of truth and there is no interpretation of anything but truth"),[51] but because of its complexity it can only be briefly alluded to here. However, one question at least deserves to be addressed because of its relevance for our purpose, namely, the question of Pareyson's perspectivism. Does Pareyson stand against perspectivism or is he, after all, a perspectivist?[52]

The answer to this question depends, of course, on what we mean by "perspectivism." On the one hand, Pareyson was always very critical of those relativistic forms of existentialism that seemed to suggest that all perspectives are equally valid. In such forms of existentialism, as Pareyson claims in a 1952 manuscript (which, in anticipating his mature critique of deconstructionism that he subsequently saw as the latest form of relativism, sounds almost prophetic), "the validity of a philosophy consists in its adherence to the personal life of which it is the expression: philosophy is nothing but a personal confession, and its value is merely biographical."[53] On the other hand, however, being a true hermeneutic thinker, Pareyson embraces perspectivism conceived of as the philosophical tenet that no perspective on the world can be taken as definitely true. In fact, if the "I" is, as we have seen, a "personal perspective" on the world, then interpretation is not a heterogeneous philosophical approach that may or may not be used, but the only authentic modality in which the "I" can express (or, even better, *live*) its relation with the world. Heidegger recognized this, but then he considered the truth as ineffable. In other words, Heidegger conceived the personal perspective of the "I" as an insurmountable *obstacle*, hence his negative ontology. It may be argued that negative ontology is the last remainder of that "inferior" subjectivism (inferior as based on the subject/object polarization and opposed to the *true subjectivism* that is one of the features of the ontological personalism Pareyson is aiming at) that Heidegger wanted to avoid in the first place. In a lucid statement that could be considered as summarizing his entire critique of Heidegger, Pareyson claims: "Only of a subject capable of turning her own very definite perspective into a condition, rather than an obstacle, can it be said that she interprets."[54] Only once the concrete "I" is taken as the condition of interpretation, while at the same time it is maintained that this makes truth inexhaustible (but not ineffable), can we engage in a philosophical project that preserves both subjective content (in the superior sense of "the most real and concrete existence") and objective validity (in the superior sense of "the most alert and accurate reflection").

CONCLUSIONS

It has already been emphasized that Pareyson's notion of "situation," which was already present in his early writings, anticipates his mature theory of interpretation. "If it be said that I am one with my situation," Pareyson writes in 1952, "it must be added that I am also, in an immediate way, a point of view, in virtue of which I can do nothing but see."[55] This is existence, namely, the "I" being one with its situation. Pareyson is clearly very receptive of Heidegger's lesson that Dasein "always understands itself in terms of its existence, in terms of its possibility to be itself or not to be itself."[56] As we have however seen, in comparison with Heidegger, Pareyson's philosophy acquires less formal and more concrete nuances: existence is thus conceived as the sole possible opening not only toward its internal structures, but also toward reality broadly conceived.[57] The impossibility to "leap out of what I am," to use Marcel's emphatic expression,[58] here becomes not an obstacle, but a condition that grounds Pareyson's notion of *personal existence*. One should not forget that Pareyson kept referring to himself as an "existentialist" even in the context of the mature expressions of his theory of interpretation. Interpretation is personal because the interpreter *is* the only possible perspective on truth.[59] Yet "personality does not mean 'subjectivity.'" Pareyson explains: "The 'subject,' as it is conceived by a certain philosophical tradition, is self-contained, and transforms everything with which she comes into contact into her own activity; the person, by contrast, is open, and always disclosed to something else or to others. The best guarantee against the danger of subjectivism is offered by the concept of person, according to which, while affirming that everything with which the person comes into contact must become interior to her, at the same time asserts her irreducible independence. Interpretation is not 'subjective,' but 'personal.'"[60]

The novelty of Pareyson's notion of the "I" as "person" resides precisely in this twofold awareness: personal existence is the only possible *perspective* on the world, but, at the same time and precisely because it is a perspective *on* the world, the world always and originally *constitutes* it. This twofold nature of existence is present in Pareyson's thought since his early writings. In a 1940 article, he claims with admirable clarity that existence is "*in-sistentia*, being inside, presence, intimacy" and, at the same time, "*ex-sistentia*, being outside, protrusion, emergence."[61] Here one can find, *in nuce*, the essential core of Pareyson's notion of person as paradoxical coincidence of relation with the self and relation with the other. The notion of person thus conceived is also, in turn, the grounding aspect of Pareyson's theory of interpretation.

In *Truth and Interpretation*, Pareyson argues: "The recognition of other perspectives must occur on the basis of the affirmation of one's own, otherwise the very nature of the perspective as such—as the personal possession of truth—will be lost."[62] In other words, the assertion of one's own perspective is the condition for the recognition of other perspectives—although even this formulation is artificial and, as it were, "didactic" because, on closer inspection, the assertion of one's own perspective and the recognition of other perspectives are one and the same. "Philosophical reflection," Pareyson remarks, "does not speak of truth directly, in which case it would be an objectifying discourse, but it always approaches truth as already interpreted." This is "the principle of hermeneutical thought," which was introduced "as much in the mature works of Hegel as in those of Schelling."[63]

It is interesting to note that the number of references to Hegel increases in Pareyson's later writings. One might even suggest that, faced with Heidegger's "*impasse* of negative ontology" and—even worse, in Pareyson's view—with the relativistic drift of deconstructionism, Pareyson shows a tendency to return to the origins of the hermeneutic tradition, to that "alert and accurate reflection" and to that need for "objective validity" that Hegel had represented. Of course, Pareyson keeps prefering other thinkers in the German idealist tradition over Hegel, such as Schelling. And yet one might wonder whether Pareyson would have evaluated Hegel's philosophy differently had he accessed it not through Gentile's eyes, as a system of progressive achievement of immanence and resolution of the individual in a purely conceptual process, but rather in light of the studies that, since the last decades of the twentieth century onward, have reinterpreted (much more appropriately, we might add) Hegel's idealism as an attempt to approach the "I" from a perspective that takes into account the role of intersubjective acts of mutual recognition for the genesis of self-conscious thought.[64] After all, as appropriately remarked by Maurizio Pagano, the theme of the "relation to others as constitutive of the subject," which is so important in Pareyson's works on the notion of "person," had been pioneered precisely by Hegel in his investigations on recognition.[65]

There is one important point about which Pareyson's strategy for overcoming the opposition between subject and object inexorably diverges from Hegel's. In *Truth and Interpretation*, in the context of an argument on the conception of freedom that favors Schelling over Hegel, Pareyson claims that Schelling has seen that "what Hegel places at the end should have been placed at the beginning, and that the unity that follows duality can only take the form of a totality, which is ultimately abstract and utterly lacking compared to the inexhaustible richness of the originary unity."[66] Hegel effectively put the unity between subject and object "at the end"; not in the sense that he sees subject and object as originally opposed (as in traditional Cartesian and post-Cartesian metaphysics), but in the sense that he thinks of the distinction between subject and object as an unavoidable step in the development of human rationality, which has to be subsequently overcome to establish that unity of subject and object that achieves a *mediated* objectivity. Pareyson is concerned that a mediated unity (the "unity following duality") necessarily takes the form of an artificial and abstract "totality," which would not do justice to the originary and concrete unity. Hence, he follows Schelling (whom he conjoins with Heidegger) in seeing Being as an event and conceiving the event, in its ontological structure, as freedom. With this move, as Aldo Magris has pointed out, Pareyson intends to overcome "the traditional antithesis between objectivism and subjectivism."[67]

> For common sense (which always uses metaphysical categories, even if it does not know that), the event is an "objective" phenomenon of the external world, whereas chosen freedom is an operation made by persons, a "subjective" phenomenon:

two things that in such terms could not be assimilated as forms of freedom. But here one is required to see things differently. Subjectivity is neither exhausted simply in the mental, psychological sphere and in self-consciousness, nor in the mere linguistic use of personal pronouns; and objectivity, in turn, should not be confused with the physical presence of a lifeless object.[68]

This is clearly a sophisticated and elegant solution. However, as a conclusion, I allow myself to ask a question that may lead to further investigation. Pareyson's solution puts a strong emphasis on the originarity of freedom as the site of the unity of subject and object. As a consequence, the philosophical enterprise is conceived as the self's struggle to relate itself hermeneutically to its originary unity with Being. This work, for Pareyson, takes primarily the form of a hermeneutic of religious experience. One might wonder if, in so doing, the objective (in the "superior" sense of the word) validity of philosophy, which Pareyson always wanted to maintain against every form of relativism, is, after all, weakened. Also, it might be objected that what is lacking here is some kind of "operational principle" that can constitute a *praxis* of existence. If existence is, as Pareyson maintained, not only "*in-sistentia*," that is, presence and intimacy, but also "*ex-sistentia*," in other words, protrusion and emergence, and if the formation of the self is both the result of an individual choice and the outcome of a collective enterprise, does that not mean that the unity of subject and object is, after all, not only at the beginning, but *also* at the end?

Pareyson did not provide an answer to this question, but we should not forget that he died before completing his *Ontology of Freedom*. It might well be that such answer could have found a place in such a work. At any rate, there is no doubt that the more general and very relevant question of the concreteness of existence out of the self in the overcoming of the subject/object opposition was indeed asked by Pareyson with an almost unprecedented clarity and rigor. Hermeneutically, sometimes asking a question is actually more important than providing an answer to it.

NOTES

1. Jeff Malpas, *Heidegger's Topology: Being, Place, World* (Cambridge: MIT Press, 2006), 356.

2. Fredrick Beiser, *German Idealism: The Struggle against Subjectivism, 1781–1801* (Cambridge: Harvard University Press, 2002).

3. See Luigi Pareyson, "Filosofia e verità," interview by Marisa Serra, in *Studi cattolici* 193 (March 1977); now in Luigi Pareyson, *Interpretazione e storia*, ed. A. De Maria (Milan: Mursia, 2007), 241–54.

4. Luigi Pareyson, *Ontologia della libertà* (Turin: Einaudi, 1995), 68. When quoting from Pareyson's work, I provide reference to the original publication, as well as to the volume (in Italian) where that publication is now included. If the passage is included in the collection of Pareyson's writings published in English with the title *Existence, Interpretation, Freedom: Selected Writings*, trans. Anna Mattei, ed. Paolo Diego Bubbio (Aurora, CO: The Davies Group Publishers, 2009), I use that translation and provide the corresponding page number (hereafter cited as EIF). If the quote is from *Verità e interpretazione*, I use Valgenti's English translation and provide the corresponding page number: Luigi Pareyson, *Truth and Interpretation*, trans. Robert Valgenti (Albany: State University of New York Press, 2013); hereafter cited as TI. In all other cases, the translation from the Italian is mine.

5. I am aware that this is not undisputed. I do not have the space here to defend this position; I argued for it at length in *God and the Self in Hegel: Beyond Subjectivism* (Albany: State University of New York Press, 2017), 153–59.

6. See Paul Redding, "Hegel, Idealism and God: Philosophy as the Self-Correcting Appropriation of the Norms of Life and Thought," *Cosmos and History: The Journal of Natural and Social Philosophy* 3, nos. 2–3 (2007): 16–31.

7. Dennis Schmidt, *The Ubiquity of the Finite: Hegel, Heidegger, and the Entitlements of Philosophy* (Cambridge: MIT Press, 1988), 50. See also Paolo Diego Bubbio, "The I and World History in Hegel," *British Journal for the History of Philosophy* 25, no. 4 (2017): 706–26.

8. Luigi Pareyson, *Esistenza e persona*, 4th ed. (Genoa: Il Melangolo, 1985), 89.

9. Luigi Pareyson, *Introduzione a Hegel* (Bari: Laterza, 1953), now in Luigi Pareyson, *Interpretazione e storia* (Milan: Mursia, 2007), 109ff.

10. *Interpretazione e storia*, 119–20.

11. Luigi Pareyson, "Critica e metafisica" (1952), in *Interpretazione e storia*, 134–44. The metaphor of the God's eye-view is used by Pareyson in "Introduzione a Hegel," in *Interpretazione e storia*, 118.

12. Luigi Pareyson, "L'etica di Kierkegaard nella 'Postilla'" [1970–71], in *Kierkegaard e Pascal* (Milan: Mursia, 1998), 129.

13. Luigi Pareyson, "Frammenti sull'escatologia," in *Ontologia della libertà*, 296.

14. Pareyson, "L'etica di Kierkegaard nella 'Postilla,'" 129.

15. Pareyson, "Frammenti sull'escatologia," 296. On this point, see Sergio Givone, "Philosophy and Novel in the Later Pareyson," pp. 185–99 of this volume.

16. Pareyson, *Ontologia della libertà*, 68.

17. *Ontologia della libertà*, 338.

18. See Nicola Abbagnano, *Storia della filosofia*, vol. VI, *La Filosofia dei Secoli XIX e XX* (Turin: UTET, 1993), 113.

19. Ibid., 115–16.

20. Maurizio Pagano, "Ripensare il soggetto, ripensare l'universale a partire da Pareyson," in *L'esistenza e il logos: filosofia, esperienza religiosa, rivelazione*, ed. Paolo Diego Bubbio and Piero Coda (Rome: Città Nuova, 2007), 143–73, here 161.

21. Luigi Pareyson, "Vita Arte Filosofia" (1947 lectures notes), now in *Interpretazione e storia*, 31–96, here 44.

22. Luigi Pareyson, *Studi sull'esistenzialismo* (Milan: Mursia, 2001), 187.

23. After all, "a philosophical 'system' does not have to be, *ipso facto*, a system of necessity." See Aldo Magris, "Il significato ontologico della libertà," in Bubbio and Coda, eds., *L'esistenza e il logos*, 118.

24. Pareyson, *Esistenza e persona*, 47.

25. Pareyson, "L'etica di Kierkegaard nella 'Postilla,'" 137.

26. "L'etica di Kierkegaard nella 'Postilla,'" 138.

27. Pareyson, *Studi sull'esistenzialismo*, 56.

28. Pagano, "Ripensare il soggetto, ripensare l'universale a partire da Pareyson," 148.

29. Pareyson, "L'etica di Kierkegaard nella 'Postilla,'"129.

30. "L'etica di Kierkegaard nella 'Postilla,'" 128.

31. Martin Heidegger, "Hegel's Concept of Experience," in *Off the Beaten Track*, ed. and trans. J. Young and K. Haynes (Cambridge: Cambridge University Press, 2002), 100–01.

32. Martin Heidegger, *History of the Concept of Time* (Bloomington: Indiana University Press), 238.

33. Christopher Fynsk, "The Self and Its Witness," *boundary 2* 10, no. 3 (1982): 185–207, esp. 186.

34. Luigi Pareyson, *Prospettive di filosofia contemporanea* (Milan: Mursia, 1993), 32.

35. Luigi Pareyson, "Genesi e significato dell'esistenzialismo," *Giornale critico della filosofia italiana* 5 (1940); now in *Studi sull'esistenzialismo*, 16; EIF, 42.

36. *Studi sull'esistenzialismo*, 16–17; EIF, 42.

37. *Studi sull'esistenzialismo*, 1; EIF, 42.

38. Pareyson, *Verità e interpretazione* (Milan: Mursia, 1971), 100; TI, 87; EIF, 153.

39. Luigi Pareyson, "L'unità della filosofia," *Filosofia* 4, no. 1 (1952): 83–96; English translation A. Di Lascia, "The Unity of Philosophy," *Cross Currents* 4, no. 1 (1953): 57–69; now in *Interpretazione e Storia*, 97–108; EIF, 50.

40. Luigi Pareyson, "Filosofia e verità"; EIF, 157.

41. Martin Heidegger, *The Fundamental Concept of Metaphysics. World, Finitude, Solitude*, trans. William McNeill and Nicholas Walker (Bloomington: Indiana University Press, 1995), 208.

42. Gianni Vattimo, "From Aesthetics to Ontology of Freedom," in this volume, pp. 159–67.

43. Pareyson, *Verità e interpretazione*, 72; TI, 62; EIF, 175.
44. Pareyson, "Esistenzialismo 1941," in *Studi sull'Esistenzialismo*, 21–34, esp. 28.
45. See Silvia Benso, "On Luigi Pareyson: A Master in Italian Hermeneutics," *Philosophy Today* 49, no. 4 (2005): 381–90, at 389n.
46. Pareyson, *Studi sull'Esistenzialismo*, 171.
47. Ibid., 156.
48. Pareyson, "Critica e metafisica," 144ff.
49. Pareyson, *Verità e interpretazione*, 117; TI, 100. Valgenti translates the Italian "*inopportunatamente e sterilmente*" as "unfortunately and hopelessly"; here I followed the translation of EIF, 196.
50. Pareyson, *Verità e interpretazione*, 117; TI, 100; EIF, 196.
51. Ibid., 53; TI, 47. Valgenti translates the claim as "of truth, there is only ever interpretation, and there is no interpretation, lest it be of truth." I think that the translation provided in EIF (161), and used here, renders better the elegance of Pareyson's Italian expression ("della verità non c'è che interpretazione, e non c'è interpretazione che della verità").
52. The question has been previously addressed by Benso, "On Luigi Pareyson," 385.
53. Pareyson, "Critica e metafisica," 144.
54. Luigi Pareyson, *Estetica. Teoria della formatività*, 1954 (Milan: Bompiani, 2005), 187; EIF, 110.
55. Pareyson, "L'unità della filosofia"; EIF, 56.
56. Martin Heidegger, *Being and Time*, trans. Joan Stambaugh, rev. Dennis J. Schmidt (Albany: State University of New York Press, 2010), 11.
57. See Benso, "On Luigi Pareyson," 384.
58. Gabriel Marcel, *Metaphysical Journal*, trans. Bernard Wall (London: Rockliff, 1952), 277.
59. As Eco remarks, "The interpretative activity (and this is, for Pareyson, the central point) is *perspectival*"; Umberto Eco, "Pareyson vs. Croce: The Novelties of Pareyson's 1954 *Estetica*," p. 75 of this volume.
60. Pareyson, *Estetica*, 226; EIF, 114.
61. Pareyson, "Genesi e significato dell'esistenzialismo," in *Studi sull'esistenzialismo*, 16; EIF, 41.
62. Pareyson, *Verità e interpretazione*, 79; TI, 68; EIF, 181.
63. Luigi Pareyson, "La filosofia e il problema del male," *Annuario Filosofico* 2 (1986); now in *Ontologia della libertà*, 161; EIF, 232.
64. This definition is mine (see *God and the Self in Hegel*, 107. See also Paolo Diego Bubbio, "Hegel, Heidegger, and the 'I': Preliminary Reflections for a New Paradigm of the Self," *Philosophy Today* 59, no. 1 [2015]: 73–90), and it has in no way the ambition to summarize the outcomes of half a century of Hegel scholarship. It is undeniable, however, that the importance of recognition has been increasingly acknowledged in the last few decades. See Ludwig Siep, *Anerkennung als Prinzip der praktischen Philosophie* (München: Alber, 1979);

Andreas Wildt, *Autonomie und Anerkennung. Hegels Moralitätskritik im Lichte seiner Fichte-Rezeption* (Stuttgart: Klett-Cotta, 1982); Robert R. Williams, *Hegel's Ethics of Recognition* (Berkeley: University of California Press, 1997). Also, for a "hermeneutic" interpretation of Hegel, see Maurizio Pagano, *Hegel: La religione e l'ermeneutica del concetto* (Napoli: ESI, 1992); Paul Redding, *Hegel's Hermeneutics* (Ithaca: Cornell University Press, 1996).

65. Pagano, "Ripensare il soggetto, ripensare l'universale a partire da Pareyson," 169.

66. Pareyson, *Verità e interpretazione*, 165; TI, 143; EIF, 204.

67. Magris, "Il significato ontologico della libertà," 115.

68. Ibid., 115.

10

From Aesthetics to Ontology of Freedom

Gianni Vattimo

ANTICIPATORY SPIRIT

More than twenty years after his passing (born on February 4, 1918, he died on September 9, 1991), one can truly say that, in the case of Luigi Pareyson, time is a gentleman. Just a few years before being stricken by a serious sickness, Pareyson's thought encountered a wide resonance, even outside academia. Since then, such resonance has increasingly amplified and deepened, so much so that in many senses one can speak today of the anticipatory, if not even the decisively prophetic character of Pareyson's philosophy. I think that today, even more than twenty years ago, one can truly recognize the not merely specialized currency [*attualità*] of his thought. The rubric "tragic thought," which he often employed in his later years to characterize his theoretical position, helps to overcome the limits of the academic horizon. Such a horizon is increasingly problematic even for the most tenacious defenders of philosophy as a specialized science charged with the custody of a tradition of texts to be kept rigorously separated from the current times [*attualità*], and therefore also from any social usefulness. Even these defenders are becoming persuaded (perhaps just so that they are not completely marginalized from cultural industry) that perhaps one should seek a less evanescent relation with daily existence, politics, religion, and the new issues raised by science and technology. This should be a relation similar to the one that was in place at the times of great systematic philosophies such as idealism (when the young Schelling, Hegel, and Hölderlin, in the Tübingen seminar where they were classmates at the end of the eighteenth century, followed the vicissitudes of the French Revolution with enthusiasm and participation). This was true also for an existentialist such as Kierkegaard (another of the great masters who constantly inspired Pareyson), who is the author of inflammatory timely polemics against the Danish Church.

Not few Italian and European philosophies of these most recent decades walk the paths that were trodden on by Pareyson, often with anticipatory spirit. I am here thinking of some Italian philosophers of the "younger" generation such as Massimo Cacciari, whose books, especially his ambitious *Dell'inizio* [*On the Beginning*],[1] unfold within the same perspective; or another philosopher of Cacciari's same generation (that is, from the 1940s), Reiner Schürmann, the author of *Heidegger on Being and Acting: From Principle to Anarchy*,[2] one of the most significant books on Heidegger in the last decades of the twentieth century. In different terms and forms, names such as Cacciari and Schürmann but also so many French philosophers in the Derridean and Heideggerian traditions (the most recent being, for example, Jean-Luc Nancy, especially with his book *The Experience of Freedom*)[3] attest to the currency of tragic thought in today's cultural circles, especially those made of young people—precisely those who, inside and outside academia, increasingly often approach also the texts of the later Pareyson.

Pareyson arrives at tragic thought by radicalizing, in a manner that goes beyond a classical figure in hermeneutics such as Gadamer, the relation between philosophy of interpretation and conception of being, which was already at the center of Heidegger's meditation. If one recognizes, with Heidegger, that our experience of the world is always an interpretation (that is, an encounter in which, as Pareyson writes, "the matter reveals itself to the extent that the person expresses him or herself") and not a passive mirroring where the subject annihilates itself in order to reflect the object more adequately, then one must speak of being too in terms that no longer belong to the metaphysical tradition. That is, one must think of being no longer as an ultimate, immutable, and completely "given" ground outside of any genuine historicity because, as the theologians who have insisted on the question of predestination know, if being (or God) is entirely actual ever since and for eternity, then becoming, history, and human freedom are purely unexplainable fictions. In order to acknowledge that truth is always interpretation (including scientific truth, because any scientific claim is verified or falsified only within the frame of paradigms that scientists possess from beforehand, from their received education, their culture, and so forth; paradigms that they then "express" in their experimental work), being must in turn be thought as event and not as a fixed structure that is given once and forever. For Pareyson, but also for Schelling, Kierkegaard, and many Christian existentialists (or Jewish ones, like Levinas), being, which is not the eternal and immutable geometric order but rather the source of interpretation and freedom, is the biblical God, who is in turn initiative, affirmative act, positivity that imposes itself against a negative possibility. A God of this kind carries evil within himself, albeit as prehistory that has been defeated. The tragedy of human existence, which is never completely free of limitations, evils, suffering, and useless abuses, finds here its most remote rooting.

That much contemporary European philosophy places itself under the sign of tragedy does not necessarily imply that tragic thought constitutes the truth of our current condition for everyone, including some of Pareyson's students. There is another aspect of Pareyson's philosophical legacy that circulates widely also among non-tragic thinkers—namely, the idea that philosophy is essentially the hermeneutics of religious experience. This means interpretation of sacred myths and writings (for Pareyson, this certainly means Jewish and Christian sacred scriptures eminently). These days many Christian philosophers, or at any rate those philosophers who wish to save the possibility of religion perhaps in the name of Wittgenstein's distinction among various "language games," tend to separate religious from philosophical discourse and ascribe to each its own rules and criteria of validity. (Yet who assigns the parts in the comedy? Who decides what the boundaries of the two different discourses are?) Conversely, Pareyson has taught us to recognize the continuity, and also the possible conflicts, between philosophy and religious tradition. Both concern themselves with the same matter; both live on a "revelation" that hides but also offers infinite and always lively possibilities of interpretation. For the "global" society in which we are increasingly living, the question of the plurality of cultures, which means also the plurality of their founding religions and myths, is crucial. On the basis of such a consideration, we are bound to acknowledge that, in this sense, Pareyson's philosophical legacy is anything but a past residue.

TRAGIC THOUGHT AND HERMENEUTICS OF RELIGIOUS EXPERIENCE

The two points of Pareyson's "currency" from which I move are not at all two separate aspects of his philosophy, or aspects that can even be separated. Pareyson reaches tragic thinking as a result of his practicing philosophy as hermeneutics of religious experience and not otherwise. This way of defining and practicing philosophy is perhaps the most essential and meaningful of his teachings. Of course, we would need a broader discourse and a more complete rereading of all of his works if we wanted to establish whether and to what extent even his proposal of an aesthetic theory of formativity, which at first appears as a phenomenology of artistic creation with no evident connections to the biblical and Christian legacy, can in fact be already definable as a hermeneutics of religious experience. The continuity and the consistency of the itinerary that goes from aesthetics to the religious interests in Pareyson's final years are, however, not difficult to see (and this is something that has been shown in an excellent manner by Francesco Tomatis). The discovery of the forming form sets thinking out toward a vision of reality that is much more aligned with idealism than with any form of realism or empiricism. The form that emerges in artistic creation as well as any event tied with human activity is the manifestation of a presence that transcends the simple relation between subject and object. Using Heidegger's idiom, we can talk about an event of being. Already for the Pareyson in his existentialist stage as a scholar of Jasper, there is no rational discourse exhaustive of this event. What Pareyson will find in Schelling and will develop in his hermeneutics of religious experience is nothing else but an unfolding of this initial existentialist position. When he retraces, in a synthetic manner, his itinerary toward the hermeneutics of religious experience, Pareyson insists on freedom as the starting point for everything else. In a sense, this is more Kierkegaard (and Barth) than Jaspers. What opens philosophy to religious experience is not so much the impossibility of theoretically embracing the totality of being, its infinity; rather, it is the abysmal "novelty" of the free act. That is, its originating out of "nothing," its pure and simple happening, its absolute "positivity" in the sense of being posed without any premise that makes it possible or necessary. Even concerning the Big Bang, whatever it may mean, we can have a discourse only after its occurrence; we can never have an explanation of what was before and of its reason why.

Philosophy, which Pareyson also calls "ontology of freedom" (the title of one of his posthumous books),[4] encounters myths when it asks the question of the provenance of freedom. It encounters myths in the most literal sense of the term—it finds myths in front of itself, and the contingency of it all manifests itself also in the fact that there is not only one myth; myths are plural, and certainly they do not offer themselves to a "rational" comparative choice. Their affinity with the realm of freedom and event consists also in their self-imposition as tales with which everyone is, in one way or another, already familiar, within which everyone "already" is. Anthropology tells us that cultures are based on myths. Even when it spurs us to study the myths of various cultures, anthropology itself knows that it is hardly the case that the one who studies myths is entirely severed from all myths. There is no "meta-culture" that can work as absolute science of cultures and their myths. We know this not (only) from anthropology but also from the concrete experience of multiculturalism we experience in late modern society, and from the failure of the pretension to find (or impose) a "rational" (that is, Euro-centric) basis that is universally valid.

Philosophy that is carried out as hermeneutics of myth is not a rationalizing interpretation; it is not a demythologization. Nor does it choose the myth to which it applies itself. What does it do with the myth then? In what sense does it provide a hermeneutics, an interpretation of the myth? What does it do, given that its program is not that of reaching a truth that is clarified, translated into logicorational terms, which are valid for all?

Here the "aesthetic" origins of Pareyson's thought come back powerfully. Interpreting a myth philosophically is not very different from reading and interpreting a work of art; the communicability and interpersonal validity of the outcome of the interpretation are not different from the ones that are attained when one comments on a work one wishes to render understandable to others. The universality that is at stake here is only the universality, always problematic, of aesthetic judgments. As Pareyson has taught us in so many pages of his *Estetica*,[5] the matter is that of the artwork's ability to build its own public, to create a community of those who appreciate it and "recognize" themselves in it.

There is no objective truth to be sought or upheld here. Pareyson does speak of "clarifying and universalizing that which [philosophy] finds in religious experience and which it makes be of interest to all human beings . . . as human beings."[6] Yet the clarifying universalizes only in the sense that it "calls" us to share by appealing to a shared humanity that cannot be presupposed as an essence, but rather is to be sought as an outcome constantly to be attained anew.

HERMENEUTICS OF MYTH AND ONTOLOGY OF ACTUALITY

It does not seem unreasonable to see in Pareyson's hermeneutics of myth another term to indicate what I think should be named "ontology of actuality." In the case of such ontology also what thinking tries to do is to grasp "the origin," the very meaning of the historical-destinal horizon within which it finds itself thrown—that is, what for Heidegger is the meaning of Being. It is well known that Heidegger understands this task mainly as listening to the poetic word in which truth "occurs." In the passage from *The Origin of the Work of Art* where the discourse is about poetic language as the place of happening of the truth, other forms of such happening are also mentioned; yet to none of these does Heidegger devote the attention that, in his entire mature production, he devotes to poetry, to aural words such as Anaximander's saying, and so forth. For Heidegger, to do ontology means to listen to the voice of Being in the place where it lets itself be heard in an eminent and inaugural way, that is, in poetry. Such listening is neither a "translation" nor a rationalization of such a word into utterances. Both for Heidegger and for Pareyson, such listening does not place us in the position of grasping an eternal "reality" as immutable as the nontemporal essences of metaphysics. If this were the case, then a logically cogent and definitive-definitory discourse should indeed be possible. The outcome of such listening within the philosophical discourse is some form of repetition of the story that the myth tells, a setting it into a form *ad homines* (this is why, ultimately, speaking of "actuality" is appropriate). It is needless to say that, both in Heidegger and in Pareyson, it is difficult to explain the sense of the hermeneutics of myths or of listening to the voice of Being in systematic or even simply didactically useful terms. Rather, one should wonder why in Heidegger the hermeneutic approach does not yield to a religious outcome as it happens in Pareyson. Heidegger's relinquishment of Christianity is a story that still remains mysterious in many senses, especially when one recalls the absolutely central importance that sacred scripture, specifically Saint Paul, had for him in the 1919–20 lecture course on the phenomenology of religion. In that course, all the central themes of *Being and Time*, from the idea of authentic temporality to the polemic against metaphysics, had already been fully delineated. Decisive in terms of his relinquishment of the Christian faith must have been for Heidegger his refusal of the metaphysical scholastic tradition: both the Catholic Church's official philosophy and all relation with ecclesiastic dogmas and discipline. The history of scholastic metaphysics is only one aspect of the involvement of Christianity in the history of late antiquity and modernity. It was therefore bound to happen that Heidegger's progressive self-distancing from metaphysics and the technical society that it produced would also drive him on a path progressively more distant from Christianity understood as an essential component of this history and this world. Pareyson's position is different because (and this certainly opens up a problem), ever since the beginning, Christianity appears to him as an alternative to modern metaphysics, especially thanks to the path on which Kierkegaard ventured. Not only this though. The very fact, contingent yet very significant, that from the beginning of Pareyson's formation, Italian culture was dominated by secular orientations (first Croce and Gentile and then, in the second half of the century, Marxism and Neo-Enlightenment) powerfully contributed to prevent that, for Pareyson, Christianity identify with modernity. The question that arises here is that of an alternative between the two positions, and Heidegger's seems ultimately to be more consistent with Pareyson's own antimetaphysical presuppositions. That is, the hermeneutics of myth can be nothing else that listening to history, be it the tale of the sacred scripture or the story of its vicissitudes in the Christian world up to the very history of the Catholic Church and other churches.

Seeing Christianity as deeply implicated in the history of modernity does not necessarily mean that one must then reject such Christianity, as Heidegger does. On the contrary; one can here observe that such a radical refusal would end up once again configuring the pretension (as we think happens in Pareyson) of a beyond-historicity of a metaphysical kind—in Pareyson, the truth kernel of Christianity escapes (but how can it be, if it is a myth?) all historical events; in Heidegger, metaphysical and ultimately nihilistic modernity, of which Christianity too is part, is opposed via a nebulous reference to a homeland that, for Heidegger and for a certain period, was Nazi Germany. I do not elaborate further on this point. I wish to reassert, though, that in both Heidegger and Pareyson the risk exists of setting aside listening to history in favor of a problematic listening to Being that is itself situated outside of history. This risk can be escaped only through a complete historicism. The issue is especially delicate for Pareyson, for whom the hermeneutics of myths means listening to the Christian myth. Pareyson is completely aware of the problem, so much so that he devotes many pages in his *Ontologia della libertà* to a discourse on eschatology that to me appears affected by serious metaphysical limitations. The limitations are such because in order to speak of ultimate things they use too many elements drawn out of Plotinus and Schelling. It is true that complete historicism must take into consideration the history of the reception of Christianity also in authors such as the ones mentioned. One should not, however, isolate such [authors] as "sources" of philosophical truths; rather, one should treat them as symptoms (I know it is an exaggerated term), as moments of a story that still needs to be situated against its own background.

What would Christianity be when read, à la Heidegger, as a moment in the history of Western metaphysics? Would it simply be the story of an error to be erased in an Enlightenment manner? Obviously not, because this would still imply reference to a supratemporal truth. Even when we read Christianity as Pareyson does, Christianity does not retain any of the features that the metaphysical tradition has ascribed to it and with which Christianity has for too long been made to coincide. Then what? If I had to express it very synthetically, I would say that, on the grounds of his hermeneutics of myth, Pareyson can certainly go to mass and say the rosary, but he cannot go to seminaries and theology schools. A myth that is listened to but not translated and reduced to metaphysical-rational terms finds its most appropriate expression in Christian prayers and certainly not in theology. The one who recites the rosary cannot truly think that he or she is truly speaking with the Virgin Mary, who would be listening somewhere (in the heaven to which she would have been bodily assumed two thousand years ago). Nor can praying to God truly mean addressing Him personally, perhaps so as to ask Him whether He would do a certain specific thing for us, whether he would bestow a "grace" on us. Or perhaps yes, it could mean precisely this, because moving in the realm of prayer means remaining within myth without "translating" it. The word "myth" here takes up again its current meaning—when we pray, we are "only" practicing a myth, as when we read Hölderlin and search in him a meaning for our existence. Ontology of actuality is this listening to one's own existential horizon, almost reviewing it, without claiming to coming to terms with it. Is this then any different from pure and simple superstition? It is only insofar as listening to myths does not turn into a magic practice, like the one proper to those who repeat some formulas so as to keep this or that disgrace at a distance or produce this or that outcome one wishes for. Under this condition, a similar view of prayer and the hermeneutic relation with myth does not at all clash with the "religious practice" such as is commanded by Christian predication. Participating in the mass, partaking in the sacraments, and praying in the various forms we have been taught does not require any metaphysical subscription to philosophical or dogmatic truths. What about at least believing that God exists? Or being "founded" on Thomas Aquinas' Five Ways? To proclaim the Creed at a certain point during the mass is much more an affirmation of belonging to the society of believers than a profession of belief in the "reality" of something. Should I truly believe, for example, that Jesus "is seated at the right hand of the Father"?

Pareyson certainly did not go so far as these "secularizing" extremes; I do not wish to attribute them to him. Yet it is certain that his orthodoxy as a "Catholic" thinker was never as devout as the Catholic Church would have liked it, and especially so in his later years. In any event, even at the level of the relation between faith and hermeneutics of myth on one side and religion as public practice, the presence of an institution such as the Church in the social and political life (especially in Italy) on the other, Pareyson's teaching is still entirely to be developed. And it is very reasonable to think of such development as alternative to the wave of fundamentalism that seems to be overwhelming us.

—Translated by Silvia Benso

NOTES

1. Massimo Cacciari, *Dell'inizio* (Milan: Adelphi, 1990).
2. Reiner Schürmann, *Heidegger on Being and Acting: From Principle to Anarchy* (Bloomington: Indiana University Press, 1987).
3. Jean-Luc Nancy, *The Experience of Freedom*, trans. Bridget McDonald (Palo Alto, CA: Stanford University Press, 1994).
4. Luigi Pareyson, *Ontologia della libertà* (Turin: Einaudi, 1995).
5. Luigi Pareyson, *Estetica. Teoria della formatività* (Milan: Bompiani, 1996).
6. Pareyson, *Ontologia della libertà*, 23.

11

Evil in God

Pareyson's Ontology of Freedom

Martin G. Weiss

INTRODUCTION: FROM EVIL TO FREEDOM TO CHRISTIANITY

Luigi Pareyson is known, along with Hans-Georg Gadamer and Paul Ricoeur, as one of the founders of philosophical hermeneutics[1] and as the academic teacher of such influential philosophers as Umberto Eco, Gianni Vattimo, and Aldo Magris, to name but a few. What is less known is that Pareyson devoted most of his later years to a meditation on the problem of evil. For Pareyson, the phenomenon of evil is not only a moral problem. It includes what Leibniz termed *malum metaphysicum*, that is, suffering and contingency, as well as the question concerning "radical evil"; in other words, the question of whether and how a rational being, given the alternative to choose between good and bad, can willingly and consciously choose evil. Pareyson is not interested in the explanation of moral evil given by Socrates, who eventually denied the existence of radical evil and declared that no one chooses evil willingly and consciously but only mistakenly, by confusing bad and good. According to Pareyson, evil is neither only an ontological *privatio boni* [privation of good] nor the result of a moral error; rather, evil is a real negative force.

In philosophy, evil has been reduced every so often to being simply a moral form of badness or some sort of ontological lack and imperfection. The impossibility of sustaining the moral argument about evil is already pointed out by Schelling,[2] who observes that the reality of evil cannot be understood as mere deficiency. Heidegger explains Schelling's point as follows: "As a lack, it is true that a lack is a not-being-present. Nevertheless this absence is not nothing. The blind man who has lost his sight will argue vigorously against the statement that blindness is nothing existent and nothing depressing and nothing burdensome. Thus, nothingness is not nugatory; but rather, something tremendous, the most tremendous element in the nature of Being."[3] Following on this Schellingian notion of evil as reality, Pareyson considers evil not just in the moral sense or within ethics, "which in truth is too narrow a domain when it comes to such an enormous and disquieting issue,"[4] but as *malum metaphysicum* [metaphysical evil] insofar as "the problem of evil finds its roots in the obscure depths of human nature and in the secret recess of the relation between human beings and transcendence."[5] The insight into the reality of evil makes it necessary to explain the connection between evil and the "first principle" or "first cause"; that is, that which since Aristotle philosophy is accustomed to calling "God." If there is only one cause, as both Aristotle and Christian philosophy claim, and evil exists, then is it not necessary to admit that the first cause, God, must also be the cause of evil?

Pareyson stresses that evil can only be conceived as chosen evil, thereby highlighting the connection between the concept of evil and the concept of freedom. Echoing Hume's concept of the naturalistic fallacy, Pareyson insists that the notions of good and evil exclude the notion of necessity. Following on Kant's idea that the only thing that could be called good is the good will, Pareyson argues that if an event occurs by necessity—in other words, it does not have the possibility to be different from what it is—we would call it neither good nor bad but a mere fact beyond good and bad. Good is thus for Pareyson something that has been chosen in the presence of a bad alternative; analogously, evil is the chosen evil, that is, an evil that has been chosen even though it would have been possible to choose the good. Schelling had already stressed that freedom is the faculty of good and evil: "For freedom as a real faculty, that is, a decided liking of the good, is in itself the positing of evil at the same time. What would something good be which had not posited evil and taken it upon itself in order to overcome and restrain it? What would something evil be which did not develop in itself the whole trenchancy of an adversary of the good? Human freedom is not the decidedness for good or evil, but the decidedness for good and evil, or the decidedness for evil and good."[6] As a way of emphasizing the connection between freedom and the problem of evil, which is crucial to Pareyson's later thought, his posthumous main work, edited by Gianni Vattimo and Giuseppe Riconda, has coherently and appropriately been titled *Ontologia della libertà. Il male e la sofferenza* [*Ontology of Freedom: Evil and Suffering*].

If evil is chosen evil, then not only moral evil, that is, bad actions, but also metaphysical evil, that is, suffering and contingency, must have their origin in an act of original freedom. According to Pareyson, this idea of an original freedom at the basis of both good and evil constitutes the core of Christianity. Thus the interpretation of the Christian narration is Pareyson's starting point in his considerations about the philosophical meaning of evil.

FROM GOD AS RADICAL FREEDOM TO THE THEOLOGY OF THE CROSS

As elucidated in his principal work on hermeneutics, *Truth and Interpretation*,[7] according to Pareyson, truth, understood as the inexhaustible origin of its interpretations, cannot be grasped by reifying concepts because truth does not exist outside its interpretations, in the same way that a piece of music does not exist outside its particular performance. The only way to "express" truth is through what Goethe, Schelling, Otto, and Kerényi called "tautegorical symbols."[8] In this specific sense, a symbol is neither a sign nor a signifier, as it is not referring to a signified outside itself. On the contrary, in a tautegorical symbol, that which is symbolized does not exist outside the symbol. To use the musical image once again, every concrete interpretation of a certain piece of music, which exists only in and as its singular interpretation (performance), could be called a symbol of this piece of music. This is so regardless of the fact that such interpretations may be infinite in number. As Pareyson writes, "a symbol is not limited to representing an object through an allusion, a referral; on the contrary, *it is* [the object] directly. It is reality itself as present and live. It is this living presentation, even better, this radical identity that we call tautegorical unity, which enables the presence, in the symbol, of that which cannot be present otherwise."[9]

Pareyson clarifies further what he intends with "tautegorical symbol" by referring to the notion of an "aesthetical idea" as developed in Kant's *Critique of Judgment*, section 49. Kant gives the example of certain symbolic attributes of ancient Greek deities, namely, Zeus' thunderbolt and eagle, which prompt an endless process of representations and reasoning, and then writes: "By an aesthetical Idea I understand that representation of the Imagination which occasions much thought, without, however, any definite thought, *i.e.* any *concept*, being capable of being adequate to it; it consequently cannot be completely compassed and made intelligible by language. We easily see that it is the counterpart (pendant) of a *rational Idea*, which conversely is a concept to which no *intuition* (or representation of the Imagination) can be adequate."[10]

A tautegorical symbol, that is, an "aesthetical idea" understood as the starting point for an endless process of thinking, is therefore a finite thing in which and as which something infinite appears. In Kant's terminology, a tautegorical symbol as an aesthetic idea is a thing well given in a sensitive intuition (*sinnliche Anschauung*), but at the same time it is also the starting point of an endless thought. The greatest difference between such a symbol and a common rational concept lies in the fact that a concept or a definition (by definition) always only grasps a defined, finite entity, whereas a tautegorical symbol makes accessible the infinite, that is, that which goes beyond rational concepts. The places one should investigate in the search for truth, which is the inexhaustible origin of its infinite interpretations, are for Pareyson neither conceptual deliberations nor formalistic calculi but mythical and religious narrations. It is mythical and religious narrations that philosophy has the task of interpreting in order to make truth accessible also to people who do not share the mythical or "religious experience" underlying these very narrations.

According to Pareyson, religious myths have tried to make sense of the phenomenon of evil for the longest time, whereas philosophy, mainly that of Hegel, has often succumbed to the temptation to trivialize and mystify evil by reducing it to a mere dialectic moment of a more rational, intelligible process. According to Pareyson, philosophy has in fact "a tendency to sacrifice the reality of the negative in favor of its intelligibility,"[11] and thus it ends up annihilating and mystifying evil. On the contrary, "evil and suffering, which have been hidden and made to disappear in the rationalized world of philosophy, are truly present in myths, that is, in art and religion, and it is there that philosophy should go and look for them so as to turn them into the object of a no longer mystifying consideration."[12] This move to religious myths is certainly made possible on the basis of Pareyson's own personal religious faith. It does not follow, however, that Pareyson would substitute philosophy with religious experience. Nevertheless, according to him, religious experience as expressed in religious myths and narratives must be taken into consideration by philosophy when it comes to the problem of evil. "More than a negation of philosophy, it is a matter of a new kind of philosophy, one based not on demonstrative reason but on hermeneutic thought."[13]

There is only one possibility for approaching myths, according to Pareyson, namely, by narrating them, which also means not explaining them in a rationalistic manner but rather trying to understand them in a philosophical, that is, hermeneutic way. What Pareyson is after is a *"hermeneutics of myths*, more precisely, a hermeneutics of *religious myths.*"[14] He clarifies: "The philosophical reflection in and on myths must abstain from a demythologization that aims at *replacing* myths with *logos* or *translating* their content into a philosophical format. It has the task of respecting myths, preserving and confirming their revelatory character, aware that myths say things that can only be said in that manner, and that it is important for philosophy that such things be said in such a way."[15] The main aim of the hermeneutics of religious experience is to make myths transparent and plausible also to those who do not share the religious experience and to make them clear to the nonbelievers, without reducing their deeper meaning.[16] Pareyson stresses that "hermeneutics is not ontic and objectifying metaphysics; rather, it is an existential ontology. As turned toward religious myths, it is neither theology nor philosophy of religion or religious philosophy but rather *philosophical interpretation of the religious experience or the religious consciousness.* Concretely, it presents itself as *philosophical rethinking of Christianity*,"[17] whereas Christianity is conceived as narration about God's self-originating radical freedom.

Pareyson's aim is to show that the Judeo-Christian religious experience, as documented in the Old and New Testaments, suggests that God, that is, the principle on which all being rests, cannot be understood as reified *ens necessarium* (necessary being), as the onto-theological tradition has claimed. Rather, God must be conceived as radical freedom. Pareyson grounds his own interpretation of God as freedom on the biblical account of God's self-revelation to Moses as it is contained in the book of Exodus.[18] In the episode of the burning bush as narrated in the Bible, God is self-revealed, in the Latin translation, as *ego sum, qui sum*.[19] Pareyson examines a variety of traditional explanations of this passage from Exodus. According to the tradition, this passage can mean "I am, the One who is" or it can also mean "I am, who I am." Whereas the first interpretation understands God as a static Being, thus yielding to "a typical conception of objectifying, ontic, and speculative metaphysics,"[20] the second refers to God as the personified God, thus yielding to various anthropomorphized concepts of God as person that Pareyson criticizes.

Pareyson considers a third interpretation of the biblical passage. For him, Yahweh has answered Moses' question with a statement that should well be rendered as "I am, who I am." In Pareyson's interpretation, what God is saying with this expression, which is "an extraordinary and astounding expression of divine irony,"[21] is "I shall not tell you my name; even, I do not want to tell you my name. You do not need to know it. Why do you ask? I am, who I am, that is: I am exactly who I want to be, and that is enough. You should not be concerned with this issue. Do not bother about it, the issue does not concern you."[22] Pareyson concludes: "God's being—His existence as well as His essence—depends on His will alone which, as arbitrary freedom, turns out to be His true and only essence."[23] This means, according to Pareyson, that God does not exist necessarily. Were God's existence necessary, this would undermine God's freedom, as God would find Himself always to preexist Himself, in principle. God would not have the possibility or choice "to be or not to be." His existence would be something that He has no choice over, leading to the paradoxical situation of an almighty God wondering about His own origin, as envisioned by Kant in his *Critique of Pure Reason*: "We cannot bear, nor can we rid ourselves of the thought that a being, which we regard as the greatest of all possible existences, should say to himself: I am from eternity to eternity; beside me there is nothing, except that which exists by my will; whence then am I? Here all sinks away from under us; and the greatest, as the smallest, perfection, hovers without stay or footing in presence of the speculative reason, which finds it as easy to part with the one as with the other."[24]

For Pareyson, God reveals Himself as absolute freedom, that is, as freedom that goes beyond existence, or better, that comes before existence. How can this be? To answer this question, Pareyson takes up Schelling's idea of a "God before God" (who has the freedom to be or not to be) and a "God after God" (that is, God after the decision to be).[25] For Pareyson, as already for Schelling, God cannot be conceived as *ens necessarium*, that is, as the being whose existence is necessary, because then God would be forced to be. This idea is incompatible with God's absolute freedom. Moreover, the onto-theological conception of God as *ens necessarium* brings up the question of what, if not God Himself, would or could cause God to be. In fact, Pareyson stresses that God (after God) is necessary not because God is forced to be by some laws of nature or logic, but because God (before God) chooses to exist even though He had the possibility to choose His own inexistence in an absolute past that was never present, as Pareyson puts it. God's freedom is indeed radical, as, according to Pareyson, it must include the freedom not to exist. Thus the possibility of total nothingness, which (if God is understood as *summum bonum*) one may call "radical evil," somehow lies in God, albeit only as never realized, as mere possibility.

Freedom as absolute freedom could not have made a choice had it not had the capacity for both evil and goodness (that is, for being and nothingness). It is chiefly here that Pareyson's perspective differs from traditional onto-theology. In other words, as primary principle and abysmal reason of reality, radical freedom comes to signify, for Pareyson, both the freedom to be, that is, affirmation, and at the same time the move toward negation and nothingness. Absolute freedom is able to choose between these two options. If we replace the notion of radical freedom—that is, the ground of reality, or the possible choice for nothingness—with the term "God," the original ambiguity of God, covered over by traditional metaphysics and theology, shines through again, according to Pareyson.[26] That is the original possibility of God to choose between positivity and negativity. God is freedom, according to Pareyson, and freedom "is in itself ambiguous in the sense that it can be positive freedom or negative freedom; the dilemma between good and evil, being and nothing simply expresses such ambiguity."[27]

Unlike traditional scholastic thought, God is not necessarily "good" because of his essence. On the contrary; God is good because he chooses to be good (that is, to exist) by rejecting the possibility of evil (that is, not to be). In this consideration of possible rejection, it is only the chosen being that becomes good. Evil is the chosen nothingness, the active negation, in light of the possibility of choosing being itself.

According to Pareyson, it is "before time" that God had the choice between good and evil, that is, the choice between his own existence and his own inexistence. This means that there is evil within God only as a choice that has never been made, as an absolute past that has never existed, with the actual choice being that in favor of goodness.[28] As Pareyson writes, "saying that God exists means to say: being and the good have been chosen forever, that is, evil and nothing have been defeated forever. The act of freedom has been an act of positive freedom; freedom has decided in favor of the good, its choice has been in favor of being. God has willed existence, which He has done by defeating the negative, that is, nothingness. [. . .] In God, evil and nothingness remain as a nonaccepted alternative, as a possibility that has been cast aside."[29]

It may be noted that, according to Pareyson, God certainly knows nothingness even when nothingness is just an option. A deity would never be free if per se it were to display the fact of goodness alone. According to Pareyson, as we have already noted, God is not good by nature or because being good would be part of His essence. God is good because He has chosen to be good, that is, He has chosen existence even if He could have chosen nothingness and therefore His own nonexistence.

Yet, with His choice of goodness, as we have seen, the possibility of evil is also being displayed, as good is simply that which had the option to turn bad. Consequently, what follows here is this: evil is also induced by God even if it stands out as a rejected option.

As a possible option, evil is being bequeathed by God.[30] Only in this sense does Pareyson talk about evil in God or, to quote Karl Barth, "the shadow side of God," that is, "the dark accompaniment to the victory over nothingness and to the choice in favor of the good, the opaque side of its positivity; the disquieting aspect of [God's] stable and certain affirmation."[31] Pareyson is fully aware, here, that the expression "Evil in God Himself" is a misguiding terminology, "a disquieting expression that requires some clarifications."[32] On the other hand, however, this clarifies best the unfathomability of evil itself. There is no other option but to engulf evil as part of the mystery of God Himself. The expression "evil in God" means that every way has been attempted to analyze evil, but there is no option other than to recognize that evil cannot be explained.[33] As Pareyson writes, "saying that evil is within God does not mean that He is the author of evil. . . . God is undoubtedly the origin of evil, but certainly He is not the realizer of evil; this is a thing that pertains only to the human being, on the level of history."[34] He further adds: "The very fact that God, as freedom, is choice in favor of the good, testifies to the presence of evil in Him as no longer a current alternative: as positive choices, all of God's operations are a victory over nothingness and evil, so that nothingness and evil persist in Him certainly as overcome, and thus in a latent form, as simply possible and yet available for the one who would want to realize them as an alternative to the divine choices, in oppositions to Him, in conscious and intentional transgression."[35]

In the book of Genesis, according to the myth of creation, God created humans in His image, that is, as free to choose between good and bad. But whereas God, put before the alternatives of good and bad, lying in Him as mere possibilities, chose to realize the good, humans, in an act of rebellion, chose to realize evil. "Human beings reawaken, within the cosmic scene, that evil that was at rest in God."[36] The reason for the human rebellion is indicated by Nietzsche: "If there were gods, how could I stand it, not to be a god?"[37] Temporal history and the accounting for it start with the choice made by human beings. "God's existence means, as we have seen, first of all that within eternity evil is a possibility that has been played out once and for all, and that has been defeated. This play has occurred, however, within eternity. Within history, the game is open again, it starts anew, and everything can happen. *Sub specie aeternitatis*, evil has been defeated, is *already* defeated, and has been defeated *forever*. In history, though, evil is quite present and real and can *still* win."[38]

Pareyson also claims, however, that the accounts of Christianity do not simply stop at this point. According to the Bible, God restricts Himself as Christ on the Cross and tries to take evil out of the world in order to save human beings. Thus Pareyson embraces the key notion of what is called *theologia crucis* [theology of the cross]. According to this interpretation of Christian teachings, the evil that was brought into the world by humans is so great that the suffering of many, indeed (one could really say) the suffering of the entire humankind, is not enough to atone for such evil. Only the suffering of God Himself would be vast enough to do so. That is why God decides, by Himself and out of His free love for human beings, to give Himself up to the uttermost possible suffering, namely, to the pain of human death.

God's self-restriction, His *kenōsis*, goes all the way up to the point of reaching God's forsakenness of God Himself. This is distinctly expressed in Christ's exclamation on the Cross: "My God, my God, why have you forsaken me?," as Mark 15:34 and Matthew 27:46 report. In this cry, Pareyson retraces a moment of atheism within God Himself. In order to save humankind, God takes on suffering, losing faith in Himself. God assumes upon Himself the horrible God-forsakenness occurring in the one moment of human death, so that He can effectively redeem humankind and at the same time give sense to human suffering, which now can be accepted as a form of solidarity with (the suffering) God. According to Pareyson, this very principle of the suffering God is explored by Alyosha Karamazov when he disputes with his brother Ivan. Pareyson thus discusses a basic principle of Dostoevsky's: "On the one hand, humankind has been freed from suffering because God has taken on these sufferings Himself; on the other hand, the meaning of human suffering is its being a co-suffering with the Redeemer who with his own suffering has taken away human suffering."[39] In the suffering of the most innocent of all, as Alyosha Karamazov remarks, God has counterbalanced the suffering of the innocents.

The "superior form of atheism" in God Himself, as Pareyson calls it, that is, God's self-denial on the cross, "this 'suicide' that we do not know whether to consider most sublime or most terrible; in any event, it is enigmatic and mysterious,"[40] is for Pareyson a clear disproving of the inferior forms of atheism occurring in the nineteenth century, which tried to prove the inexistence of God by pointing to the suffering of the innocents. Only the *theologia crucis* can be set against classic atheism. Suffering becomes a new form of *copula mundi*, a connection between

God and humankind. All prior accusations against God, such as those that maintain that God accepts without further ado the suffering of the innocent, evaporate completely when confronted with the (human) death that God Himself undergoes on the Cross. Outside of this conception, evil and suffering, according to Pareyson, are totally inexplicable, that is, unacceptable.

All religions have dealt with the problem of evil, but mostly by offering a way out of pain and suffering. According to Pareyson, Christianity too has given an answer to the problem of evil—not in order to get rid of it, but so as to give pain and suffering a sense. Christianity does not want to liberate human beings from suffering, but to make suffering meaningful, so that it can be accepted. "The matter is that of accepting suffering as inescapable, and through such an acceptance one should find a chance not only of overcoming but even of overturning it."[41] If by "meaningful" we mean that which we can both understand and accept, then we can say that the Christian narration tries to give sense to evil, pain, and suffering. Evil as evil is senseless, without meaning, and cannot be accepted. But if the framework of the Christian narration enables us to give some positive meaning to pain and suffering, as Pareyson suggests, then pain and suffering lose their evil character and become something acceptable, maybe even desirable, if seen as a way to be close to God, as the theology of the cross asserts: "Liberation from suffering consists in heightening suffering itself."[42]

It is important to emphasize that Christianity, according to Pareyson, does not see pain and suffering as an aim in itself, which one would have to pursue. According to Pareyson, the Christian narration offers only an interpretation of pain and suffering, which if shared would make it possible to understand and accept them and thus strip them of their evil character. With this claim, Pareyson undoubtedly proves to belong within the tradition of Christian thinkers. Since the very beginning, Christian theologians and mystics have been very attracted to the paradox that God Himself felt God-forsaken, and that out of love for humans God died the mortal death for human suffering as well. Eighteenth-century Italian scholar, spiritual writer, and theologian Alphonsus de' Liguori stated that God must have gone crazy because He loved humanity so much that He was willing to die for humanity.[43] The quote from Angelus Silesius that "love pulls God into death" is cited by Pareyson in this context as well as these verses: "That God is being crucified, that we can actually hurt Him/injure Him/That He will endure the disgrace which they have inflicted upon Him/That He has endured all fear/And that He can die/ Do not be surprised, this happened out of love!"[44]

CHRISTIAN TRAGIC FAITH
VERSUS CONSOLATORY ATHEISM

Through the perspective of God's suffering and dying, Pareyson argues, within the Christian context suffering has become more meaningful than ever. "Christianity alone 'understands' negativity insofar as it gives meaning to evil and finds a sense for suffering itself."[45] Still, does this assumption not appear as equally absurd as the response given by nihilism, which professes the complete nonsense and absurdity of existence? That is why, according to Pareyson, it becomes necessary to choose between absurdities. According to Kierkegaard, there is an absurdity of nonsense and there is, on the opposite, an absurdity of the paradox; for Pareyson, only the latter contains the truth.[46]

As already noted, Pareyson does not step away from a thought that would highlight his "Christian existentialism." Furthermore, he reflects upon it in a certain specific way. He reflects on the principles sustaining the atheism of yesterday and today, and, as he starts from the question of evil and the rejection of theodicy and its principles, he highlights the contemporaneity of tragic Christianity.

Classic atheism states that the reality of evil is a proof that God does not exist. This objection can only occur because of the theistic equation between God and goodness. The consequence of the objection is the rise of classic atheism; subsequently, the denial of God becomes the denial of goodness in itself and the denial of any moral standard, or, as Ivan Karamazov states: "If God is dead, everything is allowed."

In classic atheism, the point of departure is the belief in God and subsequently the painful realization of God's nonexistence. By losing God, for the classic atheist, the absurdity of this tragic world becomes evident. The heroic classic atheism, which emphasizes the tragic nature of existence, stood in sharp contrast to the light and optimistic position of nineteenth-century Christianity, which relied instead upon the reassuring securities of the eternal truths and therefore ignored the tragic nature of existence itself.

Within the twentieth century, Pareyson argues, a curious transformation has nevertheless been at work. The tragic atheism of the nineteenth century has been replaced by a more relaxed, optimistic, comforting, and consolatory form of atheism. The classic form of atheism had operated within the framework of religious thought and understandings. Contemporary (referred to as "modern") atheism, however, no longer has God as its point of departure because it operates outside all religious horizons. It does not experience the pain of being without God. On the opposite, now the absurdity of this world has become a form of reassurance that is comforting in itself. Contemporary atheism has become indifference. It does not depart from the principle of goodness as a starting point to find out then about goodness' nonexistence. Its point of departure is the nonexistence of both good and evil. All is indifferent for the contemporary atheist, and so the lack of goodness and the suffering due to the existence of evil can no longer be experienced in their radical character: "Without God, all distinction between good and evil disappears, and so do *Angst* and despair."[47] Pain is understood as as natural as pleasure, neither better nor worse than this. Within contemporary atheism, tragedy has been sacrificed. What happens just happens. There reigns a new form of *amor fati*. Any trace of tragedy has been erased because atheism today starts with the negation of all evil.[48] According to Pareyson, atheism has taken on a role of soothing, consolatory security, a function that in the nineteenth century was performed by Christian faith.

On the contrary, existentialist Christianity, or "tragic thinking," as understood by Pareyson, comprehends evil in its whole terror and teaches how to suffer for the sake of others. "Not only are the presence of negativity and God's existence not simply incompatible; on the contrary, they also demand one another; neither is thinkable without the other."[49] The experience of the negative and the encounter with the existence of God are inseparable from each other: "Were there no God, evil would not be; the very existence of evil attests to the presence of God—an offended and angry God, a suffering and redeeming God."[50] The place of the experience of good and evil, of the tragedy of existence as well as its absurdity, can only be situated within Christianity itself. Tragic thinking is today at home only within Christianity. Its core belief, so to speak, must be: There is no clearer proof of a deity than the reality of evil itself. Because evil, that is, pain and suffering, is the best connection we have with God Himself. "Only if God exists there is evil, and in itself evil indicates God."[51]

CONCLUSIONS

Pareyson's attempt to explain philosophically the meaning of evil leads him not only to a clarification of this notion—by highlighting its intrinsic connections with the concept of freedom—but also to a radical interpretation of Christianity as a religion that tries to make evil, pain, and suffering acceptable by inscribing them into a narrative of sin and redemption that permits one to see evil, pain, and suffering as something meaningful.

The Manichean answer to the question of how good and bad relate consisted in the introduction of a second equally powerful evil principle beside God. This was necessary because if God is good, he could impossibly be the cause of evil. But, as indubitably there is evil, there must exist another cause beside God. The tradition based on Plotinus, on the contrary, maintains that God is the only cause and God is good, so this tradition had to negate the reality of evil and declare it a mere privation and lack of being. The Manicheans have the merit of acknowledging the reality of evil and not reducing it to mere privation and lack of being. But they could do so only by doubling the first causal principle, ending up with two equally powerful supreme beings, one good and the other evil.

Like Schelling before him, Pareyson tries to reconcile the insight into the reality of evil with the uniqueness of the causal principle. Schelling lists three possible ways to do so: The first model is the idea of the immanence of all things in God, that is, the attempt to put everything in God, to conceive the world as a mere property of the divine substance. But, as Heidegger writes, "the possibility of immanence is most fundamentally shattered by the fact of evil. If evil really exists and if God is the ground of beings, then evil would have to be posited in the primal will itself, and God would have to be declared evil. That is impossible. From the standpoint of immanence, the only way out is a denial of the reality of evil, which . . . amounts to a denial of freedom."[52]

In the same way that the definition of freedom as the ability to choose between good and bad makes the immanence of all things in God impossible, this definition of freedom makes it impossible to reduce evil to a form of *privatio boni* because if evil is not real, that is, if it does not exist, then freedom, understood as the possibility to choose between good and evil, would also be impossible, because real choice is possible only between real alternatives.

The second attempt Schelling considers to reconcile the reality of evil with the doctrine of the sole principle consists in declaring evil only as an epiphenomenon (*concursus*) of the good. As the first principle and only cause, God cannot be evil; there cannot be a cause of evil. But as evil cannot be denied completely, this epiphenomenal model of evil conceives God not as the cause of evil, but only as that which "permits" evil, without being involved in its realization. But

> if the ground of beings as a whole is thought only as that which admits evil, this admittance is equivalent to being the cause if beings, in which evil is allowed, are essentially a consequence of the ground in their being. Or else the denial of the reality of evil comes about again, and thus the denial of freedom,

> and the whole question loses its object. Both systems, that of immanence and of *concursus*, are so posited that all positive being is understood as coming from God. If evil is something positive, though, then these systems negate themselves since God is always thought as the *ens perfectissimum*, as the highest being excluding every lack. One thus falls prey every time to the escape of conceiving evil as nothing positive in order to save the system.[53]

The third attempt Schelling considers to include evil within the system of the one principle is that of "emanation," that is, a model that conceives all things as emanations of God.

> The third way consists in allowing evil to arise only gradually in the course of increasing distance from God and in positing it only at the place of the furthest distance from God, in conceiving it as this complete removal from God. But the hopelessness of this way is easily seen. In the system of things flowing from God (system of emanation), the difficulty of unifying evil with God is not removed, but only postponed. For in order for things to be able to flow from God at all, they have to be somehow in him already. The doctrine of emanation is thrown back upon the doctrine of immanence and again gets caught in its difficulties.[54]

None of the three models put forward (the lack-theory, the immanence-theory, and the emanation-theory) succeeds in reconciling the uniqueness of the principle with the reality of evil.

In contrast, Pareyson's ontology of freedom, largely inspired by Schelling, tries to unify the Manichean insight into the reality of evil with the necessity of maintaining the uniqueness of the causing principle by differentiating between the mere possibility of evil—which has its origin in God—and the realization of evil—which has its cause in human beings. The difference between this position and the abovementioned epiphenomenal model of evil consists in the fact that, for Pareyson, God does not only allow for the realization of evil by human beings but also allows for the possibility to realize evil himself so that one must say that evil is part of God albeit only as a never chosen and yet real possibility. As Pareyson writes, "the heart of reality is not *the good* . . . but the *chosen good*, that is, freedom, which in its essential doubleness grounds the inscrutable dynamism of the universe. Not as the good but as chosen good is the originary positivity the existence of the living God."[55]

NOTES

1. See Silvia Benso's chapter in this book.
2. F. W. J. Schelling, *Philosophical Investigations into the Essence of Human Freedom*, trans. Jeff Love and Johannes Schmidt (Albany: State University of New York Press, 2009).
3. Martin Heidegger, *Schelling's Treatise on the Essence of Human Freedom*, trans. Joan Stambaugh (Athens: Ohio University Press, 1999), 101.
4. Luigi Pareyson, *Ontologia della libertà. Il male e la sofferenza* (Turin: Einaudi, 1995), 151.
5. Ibid., 152.
6. Heidegger, *Schelling's Treatise on the Essence of Human Freedom*, 156.
7. Luigi Pareyson, *Verità e interpretazione* (Milan: Mursia, 1971).
8. Pareyson, *Ontologia della libertà*, 104.
9. Ibid., 105.
10. Immanuel Kant, *Critique of Pure Judgment*, trans. J. H. Bernard, 2nd ed. rev. (London: MacMillan, 1914), 197–98.
11. Pareyson, *Ontologia della libertà*, 154.
12. Ibid., 156.
13. Ibid., 159.
14. Ibid., 161.
15. Ibid., 161.
16. Ibid., 148.
17. Ibid., 161.
18. See Exodus 3:14.
19. Pareyson, *Ontologia della libertà*, 119.
20. Ibid., 119.
21. Ibid., 122.
22. Ibid.
23. Ibid., 130.
24. Immanuel Kant, *Critique of Pure Reason*, trans. J. M. D. Meikljohn (London: J.M. Dent & Sons, 1950), 287.
25. See Schelling, *Philosophical Investigations into the Essence of Human Freedom*.
26. Luigi Pareyson, *Esistenza e persona* (Genoa: Il Nuovo Melangolo, 2002), 32.
27. Pareyson, *Ontologia della libertà*, 177.
28. Ibid., 135.
29. Ibid., 177.
30. Ibid., 181.
31. Ibid., 179.
32. Ibid., 180.
33. Ibid.
34. Ibid., 183.
35. Ibid., 185.

36. Ibid., 186.
37. Friedrich Nietzsche, *Thus Spoke Zarathustra*, trans. Thomas Common (Philadelphia: University of Pennsylvania Press, 1999), 110.
38. Pareyson, *Ontologia della libertà*, 190.
39. Ibid., 198.
40. Ibid., 200.
41. Ibid., 207.
42. Ibid.
43. "How can it be that an omnipotent God, who needs no one in order to be as happy as He is, wanted to become man and die on the cross so as to save human beings? This would be the same as believing in a God that has gone crazy for the sake of humans." See Alfonso Maria de Liguori, *Opere Ascetiche*, vol. V: *Passione del Nostro Signore Gesù Cristo* (Rome: CSSR, 1934), 31.
44. Pareyson, *Ontologia della libertà*, 201.
45. Ibid., 205.
46. Ibid., 207.
47. Ibid., 229.
48. Ibid., 232.
49. Ibid., 227.
50. Ibid.
51. Ibid.
52. Heidegger, *Schelling's Treatise on the Essence of Human Freedom*, 100.
53. Ibid.
54. Ibid.
55. Pareyson, *Ontologia della libertà*, 292.

12

Philosophy and Novel in the Later Pareyson

Sergio Givone

PREMISE

Hermeneutics neither comes after nor derives from aesthetics in the philosophy of Luigi Pareyson because, on the contrary, aesthetics is preceded and made possible by hermeneutics.[1] It is true though that in Pareyson (starting with *Truth and Interpretation*[2] but especially in *Ontologia della libertà* [*Ontology of Freedom*]),[3] aesthetics finds in hermeneutics a sort of fulfillment because it is precisely hermeneutics that gives voice to themes that Pareyson's aesthetics (his *Estetica. Teoria della formatività* [*Aesthetics: Theory of Formativity*])[4] had bracketed or even excluded from its realm. Among them are two themes: that of the truth-value of art and that of the philosophical meaning of novels. When one therefore wants to discuss philosophy and novel in Pareyson, one must make reference to the later Pareyson.

As Paolo D'Angelo has remarked in an earlier chapter in this volume, in his *Estetica*, Pareyson was involved in a confrontation with Benedetto Croce that saw Pareyson distancing himself decisively from the idea that art is simply a theoretical activity. For Pareyson, art is a making, not a knowing. Because it is a making (a making that is not simply generically formative, but one in which formativity is rather prevalent and intentional), it does not matter what its contribution to thinking is. In fact, there is art that is deeply infused with philosophy and there is art that is impenetrable to philosophy. All this, however, has no relevance to what art is. According to Pareyson, art as a style or way of forming is indeed revelatory of a world, namely, the artist's world, a spiritual world. Not for this reason, however, does such revelation have a speculative relevance because any form of knowledge or exploration of worlds, be they the artist's private world or historical worlds, is in the service of the success (or lack thereof) of the artwork and not of some alleged philosophical contents of a superior order. When the anti-Crocean disposition dissolves (in *Ontologia della libertà*), Pareyson does not hesitate to consider philosophically the artistic genre constituted by the novel.[5] He then regards the myth (the novel being nothing else than its actualized or, if one prefers, secularized form) as the place par excellence where the truth that is not matter of fact but event is manifested. This is particularly important for our theme, as we shall see.

Before we tackle the question, which is the real knot holding together philosophy and novel (and sometimes preventing us from grasping the implications), it is not unhelpful to recall of what kind of philosophy we are talking, and of what kind of novel.

PHILOSOPHY OF FREEDOM VERSUS METAPHYSICAL RATIONALISM

For Pareyson, philosophy coincides completely with hermeneutics on the ground of the principle that its object (albeit an unobjectifiable object) is truth and truth can only be interpreted, the same way that interpretation is essentially interpretation of truth. What one should still ask is whether the three stages that mark the unfolding of Pareyson's thought—ontology of the inexhaustible, tragic thought, and ontology of freedom—must be considered within a substantially homogeneous line of development or whether they are moments that imply discontinuity, turns, and leaps. With respect to this, how can we avoid noting that tragic thought is based on the idea of the profound and ineliminable contradictoriness that lies at the heart itself of being, so much so that truth must, as it were, stand contradiction? (The principle of noncontradiction, which remains valid at the logical level, reveals itself as powerless at the ontological level; in fact, it is impossible to say that reality is simultaneously contradictory and noncontradictory insofar as this is manifestly false on the ground of that principle, yet it could very well be true, as it is in fact true, that reality is itself contradictory). Conversely, in the case of the ontology of the inexhaustible there is no contradiction—two interpretations of truth, albeit deeply in disagreement, can both attain and faithfully attest the truth, each from its own peculiar perspective. In its turn, the ontology of freedom opens completely new perspectives, especially with respect to its eschatological implications that have remained barely sketched but are not thereby secondary. The question then is: Does the conception of truth that emerges here, that is, in the ontology of freedom, represent an overcoming of both the ontology of the inexhaustible and tragic thought? By reconciling the irreconcilable, by redeeming the irredeemable, the *apokatastasis* prospected by the ontology of freedom seems to postulate a truth that is beyond truth and that in any event is neither the noncontradictory truth belonging to the ontology of the inexhaustible nor the contradictory truth belonging to tragic thought.

Let us leave on the side, for now, this interpretative problem to which we must return later. What brings together Pareyson's three "philosophies," which are in fact only one philosophy because they all result in hermeneutics, is even more important than what differentiates them. Such is the rejection, which could not be stronger and sharper, of the presupposition of what Pareyson himself names "metaphysical rationalism," that is, the identity of being and thought, the transparency of being to thought, the complete resolution of being into thought. In being, there is exceedance; in reality, there is a surplus, there is a gap. It is precisely such gap that justifies not only the inexhaustibility of the true but also its disquieting contradictoriness. No interpretation can claim to say the last word on the world. Moreover, there is no interpretation that can ignore the essential: namely, that the world is the way it is not because it must be this way, but because it is the way it is even if it might be completely otherwise and even the opposite of what it is.

For Pareyson (and what follows applies not only to his ontology of freedom but also to his tragic thought and even earlier to the ontology of the inexhaustible), everything hinges on freedom because the entirety of reality depends at every moment on a gesture of assent or refusal, of affirmation or negation. Before or outside this gesture, being, which certainly is or exists, nevertheless lies in some sort of inertia that renders it similar to nothingness. Even truth depends on freedom. Truth in fact exists only where it can be recognized or misrecognized. Truth and interpretation are in such a relation of solidarity that of truth, one can only offer an interpretation; and interpretation cannot but be an interpretation of truth. Saying that truth and interpretation are one and the same, as Pareyson says in *Truth and Interpretation*, certainly does not mean claiming that truth is the object of construction, or even worse, of affabulation, in the trivial and banal sense that anyone can tell the truth the way they prefer. On the contrary, truth stands as the firmest thing there is; but it stands while offering itself to being welcomed or refused. By virtue of such an act, which is absolutely originary because it is absolutely free, truth comes to being, manifests itself, reveals its nature as ontological event.

THE ORIGINARY ACT

There is only one originary act, and it is the act of freedom—freedom as the act through which God self-originates, that is, the act of "divine origination." This act occurred before time ("before all centuries"), a time that such an act nevertheless contributes to institute. We can think of it as the gesture made by God when, once and forever, God chose being even though God could have chosen nothingness; when God chose to say "yes" to being (yes, it is good that it is, *valde bonum*) even though God could have said "no," and thus chose the good and rejected evil. The question is: Could God really choose nothingness rather than being? Is nothingness a real or a fictitious possibility? What is at stake here is philosophy even more than theology. From the assertion that God could choose nothingness, there derives a philosophy of freedom (even more, only a philosophy of freedom justifies such a choice). Conversely, the thesis according to which God could not not choose being lest a contradiction (and contradictory is also the idea that nothingness can be) makes sense only within a philosophy of necessity, which represents both the presupposition and the consequence thereof. Having opted in favor of a philosophy of freedom (because, in the end, it is a matter of an option), Pareyson does not hesitate to draw all the consequences from what in some sense appears as real philosophical faith and is attested in the "Frammenti sull'escatologia [Fragments on Eschatology]" that were published posthumously in *Ontologia della libertà*.

As confirmation of the fact that God *freely* says "yes" to being and "no" to nothingness, and therefore being could *really* be annihilated or canceled, Pareyson writes: "God could remain in his solitude, Eden could not be part of the Fall, etc., death could be the end of everything."[6] If that "yes" is free, and because freedom is its foundation there is no founding reason that imposes saying "yes," then such a "yes" must be considered as "absolutely non-deducible." That is to say, "one cannot turn it into a system, with deductions, demonstrations, logical connections, unless one builds a necessary system that in itself denies freedom." It can only find place within "a tale, a narration, a myth."[7] This implies that reality itself is finally revealed for what it is—not a matter of fact (which philosophy would describe according to objective truth, which reflects it) but a series of events (events of the unobjectifiable truth that calls for being interpreted and only lives within interpretations). "The universe is not a reality but a story, a great story that can only be narrated in a tale; it cannot be theorized either in a philosophical or theological system. Well then, what is this tale, this story? It is the tale of freedom. It is the tale of the victory of being over nothingness, of good over evil."[8] Properly, reality is not reality but rather event. It is nothing except the result of a sovereign and creative act from which everything comes. Everything, in all its parts, in all its points reflects, repeats, renews that act. Being and freedom can be converted one into the other, because being is freedom and freedom is being. The universe is a story, Pareyson claims, which therefore cannot be deduced but only narrated. This of course does not mean that philosophy should turn into a form of narration that tells the story (or the stories) of freedom. It means that philosophy finds material for reflection in the story (or in the stories, novels, myths) more than anywhere else; and moreover, it finds itself as interpretative thinking—interpretative of events and situations.

What is in question is the philosophical character of this story—whether or not this story consists in the fact that it appears as always already written, or better inscribed, within a *logos* that rules all its possible developments. Pareyson defines it as "the tale of freedom" and adds that such tale is "the story of the victory of being over nothingness, of good over evil." So what? Should we then think that the hidden core of freedom is necessity, or at least that the completion of the story *necessarily* has a triumphant feature, given that there is no greater triumph than the victory of good over evil and of being over nothingness? If this were the case, we should admit that the ontology of freedom shifts here in the direction of an ontology of necessity. Moreover, we should again call into question one of its main tenets, namely, the claim that nothingness and evil are real possibilities, as it would happen if death were to have the last word (and were, as Pareyson says, "the end of everything"); it is evident that within an ontology of necessity there is no actual room for either nothingness or evil.

According to Pareyson, and this is the ineliminable presupposition of the ontology of freedom, the thesis of the real possibility of nothingness and evil coexists with the thesis of God's victory over nothingness and evil "once and for all." The fact is that the originary act has certainly occurred once and for all, but it always occurs again anew, at every moment in history. It was a victory, and it could not have been such if those destructive powers were not real. Because the powers are real within eternity (where the victory has happened), they are also real within time (where they are far from being overcome and defeated). One thus must think that at every moment—and therefore not only "before all centuries" but "forever and ever"—the event of the universe runs on the thread of possibility—the possibility that the last word might be capable, tragically, of confuting the first.

MYTH, NOVEL

The possibility not contemplated and even rejected by metaphysical rationalism is indeed the possibility that nothingness and evil are real and actually happen, and thus reveal themselves for what they are, namely, something ultimate (evil that is overcome by good is not truly evil; nothingness that is functional to being and sets becoming into motion is not truly nothingness). Hence Pareyson engages in a great work of deconstruction (the term is the least Pareysonian, but it conveys the idea) of metaphysical rationalism so as to find an opening in such a horizon that for him could represent the end of philosophy as well as its new beginning. The encounter of philosophy with the novel is simply an episode in such a search, but certainly one of the most fruitful and bearer of consequences. One could even see in it an outcome of the "ecstasy of reason" that for Pareyson, the Schellingean Pareyson, constitutes an essential tenet because it is the key to understanding what Hegel's thought is and is not.

Metaphysical rationalism is ultimately, according to Pareyson, a philosophy of identity. It is not, however, simply a philosophy of identity where, as in Parmenides, identity excludes all difference. Rather, it is a philosophy of identity in which identity, as in Hegel, in the end reappropriates the difference that it itself has posited. And what constitutes difference, according to Hegel, if not evil and nothingness? Nothingness that opposes being (completely "abstract" opposition, and completely meaningless if it were not for the fact that it is from there that becoming, the true engine of the entire process, emerges) and evil that is destined to turn itself into its contrary (in fact, the "immense power of the negative" is entirely aimed at the edification of the system in which phenomenology is converted into an encyclopedia that even includes the closure of the circle). Evil is resistance of the dead weight (*das Tode*), of the absurd, and of the meaningless that are however destined to be brought back within the domain of reason. Therefore in

Hegel, evil and nothingness constitute the difference that denies itself. This is the case not only in the end, but also at the beginning, when nothingness coincides with being and evil simply is not.

Conversely, for Pareyson, the difference is originary and cannot be taken away. It remains at the heart of being because being is one and the same as freedom; being is an act of freedom, the event of freedom. Being never coincides with itself; being is never what it is simply by reason of the fact that it cannot not be or be otherwise. On the contrary, being could not be; or it could be otherwise. Nothing binds it to being the way it actually is, least of all identity, which is to say, necessity. Yet if nothing binds being, if such nothingness is the ground of being, then there will be no "yes" to being (whether stated by God or by the human being) that does not occur in the shadow of evil; which means, that does not entail the real possibility of evil. It may very well be that such a possibility is always "overcome and defeated" by God, whereas the human being always succumbs to it; as Pareyson says, no one revamps and reactivates it as much as the human being. This is the case in eternity, though. Within time, what else can we say except that God (and this is true especially for the Christian God, with whom Pareyson is concerned) does not keep freedom for himself alone but rather places it in the hands of human beings, and therefore shares their destiny?

In any event, it is a matter of something that happens: acts, events, decisions. This something is not at all casual, it has its own logic; it arranges itself according to a thread or plot and, moreover, refers to an ideal and higher world, as though everything that belongs to one's experience attains the universal through a symbolic way. There is a word, a figure with which to say all this—myth. According to Pareyson, myth is to be understood not in the sense of fable, legend that has nothing to do with reality, with truth. On the contrary, myth is "possession of deep truth in the only way in which truth lets itself be captured."[9] What is a myth if not the gathering of the idea into a plot (plot of *logos*, *logos* as plot), an idea that cannot be deduced but only narrated? From this perspective, the novel (at least the novel that lets the ideal world transpire in the real world) appears to Pareyson as a form of myth—the form that myth has taken up in modernity and in our current times.

THE REALITY OF EVIL AND OF NOTHINGNESS

What novel, though? Dostoevsky's, naturally. It is true that in Dostoevsky's novels one finds characters who, like Ivan Karamazov, could definitely "enter as a chapter in a history of contemporary philosophy."[10] It is also true, though, that "Dostoevsky's novels are . . . positions of problems and contrasts of ideas, and his heroes are real 'personified ideas.'"[11] Yet there is more. There is the fact that "Dostoevsky's art, which he used to call a 'superior realism,' is already in itself an interpretation of reality, so that reality becomes imagination and imagination a higher reality. On the one hand, reality, seen precisely in its most real and visible features, becomes transparent to a deeper and more intense reality of a spiritual nature; on the other hand, true reality is only the hidden and spiritual reality that has no other way to manifest itself except by transpiring through visible and everyday reality."[12] It is not that Dostoevsky's characters, Pareyson remarks, are uprooted or restless souls with nothing to do. Even if it might look that way, each of them has or has had his or her own professional life, and their thoughts do not dwell in the hyperuranium but on earth, entail radical decisions, actions that are often ruinous and sometimes saving, gestures in which their lives come to be at stake. Everything becomes story, everything is story, event, narration. "Events precipitate, consequences press, conclusions loom over . . . Every day is a knot of events, every minute is fraught with destiny."[13]

The same holds true, albeit with due proportions, for the other authors Pareyson has loved: Herman Melville and Flannery O'Connor over the rest, but one should add at least Bernard Malamud, Isaac Singer, and Thomas Hardy. One may have to do, as in Melville's case, with Pierre, a man capable of the cruelest ambiguities, who knows that responsibility is the most controversial and controvertible thing not because it is empty and vain but because it has its vanishing point in infinity. Or, as in O'Connor's case, one may have to do with Hazel Motes, the drifter without art or skills who wanders wearing, whether it rains or shines, an awful raincoat from which the price tag still hangs; the mad prophet who announces a new Christianity without Christ, without redemption, without sacrifice until he realizes that he himself is Christ; he himself is the one destined to take world's evil upon himself. Or, as in the case of Singer, one may have to do with the pious Israelite who all of a sudden finds himself guilty of a shameful guilt, and even before realizing how this could have happened, he observes the collapse of all his reassuring moral certainties and realizes not without dismay that the question of good and evil is a metaphysical more than an ethical question. Well, all these novelistic situations perfectly fit the concept of "cosmotheandric tragedy" and "peripaty" with which Pareyson designates the event that implies God, human beings, and the world, where it becomes clear what believing or not believing in God means, where the sense of the world not only is revealed to but also is fulfilled in the human being.

> What is this tale, this story? It is the tale of freedom. It is the story of the victory of being over nothingness, of good over evil. This story is no more divine than human, no more protological than eschatological. It is the story of God's implication with nature and the human beings, it is the story of the cosmotheandric tragedy . . . and, what a happy coincidence, I realize this now—it is precisely in five acts, according to the division I have drawn of the various epochs. It is the biography of evil: birth, growth, death of evil. It is the great event of the good, the odyssey of the good, the difficult advent of the good.[14]

In this passage, Pareyson refers to the ideal and eternal story of freedom, that is, to the story of the universe ("I have said it many times that the universe is not a reality but an event"),[15] which is not exactly the story that unfolds in this or that specific novel given that all novels represent, if anything, a reflection of that story, a plot that unfolds starting from the prologue in heaven. The philosophy of freedom allows for no doubts regarding the ontological primacy of good over evil, that is, the fact that the good is destined to triumph over evil. There is no novel though that, representing the reality of evil, does not evoke evil as the terrifying and terrible reality that *actually* can win over the good or has even won over it. This can be explained with the consideration that, "from the perspective of the human being within history, the story of eternity appears on the one hand as successive, on the other as simultaneous."[16] In other words, within eternity the victory of good over evil is an event that has happened *once and forever*, whereas within time it is an event that occurs *time after time and always*, and one must speak in the plural about those that are "the ineducible facts of freedom." One can think of (the event of) creation, (the event of) the Fall, and (the event of) redemption. "Always" means that "God always creates and the human being always falls," that is, at every moment; likewise, "redemption certainly occurs in the historical world, in the incarnated God, yet it is God who suffers and dies, and this occurs eternally: God always suffers and dies, will still suffer and die at the end of times."[17] This entails the reality of evil and nothingness.

TWO OBJECTIONS

An aside should be made, and we should confront two objections that are offered by Giuseppe Riconda and Gianni Vattimo, respectively. These are objections made on the basis of philosophical perspectives that both emerge out of Pareyson and nevertheless deeply diverge from him. I consider them from the angle, perhaps a bit narrow, of the theme in question. Riconda has said that "One should not flirt with nothingness!" And Vattimo has claimed that "Evil does not exist!"

What Riconda means (Riconda as interpreter of Pareyson, that is) seems to be clear to me. His is an invitation to hold onto the perspective of eternity (lest one drift into an equivocal form of nihilism) because nothingness is certainly functional to being insofar as being is freedom (without nothingness, being would be necessity, that is, the being that necessarily is). But nothingness *is not if not as* a function of this being. Albeit real, nothingness has no autonomy; it is not even a power because freedom *alone* is power of good and evil, freedom *alone* institutes the good while refusing itself to evil. Freedom may have nothingness as its foundation, yet the assent that freedom gives to the good is given to the good that freedom's own "yes" institutes in a nonarbitrary way given that it is a "yes" that is simultaneously generator of and generated by the good. To emphasize nothingness, to give it too much relevance—in sum, to flirt with nothingness—means to relinquish the standpoint of eternity with the risk of undermining Pareyson's grandiose meontology and offer a more or less trivially nihilistic version of it. These remarks are well grounded, indeed. Yet, I wonder, is not the risk that of not taking nihilism seriously enough, or at least of not taking seriously enough the possibility of nihilism inherent in meontology? Does this way not eliminate the possibility that creation and redemption may fail? Is such a possibility of failure not replaced with their self-configuration as necessary moments in a story that within eternity is always self-identical? What gives reason to puzzle is the fact that, in the originary act with which God says "yes" to being, thereby defeating evil and pushing nothingness back into nothingness, Riconda sees a trait that would render Pareyson's thinking close to the position espoused by Emanuele Severino.

What Vattimo means (Vattimo as interpreter of Pareyson, that is) also seems clear to me. Vattimo alludes not so much to evil as to Evil, that is, to evil as a metaphysical reality. This is the kind of evil that for Vattimo does not exist. It is as if Vattimo, by analogy with the truth, were to say: If truth is only in the interpretations of it that are given, the same holds true also for evil, which therefore has no metaphysical reality and is rather exclusively a matter of those who suffer from or do it—a type of negative limit; nothing else, ultimately, than our mortal condition, and thus an evil that is not truly evil. I would like to remark to Vattimo: Certainly in Pareyson truth does not exist other than in its interpretations, but this does not take away the fact that it is itself the truth; it remains firmly such, no matter where, in heaven or on earth, and it cannot be halved or reduced to an *outcome of power*, as you say. The same holds true for evil. Evil does not exist except when someone evokes it, awakens it, or even beforehand posits it by negation. Yet evil is. One might want to say: it is in being, whose severing and opposing principle it constitutes. Evil is a metaphysical reality even before being a historical one. If we take this away, what is left? No longer evil but simply this or that malaise or state of uneasiness.

PHILOSOPHY AND NOVEL

Let us go back to our starting point and ask: Why does the novel need philosophy, and why does philosophy need the novel? Moreover, in what sense can we aptly say that philosophy has a vocation toward the novel, and the novel has a vocation toward philosophy? We need hardly remark that we are not speaking about the *roman philosophique*. Pareyson is very little concerned with a novel whose goal would be an illustration and divulgation of philosophical themes, according to the tenets of a poetics of an Enlightenment nature. For Pareyson, and as we have seen in the case of Dostoevsky, the novel is made of characters who are the incarnation of ideas and plots that arise out of behaviors in which the sense or non-sense of existence are at stake. The novel is nothing other than myth, that is, a place revelatory of truth according to the only way in which truth can manifest itself. In its turn, the content of philosophy is not theorems but events, acts that can in no way be deduced but can only be accompanied and enlightened by thought in the real movement of their happening. That is why philosophy and novel are co-essential.

It is interesting to note that metaphysical rationalism, not unlike the ontology of freedom, places the novel in relation with philosophy as knowledge of the historical and metahistorical reality of the human being, and even considers the form of the novel as an essentially philosophical matter. What is Hegel's *Phenomenology*, as it has been widely said and repeated, if not the great novel of Spirit? Starting from the opposition between being and nothingness, consciousness erupts into the world and makes a journey that is a *peripaty*, which Pareyson defines as the event that implicates human beings and God and moves from creation to redemption through the Fall. Interiority appropriates exteriority; it appropriates that which lies in a state of alienation but which is originarily its own, and which must return to being its own, as it will necessarily happen according to what philosophy attests step by step. The other is other only in appearance though. In reality, everything belongs to consciousness and is for consciousness. There is nothing that is not spiritual content. The fact that this truth comes to light through a long and fatiguing process ("the fatigue of the concept") does not eliminate the fact that the initial truth is ultimately the final truth. The initial figure is the opposition of being and nothingness, which has its ground in the identity of opposites. The final figure is self-consciousness, that is, the consciousness of the identity of the self and what is other than the self. At the origin, identity is the poorest and emptiest thing; but in the end, it is the richest and fullest. Yet it is the same thing. It is identity; that is, it is the unfolded and completed (which means exhaustively narrated) truth of an identity that has overcome and sublated not only difference but also contradiction, gathering itself as in a circle that binds the alpha and the omega. Hegel's *Phenomenology*, the novel of Spirit, gives way to the *Encyclopaedia*, which is to say, after the novel of novels has seen its light, there is no longer room for any other novel because philosophy has devoured them all.

What can be not inappropriately applied here is the lapidary sentence that Pareyson has left in the abovementioned "Frammenti sull'escatologia": "If freedom is the heart of reality, this is the reason why the center of reality is dialectical, contrast conflict contradiction, living contradiction. What happens to the principle of contradiction? At the center of reality is not the principle of contradiction but contradiction itself. Hegel is simultaneously right and wrong—he sees well, he thinks poorly."[18] Hegel "sees well" because he sees that "the center of reality is dialectical," and therefore everything is "contrast conflict contradiction, living contradiction." Yet not only has he thought that all this is deducible from out of the intrinsically contradictory identity of being and nothingness, but he also has thought of eliminating contradiction, taking movement away and pacifying it in the quiet of the retrieved identity; and, naturally, he has thought in terms of necessity—therefore, he "thinks poorly." And he ends up dissolving, as it were, important acquisitions like the one that attributes the form of the novel to philosophical discourse. Once Spirit has triumphed, it no longer knows what to do with the novel. Hegel proclaims the death of the novel. By consigning the novel to the past, he proclaims the death of Romantic art, which is precisely the art of the novel. We know what Hegel thought of the novelists of his times—he would have gladly sent all of them to Hell. Is this not what they want (so claims Hegel)? The novel of his times, devoted to the exploration of spiritual dimensions from which there is no return, such as death and madness, seemed to him as an inevitably disastrous attempt. According to Hegel, when consciousness is not guided by self-consciousness as by its polar star, there is *exodus* but not *nostos* [return], and it is a meaningless, wretched journey of perdition into the regions that Plato would have called "the folds of dissimilarity," where difference has lost the way of identity.

What happens to the principle of contradiction, asks Pareyson? And what happens to identity? Against Hegel, and following Schelling, Pareyson does not hesitate to maintain the transcendence of reality over that which can be thought of it. Pareyson opposes the conversion of the real into the rational (and vice versa) with the ecstasy of reason. In being, everything is event; the event is not because it has to be, according to reason, but because it is freely. In being, everything is thus "contrast conflict contradiction" without reason ever becoming capable of appropriating all of this. Albeit valid at the logical level, the principle of contradiction has little validity at the ontological level when reality is intimately and originarily contradictory. What "living contradiction" is greater than the one within God, who can do everything and yet cannot oppose and defeat evil except by taking it out of the divine depths (and if not out of there, then out of where?), that is, by positing it through the gesture that negates it? Are human beings not a "living contradiction," because they know the good by virtue of evil and do evil because there is good? And they enjoy joy only through suffering and pain? And they can also return to God but only because they have relinquished God first, and all this without implying that guilt is necessary? These are events, acts, or, as Pareyson calls them, "operations" that can only be narrated but are never deduced, whether the narration is myth or religious revelation. From Schelling Pareyson retrieves and develops the idea of the ecstasy of reason, according to which myth and revelation confront philosophy as something ineducible that offers itself to thought so as to be interpreted and universalized.

It is not by chance that mysticism, which, according to Pareyson's interpretation, both Hegel and Spinoza[19] would want to constrain within the limits of a philosophy of identity and hence of a metaphysics that eliminates all contradiction from reality, has elaborated a symbolic and metaphorical language that retains an incomparable literary and speculative value. The fact is that it is a religious experience. And experience wants to be attested, even when words founder in ineffability and silence. What we encounter here is the paradox of a word that is beyond all words. This paradox marks the originary noncoincidence of being and the thought that thinks being. That is why mysticism resorts to symbols and metaphors. Mysticism is much deeper than any philosophy of identity. Whether the reference is to "God beyond being" or to a God who is "nothingness and super-nothingness," or whether its object is "the birth of God in the soul," "God who loves himself in the human being," "the human being who, if he or she were not, then God too would not be,"[20] in all events what is at stake here is an unobjectifiable truth. Moreover, it is a truth that offers itself to two modalities of discourse that cannot be homologated. "Whereas mythical discourse speaks to the religious consciousness, hermeneutic discourse speaks to the philosophical mind, and a religious given is at the same time faith-content, very private or ecclesial, and a problem of sense, philosophical and universal."[21] Thus writes Pareyson with respect to religious experience and its communicability. This can be brought back to the theme of narration and the novel by saying that if, on the one hand, there is the hermeneutic discourse, on the other there is mythical discourse. That is to say, on the one hand there is philosophy and on the other there is the novel. Two wings for the same fly. We need both. And each needs the other.

—Translated by Silvia Benso

NOTES

1. This is what I have claimed in Sergio Givone, "Hermeneutics and Aesthetics," in *Annuario Filosofico* 26 (2010): 127ff., where I have tried to show that, from this perspective, Pareyson's thought is the specular reversal of Gadamer's.

2. Luigi Pareyson, *Truth and Interpretation*, trans. Robert T. Valgenti (Albany: State University of New York Press, 2013).

3. Luigi Pareyson, *Ontologia della libertà. Il male e la sofferenza* (Turin: Einaudi, 1995).

4. Luigi Pareyson, *Estetica. Teoria della formatività* (Turin: Istituto di Filosofia, 1954).

5. This holds true not only for the novel but also for the work of art in general. Pareyson, for example, loved to say that Mozart's music is superior to Haydn's as for aesthetic quality, but Haydn's is "much deeper."

6. Pareyson, *Ontologia della libertà*, 303.

7. Ibid., 52.

8. Ibid., 79.

9. Ibid., 26.
10. Luigi Pareyson, *Dostoevskij. Filosofia, romanzo ed esperienza religiosa* (Turin: Einaudi, 1993), 179.
11. Ibid., 20.
12. Ibid., 13.
13. Ibid., 15–16.
14. Pareyson, *Ontologia della libertà*, 79.
15. Ibid., 78.
16. Ibid., 80.
17. Ibid.
18. Pareyson, "Frammenti sull'escatologia," in *Ontologia della libertà*, 296.
19. With respect to mysticism and the interpretation of it offered by Hegel, Pareyson writes: "It is clear (it helps to repeat it) that these expressions cannot be simply carried over into a philosophical context nor can they be translated into an objectifying language without deforming them as for their meaning and misunderstanding them in their intent. Only when they are considered as an indirect and allusive discourse can they be preserved in their genuine tenor, which is religious and mystical, and therefore unrepeatably existential. This is possible through a philosophical reflection of a hermeneutic character capable of maintaining the religious nature and at the same time universalizing the meaning of it through a communication that is rational and existential at the same time. But when interpreting Eckhart's thought, Hegel has not proceeded on a similar path. The thesis according to which if God were not I too would not be, and if I were not God too would not be has appeared to Hegel as a true metaphysical coincidence of the two terms" (Pareyson, "Frammenti sull'escatologia," 241). With respect to Spinoza, "The inconveniences of a pure and simple translation or transcription of mysticism into philosophy are known, as is taught very clearly by the case of Spinoza, who has metaphysicalized Saint Paul's dictum '*in illo vivimus, movemur et sumus*' and has drawn out of it the most extreme pantheism of all times" (Pareyson, "Frammenti sull'escatologia," 236).
20. These are all references from Meister Eckhart and Angelus Silesius, in Pareyson, "Frammenti sull'escatologia," 236ff.
21. Ibid., 236.

Bibliography

PAREYSON'S WORKS IN ITALIAN

The following list is limited to books. For a more comprehensive bibliography (including articles, contributions, edited volumes, conference papers, etc.), one should consult Francesco Tomatis, *Bibliografia pareysoniana* (Turin: Trauben, 1998) and *Pareyson: vita, filosofia, bibliografia* (Brescia: Morcelliana, 2003).

La filosofia dell'esistenza e Carlo Jaspers. Naples: Loffredo, 1939; Genoa: Marietti, 1997.
Studi sull'esistenzialismo. Florence: Sansoni, 1943; Milan: Mursia, 2001.
L'estetica dell'idealismo tedesco I. Kant. Turin: Istituto di Filosofia, 1949; Milan: Mursia, 2005.
L'estetica dell'idealismo tedesco II. Schiller. Turin: Istituto di Filosofia, 1949. Milan: Mursia, 2005.
Esistenza e persona. Turin: Taylor, 1950; Genoa: Il Melangolo, 1992.
Fichte. Turin: Edizioni di Filosofia, 1950; Milan: Mursia, 1976.
Estetica. Teoria della formatività. Turin: Edizioni di Filosofia, 1954; Milan: Bompiani, 1996.
L'estetica e i suoi problemi. Milan: Marzorati: 1961.
L'Estetica di Schelling. Turin: Giappichelli, 1964; Milan: Mursia, 2003.
L'etica di Kant nella prima fase del suo pensiero. Turin: Giappichelli, 1965; Milan: Mursia, 1998.
Teoria dell'arte. Saggi di estetica. Milan: Marzorati, 1965.
L'etica di Pascal. Turin: Giappichelli, 1966.
Conversazioni di estetica. Milan: Mursia, 1966.
I problemi dell'estetica. Milan: Marzorati, 1966.
Il pensiero etico di Dostoievski. Turin: Giappichelli, 1967.
L'estetica di Kant. Milan: Mursia, 1968, 1984.
Etica ed estetica in Schiller. Turin: Giappichelli, 1969; Milan: Mursia, 1983.
Essere e libertà. Turin: Giappichelli, 1970.
L'etica di Kierkegaard nella "Postilla." Turin: Giappichelli, 1971; Milan: Mursia, 1998.

Verità e interpretazione. Milan: Mursia, 1971, 2005.
Filosofia dell'interpretazione. Edited by Marco Ravera. Turin: Rosenberg & Sellier, 1988.
Filosofia della libertà. Genoa: Il Melangolo, 1989.
Heidegger: La libertà e il nulla. Naples: ESI 1990.
Dostoevskij. Filosofia, romanzo ed esperienza religiosa. Turin: Einaudi, 1994.
Ontologia della libertà. Il male e la sofferenza. Edited by Aldo Magris, Giuseppe Riconda, and Francesco Tomatis. Turin: Einaudi, 1995.

PAREYSON'S WORKS TRANSLATED INTO ENGLISH

"The Unity of Philosophy." *Cross Currents* 4 (1953): 57–69.
"Pointless Suffering in *The Brothers Karamazov*." *Cross Currents* 37, nos. 2–3 (1987): 271–86.
Existence, Interpretation, Freedom: Selected Writings. Edited by Paolo Diego Bubbio. Translated by Anna Mattei. Aurora, CO: The Davies Group Publishers, 2009.
Truth and Interpretation. Translated by Robert T. Valgenti. Albany: State University of New York Press, 2013.

ARTICLES, BOOK CHAPTERS, AND REVIEWS ON PAREYSON IN ENGLISH

Benso, Silvia. "On Luigi Pareyson: A Master in Italian Hermeneutics." *Philosophy Today* 49, no. 4 (Winter 2005): 381–90.
Bredin, Hugh Terence. "The Aesthetics of Luigi Pareyson." *The British Journal of Aesthetics* 6 (1966): 193–203.
———. "Review of *L'esperienza artistica. Saggi di storia dell'estetica*." *The British Journal of Aesthetics* 16 (1976): 87–90.
Brown, Merle E. "On Luigi Pareyson's *L'estetica di Kant*." *Journal of Aesthetics and Art Criticism* 29 (1971): 403–10.
Carravetta, Peter. "Introduction to the Hermeneutics of Luigi Pareyson." *Differentia* 3/4 (1989): 217–41.
———. "Form, Person, and Infinite Interpretation: Luigi Pareyson, *Existence, Interpretation, Freedom. Selected Writings*." *Parrhesia* 12 (2010): 99–108.
Franke, William. "Existentialism: An Atheistic Or a Christian Philosophy?" In *Analecta Husserliana: The Yearbook of Phenomenological Research Volume CIII: Phenomenology and Existentialism Book One: New Waves of Philosophical Inspirations*. Dordrecht: Springer Science + Business Media, 2009, 371–94.
Gherardi, Silvia, and Antonio Strati. "Luigi Pareyson's *Estetica: teoria della formatività* and Its Implications for Organization Studies." *Academy of Management Review* 42, no. 4 (2017): 745–55.

Harmon, Justin. "Adventures of Form: Italian Aesthetics from Neo-Idealism to Pareyson." *Annali d'Italianistica* 29, no. 1 (2011): 363–79.
Harris, Henry Silton. "Review of *Fichte. Il sistema della libertà.*" *Journal of the History of Philosophy* 18 (1980): 97–98.
Kretsch, Robert Winston. "Review of *L'estetica e i suoi problemi.*" *Journal of Aesthetics and Art Criticism* 21 (1962): 104–5.
Lazea, Dan. "The Ontological Personalism of Luigi Pareyson: From Existentialism to the Ontology of Liberty." *Appraisal: A Journal of Constructive and Post-Critical Philosophy and Interdisciplinary Studies* 6, no. 1 (2006): 7–16.
Lippman, Edward Arthur. "Review of *Estetica. Teoria della formatività.*" *The Journal of Philosophy* 52 (1955): 791–96.
Munro, Thomas. "Review of *I problemi dell'estetica.*" *Journal of Aesthetics and Art Criticism* 26 (1968): 396–97.
———. "Review of *L'esperienza artistica. Saggi di storia dell'estetica.*" *Journal of Aesthetics and Art Criticism* 33 (1975): 464–65.
———. "Review of *L'interpretazione dell'opera d'arte.*" *Journal of Aesthetics and Art Criticism* 15 (1956): 255–56.
———. "Review of *L'interpretazione dell'opera d'arte.*" *The Journal of Philosophy* 53 (1956): 814–19.
———. "Review of *Teoria dell'arte. saggi di estetica.*" *Journal of Aesthetics and Art Criticism* 25 (1966): 219–20.
———. "Review of *Verità e interpretazione.*" *Journal of Aesthetics and Art Criticism* 30 (1972): 570.
———. "Review of *Verità e interpretazione.*" *The Journal of the History of Philosophy* 70 (1973): 132–33.
Romanell, Patrick. "Review of *Estetica. Teoria della formatività.*" *Philosophy and Phenomenological Research* 16 (1956): 572–73.
Savile, Anthony. "Review of *I problemi d'estetica.*" *The British Journal of Aesthetics* 7 (1967): 389–90.
Schaper, Eva. "Review of *L'estetica di Kant.*" *The British Journal of Aesthetics* 9 (1969): 198–99.
———. "Review of *L'estetica e i suoi problemi.*" *The British Journal of Aesthetics* 3 (1963): 77.
Sepper, Dennis L. "After Fascism, After the War: Thresholds of Thinking in Contemporary Italian Philosophy." *American Catholic Philosophical Quarterly* 80, no. 4 (2006): 603–19.
Tomatis, Francesco. "Luigi Pareyson: Good, Evil, Free Will." *Annali d'Italianistica* 29, no. 1 (2011): 131–40.
Valgenti, Robert T. "The Primacy of Interpretation in Luigi Pareyson's Hermeneutics of Common Sense: A Response to D. Di Cesare's 'U-Topias of Understanding.'" *Philosophy Today* 49, no. 4 (Winter 2005): 333–41.
———. "The Tradition of Tradition in Hermeneutics." In *Consequences of Hermeneutics*. Edited by Jeff Malpas and Santiago Zabala, 66–80. Evanston, IL: Northwestern University Press, 2010.

Vattimo, Gianni. "Pareyson: From Aesthetics to Ontology." In *Art's Claim to Truth*. Edited by Santiago Zabala, 77–89. New York: Columbia University Press, 2008.

Zawadzki, Andrzej. "*Scriptura Aliquo Modo Cum Legentibus Crescit*: The Idea of Infinite Interpretation and Its Christian Roots." In *Hermeneutics—Ethics—Education*. Edited by Andrzej Wiercinski, 49–56. Berlin: LIT Verlag, 2015.

Contributors

Lauren Swayne Barthold teaches philosophy at Endicott College and is research fellow at Essential Partners (Cambridge, MA). She is the author of *Gadamer's Dialectical Hermeneutics* (2010) and *A Hermeneutic Approach to Gender and Other Social Identities* (2016), the *Internet Encyclopedia of Philosophy* article on Hans-Georg Gadamer, as well as numerous articles on hermeneutics. Her recent work seeks to apply hermeneutic theory to contemporary problems and issues. Her current manuscript, *Civic Dialogue*, brings together Buber, Gadamer, deliberative democracy theory, feminist theory, and the work of dialogic practitioners to develop an interdisciplinary model of dialogue as a form of civic discourse particularly suited to highly polarized situations.

Silvia Benso is professor of philosophy at Rochester Institute of Technology, Rochester, New York. Among her areas of interest are ancient philosophy, contemporary European philosophy, the history of philosophy, ethics, and aesthetics. She is the author of *Thinking After Auschwitz: Philosophical Ethics and Jewish Theodicy* (1992, in Italian), *The Face of Things: A Different Side of Ethics* (2000), *Viva Voce: Conversations with Italian Philosophers* (2017), and the co-author of the volume *Environmental Thinking: Between Philosophy and Ecology* (2000, in Italian). She has also co-edited various volumes such as *Contemporary Italian Philosophy: Between Ethics, Politics and Religion* (2007); *Levinas and the Ancients* (2008); and *Between Nihilism and Politics: The Hermeneutics of Gianni Vattimo* (2010). During the past decade, she has devoted herself to the promotion of Italian philosophy and is the general co-editor for the SUNY Press Series on Contemporary Italian Philosophy. Most recently, she has been the co-founder of a new philosophical organization dedicated to the study of Italian philosophy: SIP, the Society for Italian Philosophy.

Paolo Diego Bubbio is associate professor of philosophy in the School of Humanities and Communication Arts at Western Sydney University, Australia. His areas of interest include the relationship of the post-Kantian tradition (from Kant to Nietzsche) to the later movements of European philosophy, such as existentialism and hermeneutics, and issues in philosophy of religion. He is the author of *Sacrifice in the Post-Kantian Tradition: Perspectivism, Intersubjectivity, and Recognition* (2014); *God and the Self in Hegel: Beyond Subjectivism* (2017); and the editor of Luigi Pareyson, *Existence, Interpretation, Freedom: Selected Writings* (2009). He also authored two monographs in Italian and co-edited several collections of essays in both Italian and English, including *L'Esistenza e il Logos: Filosofia, Esperienza Religiosa, Rivelazione* (2007, a collection of essays on Pareyson's thought co-edited with Piero Coda); and *Religion After Kant: God and Culture in the Idealist Era* (2011, co-edited with Paul Redding).

Antonio Calcagno is professor of philosophy at King's University College in London, Canada. Co-director of the Centre for Advanced Research in European Philosophy, he is also the author of *Lived Experience from the Inside Out: Social and Political Philosophy in Edith Stein* (2014); *Badiou and Derrida: Politics, Events and Their Time* (2007); *The Philosophy of Edith Stein* (2007); and *Giordano Bruno and the Logic of Coincidence* (1998). He is the editor of *Contemporary Italian Political Philosophy* (2015), which appears in SUNY Press' Contemporary Italian Philosophy series.

Paolo D'Angelo is professor of aesthetics at the University of Roma Tre in Rome, Italy. After graduating from the University of Rome "La Sapienza," he received his PhD from the University of Bologna. He is part of the editorial board for the journals *Rivista di Filosofia, Cultura Tedesca, Studi di Estetica, Estetica,* and *Paradigmi*. He has been vice president of the Società Italiana di Estetica (SIE). His main areas of interest include aesthetics of the visual arts, environmental aesthetics, analytic aesthetics, history of aesthetics, German philosophy, and contemporary Italian philosophy. Some of his books are translated into Spanish and Portuguese. An English translation of his book *Ars est celare artem* is forthcoming in 2017 with the title *Sprezzatura. The Art of Concealing Art*. Among his most recent books are *Il problema Croce* (2015); *Filosofia del paesaggio* (2014); *Le nevrosi di Manzoni* (2013); *Estetica* (2011); *L'estetica italiana del Novecento* (2007); *Cesare Brandi. Critica d'arte e filosofia* (2006); *Ars est celare artem. Da Aristotele a Duchamp* (2005); *Estetismo* (2003); and *Estetica della Natura* (2001).

Massimo Cacciari is professor (emeritus) of aesthetics at the Università Vita-Salute San Raffaele in Milan, Italy, after having taught at the Universities of Venice (Italy) and Lugano (Switzerland). He has been among the founders of some of the most important philosophical, political, and cultural journals in Italy: *Angelus Novus*, *Contropiano*, *Laboratorio Politico*, *Il Centauro*, and *Paradosso*. He served three times as mayor of Venice and was also a member of the European Parliament in 1999. Among Cacciari's publications, some of which appeared only outside Italy, are *Krisis* (1976); *Dallo Steinhof* (1980); *Icone della legge* (1985); *L'angelo necessario* (1986; English translation 1994); *Zeit ohne Kronos* (1986); *Drama y duelo* (1987); *Méridiéens de la decision* (1992); *Geofilosofia dell'Europa* (1994); *L'Arcipelago* (1996); *Le dieu qui danse* (2000); *Hamletica* (2009); *The Unpolitical* (2009); *Doppio ritratto. San Francesco in Dante e in Giotto* (2012); and *Il potere che frena* (2013; English translation forthcoming, 2018). His main philosophical proposal can be found in the triptych *Dell'inizio* (1990), *Della cosa ultima* (2004), and *Labirinto filosofico* (2014).

Umberto Eco was professor (emeritus) at the University of Bologna, Italy. A novelist, literary critic, semiotician, and philosopher, he wrote many books, both fictional and scholarly in content. Most of them have been translated in all major languages. Among his numerous philosophical works translated into English are *The Open Work* (1989), *A Theory of Semiotics* (1976), *The Role of the Reader* (1979), *Semiotics and the Philosophy of Language* (1984), *The Limits of Interpretation* (1990), *Interpretation and Overinterpretation* (1992), *Kant and the Platypus* (1999), *History of Beauty/On Beauty* (2004), and *On Ugliness* (2007). In addition to having taught at various universities around the world and having been granted many international honorary degrees, prizes, and awards, Eco was a member of the prestigious Italian *Accademia Nazionale dei Lincei*. He died on February 19, 2016.

Sergio Givone has been professor (now emeritus) of aesthetics at the University of Florence, Italy, since 1991. Before that date, he taught at the Universities of Perugia and Turin. He is the author of numerous publications, some of which have been translated into French, Spanish, German, and Catalan. Among them are *Hybris e melancholia* (1974); *Dostoevskij e la filosofia* (1986); *Disincanto del mondo e pensiero tragico* (1988), *Storia del nulla* (1995), *Metafisica della peste* (2012), and *Luce d'addio. Dialoghi dell'amore ferito* (2016). He is also the author of three novels: *Favola delle cose ultime* (1998), *Nel nome di un dio barbaro* (2002), and *Non c'è più tempo* (2008).

Contributors

Dennis J. Schmidt is research professor and head of philosophy at Western Sydney University, Australia. His publications include *Idiome der Wahrheit* (2015), *On Word and Image* (2013), *Lyrical and Ethical Subjects* (2005), *On Germans and Other Greeks* (2001), and *The Ubiquity of the Finite* (1988). He has co-edited *Hermeneutische Wege* (2000) and *Difficulties of Ethical Life* (2008); his translations include Ernst Bloch's *Natural Law and Human Dignity* (1986) and the revised edition of Martin Heidegger's *Being and Time* (2010). He is the editor of the SUNY Press "Series in Continental Philosophy," which now has 164 volumes in print.

Brian Schroeder is professor of philosophy and director of religious studies at Rochester Institute of Technology, Rochester, New York. He has published widely on contemporary European philosophy, the history of philosophy, environmental philosophy, Buddhist philosophy, the Kyoto School, social and political philosophy, and the philosophy of religion. Among his publications are *Altared Ground: Levinas, History and Violence* (1996); *Pensare ambientalista: Tra filosofia e ecologia* [*Environmental Thinking: Between Philosophy and Ecology*] (2000); and *Atonement of the Last God: Apocalypse, Eschatology, and the Transfiguring of Evil* (forthcoming). He is co-editor with Silvia Benso of the SUNY Press Series in Contemporary Italian Philosophy. Currently an associate officer of the Comparative and Continental Philosophy Circle, Schroeder is formerly co-director of the Society for Phenomenology and Existential Philosophy, co-director and chair of the board of directors of the International Association for Environmental Philosophy, director of the Collegium Phaenomenologicum, and executive committee member of the Nietzsche Society.

Robert T. Valgenti is professor of philosophy at Lebanon Valley College, Annville, Pennsylvania. His research and publications cover the areas of hermeneutics, contemporary Italian philosophy, and the philosophy of food. He has translated into English Luigi Pareyson's *Truth and Interpretation* (2013), Gianni Vattimo's *Of Reality* (2016), and Gaetano Chiurazzi's *The Experience of Truth* (2017). He is the founder of E.A.T. (Engage, Analyze, Transform), an undergraduate research group whose interventions aim to improve the ethical, environmental, cultural, and nutritional profiles of the college dining experience.

Gianni Vattimo has taught aesthetics at the Università di Torino, where he later became professor (now emeritus) of theoretical philosophy. He has been a visiting professor at various universities in the United States and elsewhere. He also served as an elected member of the European

Parliament in Brussels. Among his many publications that have been translated in English are *The End of Modernity* (1988); *The Transparent Society* (1992); *The Adventure of Difference: Philosophy after Nietzsche and Heidegger* (1993); *Beyond Interpretation: The Meaning of Hermeneutics for Philosophy* (1997); *Religion* (with Jacques Derrida, 1998); *Belief* (1999); *Nietzsche: An Introduction* (2002), *After Christianity* (2002); *Nihilism and Emancipation* (2004); *The Future of Religion* (with Richard Rorty, 2005); *Dialogue with Nietzsche* (2006); *After the Death of God* (with John D. Caputo, 2007); *Not Being God* (2009); *Christianity, Truth, and Weakening Faith* (with René Girard, 2010); *The Responsibility of the Philosopher* (2010); *Art's Claim to Truth* (2010); *A Farewell to Truth* (2011); *Hermeneutic Communism* (with Santiago Zabola, 2011); and *Of Reality* (2016).

Federico Vercellone is professor of aesthetics at the University of Turin, Italy. His works mostly deal with the relation between aesthetics and contemporary hermeneutics, the history of nihilism in European thought, and the tradition of German Romanticism. His most recent research focuses on the theory of image, visual studies, and the notion of morphology, providing a multidisciplinary approach to the concept of form, image, and phenomenon. He is the director of CIM, a center for research on morphology. Vercellone is the author of more than 200 books, edited books, essays, articles, and reviews. Many of them have also been translated into English, French, German, Spanish, and Portuguese. His most recent books include *Le ragioni della forma* (2011); *Anschauung Denken. Zum Ansatz einer Morphologie des Unmittelbaren* (2011, co-authored with O. Breidbach); *Dopo la morte dell'arte* (2013); *Thinking and Imagination: Between Science and Arts* (co-authored with O. Breidbach; English translation, 2014); *Il futuro dell'immagine* (2017); and *Beyond Beauty* (English translation, 2017).

Martin G. Weiss is assistant professor of philosophy at the University of Klagenfurt, Austria. His research areas include hermeneutics, phenomenology, German and Italian philosophy, as well as bioethics and biopolitics. Among his publications are *Die Hermeneutik des Unerschöpflichen. Das Denken Luigi Pareysons* (2004); *Gianni Vattimo. Einführung. Mit einem Interview mit Gianni Vattimo* (2012, 3rd edition); and *Suspect Families. DNA Analysis, Family Reunification and Immigration Policies*, edited with T. Lemke, T. Heinemann, I. Helen, and U. Naue (2015).

Index

Abbagnano, Nicola, 12, 155
abyss, 9, 89
actualism, 143
actuality, 49, 163, 164, 166
Alighieri, Dante, 63, 71, 74, 76, 207
alterity, 105, 108, 112, 116, 117, 119
ambiguity, 15, 18, 22, 93, 144, 175
Anaximander, 164
Aquinas, Thomas, 166
Arendt, Hannah, 132
Ariosto, Ludovico, 50, 59
Aristotle, x, 124, 170
artist, 4, 7, 14, 43, 46–54, 57, 63–65, 72, 73, 96, 98–100, 102, 107, 109–112, 114, 115, 118, 186
artistry, 113, 116, 118
atheism, 8, 15, 18, 21, 22, 177, 179, 180
author, 7, 20, 25, 39, 44, 50, 51, 55, 62–64, 67, 69, 72, 77, 93, 160, 165, 176, 192
avant-garde, 53

Barth, Karl, 14, 19, 25, 162, 176
Berdyaev, Nikolai, 2, 24
Bible, 173, 177
Buonarroti, Michelangelo, 64

Cartesian, 7, 130, 140, 141, 145, 146, 152

choice, 15, 18, 21, 23, 27, 31, 40, 46, 48, 51, 79, 108, 109, 111, 112, 114, 117, 118, 132, 140, 153, 162, 174–176, 181, 188
Christ, 18, 26, 177, 192
Christianity, 15, 21–23, 164, 165, 166, 169, 171, 173, 177–180, 192, 209
community, v, 5, 6, 91, 105, 106, 115–119, 121, 134, 163
congeniality, 55
consciousness, 31, 39, 95, 96, 139, 141, 143, 153, 173, 195–198
consumer, 54, 55, 67, 99
contingency, 8, 162, 169, 171
contradiction, 18, 35, 142, 186–188, 196, 197
cosmotheandric, 192, 193
Croce, Benedetto, v, 2, 4, 5, 14, 43–51, 53–56, 59–68, 78, 93, 96–98, 1001, 103, 106, 142, 165, 185, 206
cue, 68, 70, 71, 97, 98
Cusa, Nicholas of, 72

decision, 15, 18, 31–34, 36, 39, 41, 132, 134, 174, 191, 192, 207
deconstruction, 69, 190
deconstructionism, 19, 69, 149, 151
deflationism, 124, 127

Derrida, Jacques, 69, 206, 209
Descartes, René, 139
dialectic, 4, 21, 33, 37, 38–41, 50, 68, 69, 77, 107, 109, 112, 113, 115, 142
dialogue, 9, 17, 20, 23, 24, 106, 116, 119, 127, 130, 133, 134, 136, 137, 140, 205, 209
dogmatism, 1, 17, 18, 55
Dostoevsky, Fyodor, ix, 2, 8, 15, 18, 22, 24, 93, 101, 177, 191, 192, 195
duality, 37, 152

Eco, Umberto, v, 2, 4, 5, 12, 26, 57, 60, 96, 102, 169, 207
ecstasy of reason, 190, 197
emanation, 77, 182
empiricism, 162
enlightenment, 31, 165, 195
Esposito, Roberto, 118, 121
ethics, 27, 49, 57, 110, 116, 149, 157, 170, 204, 205, 209
event, x, 95, 118, 125, 152, 161, 162, 165, 170, 186, 188–193, 195–198, 205
evil, vi, ix, 7, 8, 15, 18–22, 27, 77, 132, 135, 161, 169–182, 188–195, 197, 203, 208
execution, 4, 51, 54, 97, 101
exemplarity, 6, 38, 54, 106–109, 111–115, 119
existentialism, ix, 3, 13, 14, 16, 17, 21, 25, 29, 30, 47, 61, 140, 143, 144–146, 149, 179, 202, 203, 206
exodus, 173, 183, 197
expression, 4–7, 14, 46–50, 56, 63, 64, 66, 67, 74, 85, 87–90, 97, 108, 113, 115, 116, 123, 125–127, 129, 136, 149, 166, 176

falsehood, 125, 135–137
feeling, xiii, 5, 40, 48, 49, 74, 87, 89–91, 97
Feuerbach, Ludwig, 19, 21, 144

Fichte, Johann Gottlieb, ix, 2, 14, 140, 141, 157, 201, 203
filler, 4, 70, 73–76, 78, 79
finitude, 37, 39–41, 108, 130, 135, 155
Flaubert, Gustave, 64
formativity, 3, 4, 6, 7, 14, 38, 43, 46–48, 51, 53, 54, 61, 65–67, 70, 78, 93–96, 98, 106, 108, 115, 118, 119, 162, 185
formed form, 4, 51, 71, 78, 101, 108–110
forming form, 4, 71, 99–101, 162
fragment, 31, 32, 71, 75, 78, 188

Gadamer, Hans-Georg, xii–xiv, 2, 3, 6, 11, 12, 15, 24, 25, 27, 58, 95, 99, 101, 102, 105, 124–126, 137, 147, 160, 169, 198, 205
Genesis, 50, 115, 152, 176
Gentile, Giovanni, 13, 14, 44, 46, 55, 62, 95, 102, 106, 142, 143, 152, 165
gnosticism, 77
Goethe, Johann Wolfgang von, 52, 53, 94, 95, 101, 102, 171
Gramsci, Antonio, 14
ground, 9, 18, 30, 32, 33, 35, 36, 68, 91, 92, 95, 101, 105, 114, 115, 120, 160, 175, 181, 191, 208
Guzzo, Augusto, 12–14, 94

Hardy, Thomas, 192
Hegel, Georg Wilhelm Friedrich, vi, xiii, 2, 6, 7, 14, 16, 19–21, 27, 28, 71, 88, 91, 94–96, 139–145, 151, 152, 154–157, 160, 172, 190, 191, 195–197, 199, 206
Heidegger, Martin, vi, x–xiv, 2, 6, 7, 11, 14–16, 24, 27, 40, 89, 90, 106, 124, 125, 128, 137, 139, 140, 145–156, 160, 162, 164, 165, 167, 170, 181, 183, 184, 202, 208, 209
Heraclitus, 35
historicism, 4, 20, 106, 107, 165

Index

historicity, 16, 97, 141, 146, 160, 165
Hölderlin, Friedrich, 160, 166
Hume, David, 170

idealism, ix, 4, 14, 44, 46, 61, 86, 90, 107, 140, 142–145, 152, 154, 160, 162, 201, 203
identity, 5, 24, 49, 50, 94, 96, 101, 105, 119, 124, 141, 142, 148, 171, 187, 190, 191, 196–198
ideology, 6, 25, 116, 125, 126, 131–134, 136
imagination, xiv, 5, 23, 64, 84–91, 112, 172, 192, 209
imitation, 67, 106, 107, 109–111, 114, 116–118, 125
immanence, 5, 16, 83, 143, 152, 181, 182
individuality, 31, 56, 143
ineffability, 125, 127, 128, 198
inexhaustibility, xi, xii, 1, 2, 8, 9, 15, 17, 18, 20, 25, 127–129, 132, 134, 136, 149, 187
inexhaustible, iii, v, xi, 1, 8, 9, 15, 17, 20, 37, 100, 116, 128, 129, 135, 138, 149, 150, 152, 171, 172, 186, 187
infinity, 31, 37, 39–41, 70, 101, 162, 192
initiative, 3, 30, 32–37, 39–42, 148, 161
intersubjectivity, 91, 206
intuition, 4, 5, 46–50, 56, 62–65, 71, 85–89, 96, 97, 99, 172
invention, 51, 70, 94, 95, 98, 107, 108, 118
Iser, Wolfgang, 69, 101, 103

Jaspers, Karl, ix, 2, 13, 14, 24, 26, 30, 42, 47, 140, 146, 162, 201
judgment, x, xiii, 5, 33, 55, 62, 69, 75, 81–91, 107, 109, 119, 163, 171, 183

Kabbalah, 77

Kant, Immanuel, v, xiii, 2–4, 14, 23, 24, 30, 44, 47, 75, 81–83, 86, 87, 89–92, 120, 141, 145, 170–172, 174, 183, 201–203, 206, 207
Kierkegaard, Søren, 2, 14, 16, 19–22, 24, 142, 144, 145, 154, 155, 160–162, 165, 179, 201
kindredness (*congenialità*), v, 5, 6, 105–119, 121

language, ix–xiii, 14, 22, 58, 65, 74, 87, 115, 124, 126, 161, 164, 172, 197, 199, 207
law, x, xi, 36, 37, 51, 65, 69, 84, 88, 99, 117, 174, 208
legality, 7, 66, 75
Leibniz, Gottfried Wilhelm, 169
Leopardi, Giacomo, 79, 86, 91
Lévi-Strauss, Claude, 69
Levinas, Emmanuel, 161, 205, 208
literature, xiii, 45, 67
Locke, John, 31

Magris, Aldo, 26, 152, 155, 157, 169, 202
Malamud, Bernard, 192
Marcel, Gabriel, 2, 14, 24, 146, 147, 150, 156
Maritain, Jacques, 14, 24
Marx, Karl, 19, 23, 29, 45
Marxism, 21, 165
materiality, 48, 65, 67, 77
matter 4, 47, 57, 65, 98, 148, 160
Melville, Herman, 192
memory, xi, 63
meontology, 27, 194
metaphor(ical), xiii, 6, 73, 126, 154, 197, 198
metaphysics, 12, 15, 17, 29, 61, 68, 78, 117, 118, 121, 124, 140, 141, 145, 148, 152, 155, 164, 165, 173, 175, 197
music(al), xiii, 47, 54–56, 66, 67, 171, 198
mysticism, 9, 77, 197–199

Index

myth(ical), 5, 8, 14, 19, 22, 24, 93, 161–167, 172, 173, 176, 186, 189–191, 195, 197, 198

necessity, xiii, 8, 21, 35, 38, 52, 63, 65, 73, 82, 86–88, 100, 132, 136, 142, 155, 170, 182, 188, 189, 191, 194, 196
neo-idealism, 142, 143, 203
Nietzsche, Friedrich, xiii, 22, 52, 59, 70, 89–91, 119, 176, 184, 206, 208, 209
nihilism, 16–18, 21, 22, 109, 118, 179, 194, 205, 209
nothingness, 8, 170, 174–176, 187–191, 193–196, 198
Novalis, 14
novel(ist), vi, 8, 24, 73, 93, 101, 154, 185, 186, 189–193, 195–198, 207

O'Connor, Flannery, 192
objectivism, 1, 127, 137, 139, 140, 143, 145, 147, 152
objectivity, 12, 69, 70, 116, 131, 141, 143–145, 152, 153
ontology of freedom, vi, 3, 4, 7, 8, 15, 17, 18, 77, 153, 155, 159, 162, 169, 171, 182, 185–187, 189, 195
ontotheology, 8, 21, 175
origin, vi, xii, 6, 8, 20, 25, 34, 35, 52, 73, 77, 106, 109, 111, 112, 117, 119, 120, 123, 124, 127, 129, 132, 133, 144, 151, 164, 171, 172, 174, 176, 182, 196
originality, xi, 24, 54–56, 110, 111, 114, 117

Pagano, Maurizio, 26, 145, 152, 155, 157
painting, xiii, 44, 50, 63, 64, 67
paradox(ical), 16, 91, 108, 115, 129, 139, 151, 174, 178, 179, 198
Parmenides, 190

Pascal, Blaise, 2, 14, 24, 154, 201
passivity, 37, 54, 65, 87, 89, 99, 100
Peirce, Charles Sanders, 12, 61
perception, 106
performance, 54–56, 60, 66, 67, 69, 70, 72, 97, 101, 111, 171
Perniola, Mario, 2, 26, 57
personalism, 16, 17, 25, 27, 29, 31, 32, 41, 42, 47, 100, 121, 149, 150, 203
personality, 4, 39, 41, 48, 49, 54, 57, 66–68, 70, 110, 111, 114, 151
personhood, 2, 3, 29–32, 37, 39–41, 100
perspectivism, 1, 19, 149, 206
Petrarca, Francesco, 50
Plato, 75, 76, 96, 130, 137, 197
pleasure, xiii, 84, 88, 89, 91, 180
Plotinus, 165, 181
poetics, 4, 53, 54, 64, 96, 195
poetry, 22, 57, 65, 67, 71, 76, 164
politics, 1, 62, 105, 117, 119, 159, 205, 206, 209
potentiality, 49
producer, 52
production, 6, 14, 35, 38, 46, 47, 51–53, 63, 65, 94, 95, 97, 102, 106, 108, 110, 114, 164

Rancière, Jacques, 119
rationalism, 27, 143, 186, 187, 190, 195
rationality, 24, 131, 132, 143, 152
realism, 127, 162, 192
reason, xiii, 5, 6, 24, 39, 82–84, 86–91, 117, 124, 125, 131, 132, 134, 142, 144, 173–175, 183, 190, 197
receptivity, 54, 87, 89
relationality, 41, 144
relativism, 1, 17, 106, 115–118, 127, 137, 149, 153
religion, ix, 1, 12, 14, 21–24, 159, 161, 164, 167, 172, 173, 178, 180, 205, 206, 208, 209

Renaissance, 72
responsibility, 38, 39, 100, 108, 119, 132, 192, 209
revelation, xii, 1, 6, 8, 17, 18, 22, 37, 71, 111, 115, 123, 126, 132, 133, 161, 173, 186, 197
revelatory, 11, 18, 22, 26, 112, 115, 116, 128, 173, 186, 195
Ricoeur, Paul, xii, xiii, xiv, 2, 3, 11, 12, 15, 23–27, 147, 169
Riconda, Giuseppe, 171, 194, 202
romanticism, 2, 14, 52, 72, 74, 86, 93, 209
Rorty, Richard, 125, 137, 209
rule (the), xi, 6, 51, 54, 71, 96, 101, 110, 111, 134, 161

Sartre, Jean-Paul, 41, 146
Schelling, Friedrich Wilhelm Joseph, ix, xiii, 2, 7, 14–16, 22, 24, 26, 89, 92, 94, 101, 102, 140, 151, 152, 160–162, 165, 170, 171, 174, 181–184, 190, 197, 201
schematism, 5, 84–87
Schiller, Friedrich, 14, 24, 201
Schleiermacher, Friedrich, x, 11
Schopenhauer, Arthur, xiii, 90
Severino, Emanuele, 194
Silesius, Angelus, 178, 199
Singer, Isaac, 192
singularity, 3, 30–33, 38, 88–91, 106–111, 113
situation, 3, 30–33, 35, 37–41, 46, 107, 112, 115, 133, 135, 141, 146–148, 150, 174, 189, 192, 205
society, 16, 36–38, 112, 113, 161, 163, 164, 166, 205, 208, 209
Socrates, 130, 131, 137, 138, 169
solidarity, 3, 17, 29, 30, 113, 114, 117, 123, 137, 177, 187
Spirit, 16, 30, 31, 47, 67, 71, 95, 97, 111, 114, 120, 143, 159, 160, 195, 196
Spiritualism, 25

spirituality, 48, 49, 112
Stravinsky, Igor, 64
structure, x, xi, 4, 5, 27, 35–37, 57, 70–73, 82, 83, 94, 146, 148, 150, 152, 161
style, 43, 49, 57, 71, 111, 186
subjectivism, 1, 7, 127, 139–143, 145–152, 154, 206
subjectivity, 6, 7, 54, 70, 143–145, 151, 153
sublime, 74, 84, 86, 89, 90, 177
substance, 30, 38, 39, 85, 117, 181
suffering, 7, 13, 15, 18, 19, 22, 23, 26, 57, 78, 161, 169, 171, 172, 177–180, 197, 202
symbol(ic), 22, 23, 171, 172, 191, 197, 198

taste, 6, 84, 87, 112, 114, 117–119
technics, 131, 134
technique, 38, 43, 64, 65, 67, 97, 98, 108, 113, 132
technology, 112, 160
tension, 6, 19–21, 39, 40, 52, 73, 86, 108, 109
theater, 54, 55, 57
theology, x, 21, 71, 166, 171, 173, 175, 177, 178, 188
Tilgher, Adriano, 65
totality, 1, 31, 32, 34, 36, 38, 71–73, 81, 82, 134, 142, 146, 152, 162
tragedy, 22, 26, 27, 161, 180, 192, 193
tragic, 11, 15, 18, 19, 21, 22, 26, 57, 90, 91, 101, 135, 159–162, 179, 180, 186, 187
transcendence, v, 3, 16, 17, 21, 22, 25, 29, 30, 35, 36, 40, 41, 55, 170, 197
transcendental, 5, 16, 82–87, 89, 118
translation, ix–xi, xiii, 2, 12, 47, 55, 56, 60, 66, 67, 164, 173, 199
trial, 51, 65, 66, 68, 94, 98

uniqueness, 24, 32, 39, 107, 108, 110, 120, 139, 181, 182

unity, 5, 26, 34, 37, 67, 72, 84, 86–88, 99, 101, 120, 126–128, 137, 130, 140, 145, 152, 153, 155, 171, 202
universality, 25, 31–33, 38, 39, 87, 110, 112, 116, 143, 163
user, 52

Valéry, Paul, 2, 52, 64, 65, 69, 96, 101–103

value, 5, 6, 32, 33, 36–39, 50, 51, 58, 75, 84, 85, 88, 91, 106, 110, 141, 149, 185, 197
Vattimo, Gianni, 2, 4, 7, 12, 13, 24, 26, 28, 57, 109, 110, 118, 119, 121, 148, 155, 169, 171, 194, 195, 204, 205, 208, 209
Vico, Giambattista, ix, 106, 107, 120

wonder, 89

www.ingramcontent.com/pod-product-compliance
Lightning Source LLC
Chambersburg PA
CBHW020653230426
43665CB00008B/414